YOU GOTTA BE DIRTY

THE OUTLAWS MOTORCYCLE CLUB IN & AROUND WISCONSIN

(Print Edition Only)

Badger Wordsmith, LLC
Published in Marinette, WI

MICHAEL GROGAN

YOU GOTTA BE DIRTY: THE OUTLAWS
MOTORCYCLE CLUB IN & AROUND WISCONSIN

The author has done his best to present accurate and relevant information in this book. In instances where opinions and/or speculation are offered, these views and opinions, unless attributed, are solely those of Michael Grogan.

ISBN: 978-0692774366

Author: Michael R. Grogan
             M.A. — History

YOU GOTTA BE DIRTY:
THE OUTLAWS MOTORCYCLE CLUB IN & AROUND
WISCONSIN (Print edition only)

Michael Grogan
Twitter: @PredicateActs
Crimes and offenses—United States—non-fiction
Organized crime and offenses—United States—non-fiction

CONTENTS

ACKNOWLEDGEMENTS

This book would have never come to fruition without the support and encouragement of several persons. To fill in some gaps pertaining to this research, I had the privilege to interview Milwaukee Police Department (MPD) Lieutenant Charles Berard, a thirty-nine-year law enforcement veteran and a walking encyclopedia of the Outlaws Motorcycle Club in and around Wisconsin. I would also like to thank retired MPD Detective Roger Hinterthuer, who met with me and also granted permission for portions of his book, *Justice Delayed is Justice Denied*, to be liberally paraphrased and quoted. Roger's intimate knowledge of several high profile investigations supplemented the dozens of primary sources used to complete this project.

Retired Lieutenant of Detectives Steve Spingola also provided some valuable details regarding the MPD's organizational structure in the 1970s and 1980s. Steve resided in the same neighborhood and attended some of the same schools as Larry Anstett — the fifteen-year-old *Milwaukee Sentinel* paperboy tragically killed by an explosive device left for an Outlaws' rival.

Two members of academia further contributed to the quality of this research. Dr. James Oberly's guidance was very helpful. His research on government surveillance during the turbulent 1960s pointed me towards the various countercultures of that period. Dr. Randy McBee, the author of *Born to be Wild: The Rise of the American Motorcyclist*, offered several good suggestions for this project.

I would also like to thank the representatives of the Federal Bureau of Investigation, the United States Attorney's office, the U.S. National Archives at College Park, the Wisconsin Department of Justice, the Milwaukee County Clerk's office, the Rockford Police Department, the Sheboygan County Clerk's office, and the Kenosha County Sheriff's Department for tracking down hundreds of pages of records, many of which are decades-old.

The assistance offered by these individuals and organizations improved the quality of this work, and I am thankful for their efforts.

GLOSSARY

AMA:	American Motorcycle Association
AOA:	The American Outlaw Association, a group that comprises all chapters of the Outlaws Motorcycle Club in the United States.
Charlie:	The club logo of the Outlaws Motorcycle Club
Chop-Shop:	A garage where stolen vehicles are disassembled for parts
Church:	A term used for weekly or bi-weekly motorcycle club meetings
Citizens:	The ninety-nine percent of motorcyclists who live within the law
DCI:	Department of Criminal Investigation, a division of the Wisconsin Department of Justice.
HAMC:	The Hells Angels Motorcycle Club
MPD:	Milwaukee Police Department
OMC:	Outlaws Motorcycle Club
OMGs:	Outlaw Motorcycle Gangs — a term which encompasses all one-percent motorcycle clubs worldwide.
One-Percent:	The one-percent of motorcyclists who live outside the law
OPBOB:	One-Percenter Brotherhood of Outlaw Bikers
TEU:	The Milwaukee Police Department's Tactical Enforcement Unit
SAS:	The MPD's Special Assignment Squad

INTRODUCTION
COVER AND CONCEALMENT

Seated in the witness box at a federal courthouse in Milwaukee, Todd Leifker found himself in a spot he likely never imagined. Previously tucked away out of state, the two-bit burglar and drug trafficker told the Court that he and a friend had been common criminals, but "we was never killers before he joined the Outlaws" Motorcycle Club. The moral code of the outlaw biker, Leifker testified, is premised on cover and concealment. Righteous bikers cover for each other by intimidating witnesses or killing adversaries, and then conceal the evidence from the criminal justice system.[1]

As is the case with any article of faith taken to an extreme, the concept of brotherhood sometimes fosters corruption. In many locales, miscreants and street toughs have certainly left their marks. Newspaper accounts of such debauchery often leave readers shaking their heads. Yet when reprobates band together, their brand of brotherhood reinforces a collective depravity, which, if left to fester, undermines the rule of law.

Three decades have passed since Dr. James Mathies, a psychologist with the Wisconsin Department of Corrections, told a reporter that those who join outlaw motorcycle clubs "have a lot of questions about their own adequacy and their own abilities. They have a history of not doing well in school and not doing well in society. They compensate for that, somewhat, from the support from their peer group."[2]

Hardcore bikers live and sometimes die for their organization's brotherhood, and proudly refer to themselves as "one-percenters" — the one-percent of motorcyclists that live outside the law. Hundreds of such clubs exist in the United States and Canada, but only a handful, including the Outlaws (OMC), comprise the big-four — the most radical of all one-percent motorcycle clubs.[3]

Unraveling the past of a group of one-percent bikers is a challenging experience. In his book, *That Noble Dream*, historian Peter Novick notes that authoring a history is akin to "nailing jelly to a wall." The task is more difficult when an organization makes few, if any, records available for public consumption and when some of its members engage in criminal activity.[4]

Still, recovering the history of the Outlaws Motorcycle Club is a worthwhile endeavor. "The most valuable characteristic of historical thinking," wrote the late Forrest McDonald, "is that, if employed imaginatively, it can enable us to see things around us that would otherwise be invisible." As a conservative academic, McDonald believed that contemporary historians "fail the laity" when they seek to "redress an imbalance" of a historically neglected group or "wish to further a political or ideological agenda."[5]

Readers can rest assured that the focus of this cultural history is non-ideological. The government documents, newspaper reports, and other primary sources generally speak for themselves. So does the book's title. In 1966, an original founder of the OMC's Milwaukee chapter, John Bisenius, explained a rule of the club to the press as: "You gotta be dirty."[6]

There are, however, two matters that this book does address. The first component is the government's response to the Outlaws Motorcycle Club. In 1964, when the Outlaws initially appeared in southeastern Wisconsin, the leader of the Milwaukee Police Department's (MPD) Special Assignment Squad — a unit that conducted long-term surveillance of *La Cosa Nostra*, the New Left, and the Black Panthers — concluded that the club did not pose a threat to the city's political establishment. Instead, the MPD saw the OMC as a facilitator of public disorder.[7]

Police officials later assigned a street-level tactical enforcement team to monitor and suppress the activities of the club. After a *Milwaukee Sentinel* paperboy was killed by an explosive device left for an Outlaws' rival, the MPD realized its "Houston, we've got a problem" moment. In light of the grisly murder, law enforcement ratcheted-up the pressure. As the rules of engagement changed, and members of law enforcement found themselves subjected to threats and acts of violence, rank-and-file police officers, on occasion, operated on the periphery and/or, arguably, outside the scope of the justice system.[8]

Due to political pressures that were brought to bear, law enforcement's response to the activities of the Outlaws Motorcycle Club steadily evolved. In 1984, the MPD's long-serving police chief, Harold Breier, retired. Four months later, the Milwaukee Fire and Police Commission named Robert J. Ziarnik, a thirty-three year veteran of the department, the city's next chief of police. Shortly thereafter, the MPD "halted political surveillance and promised to destroy all political files." By department order, the Special Assignment Squad (SAS) was folded into the newly formed Criminal Intelligence Division, which kept tabs on organizations involved in criminal, not political, activity. The change of leadership at the MPD further resulted in an increased willingness to work in concert with state and federal agencies. Over time, this subtle shift in organizational philosophy, which persisted long after Ziarnik's resignation, had a devastating impact on the Outlaws Motorcycle Club in Wisconsin.[9]

Another element of this research takes issue with the leniency of the criminal justice system in the 1960s and 1970s. For whatever reasons, members of the Milwaukee County judiciary, and even some of those employed with the Milwaukee County District Attorney's office, failed to see the OMC as a criminal enterprise. In many instances, low bail for serious charges, such as sexual assaults, shootings, and murders, became the norm. In several high profile cases, Outlaws free on bond reoffended and, after being charged with additional crimes, were freed again. The press finally took notice after two *Milwaukee Sentinel* employees became shooting victims.[10]

Today, the merits of diversion programs for criminal offenders, even those with gang affiliations, are, once again, being debated in the public square. This book will illustrate how members of the Outlaws Motorcycle Club, for the most part, gamed a lenient justice system. Nearly thirty years passed before federal prosecutors used sweeping racketeering statutes to punch a hole through the OMC's wall of silence.

The first two chapters of this book explore the evolution and the subculture of outlaw motorcycle gangs (OMGs) in the United States. Although renegade motorcyclists see themselves as contemporaries of nineteenth century equestrian bandits, outlaw bikers thrive in urban environments. Yet, like the James gang, the fighting readiness of one-percent bikers is, in many instances, an off-shoot of their memberships' military or quasi-military experiences. By examining the norms, customs, and traditions of OMGs, it is possible to trace the migration of this dangerous, complex, and narcissistic ideology to Wisconsin.

Chapters Three through Ten are dedicated to the transmutation of the Outlaws Motorcycle Club in Wisconsin. In the mid-1960s, three Midwestern-based motorcycle groups merged to form the Outlaws Nation. This union enabled the Outlaws to gain a foothold in Milwaukee, the home of the Harley-Davidson Motor Company. Just four years later, as the OMC's Milwaukee chapter sought dominion over the state's other one-percent clubs, the organization gradually morphed from a group of ruffian tormentors to deadly eradicators. When the Heaven's Devils Motorcycle Club refused to acquiesce to the Outlaws' demands, a decade-long confrontation resulted in several fatalities.

The remaining chapters examine the tumultuous events of the 1990s, a period when the OMC orchestrated a guerrilla-style offensive in an effort to beat back the expansion of the world's largest one-percent motorcycle club — the Hells Angels (HAMC). During this period, the HAMC began courting the Hell's Henchmen Motorcycle Club, a group with chapters in Chicago, Rockford, and South Bend, Indiana. The HAMC's bold move into OMC turf touched off a seven-year conflict that was exacerbated by a barroom beating in Janesville, Wisconsin. The brazen attacks and the retaliatory responses that followed, drew the ire of local, state, and federal law enforcement officials, who subsequently assembled a task force to search for predicate acts of racketeering. During this period, the OMC's command-and-control structure, organizational motivations, and tactics prompted the group to transition from a racketeering-based organization to an at-will urban terrorist network.

While wide-ranging, this history of the Outlaws Motorcycle Club is only as comprehensive as the available information. S o m e police reports and search warrant affidavits are no longer available. The *Privacy Act* also prohibits federal agencies from releasing information that pertains to living persons without a waiver. The existing material has produced a cogent, fast-paced narrative that captures the essence of the subculture absent pages of the mindless fluff.

[1]*Milwaukee Journal Sentinel*, April 21, 2000, p. 3B.

[2]*Milwaukee Sentinel*, May 10 1980, p. 1.

[3]Northwestern University Traffic Institute, "Outlaw Motorcycle Gang Investigations," unpublished manual (1995), 2 (held by author).

[4]Peter Novick, *That Noble Dream: The "Objectivity Question" and the American Historical Professional* (Cambridge, UK: Cambridge University Press, 1988), 1.

[5]Forrest McDonald, *Recovering the Past: A Historian's Memoir* (Lawrence Kansas: University of Kansas Press, 2004), 10-11.

[6]*The Lincoln Star* (Lincoln, Nebraska), January 10, 1966, p. 6.

[7]Steve Spingola, retired Milwaukee Police Department Lieutenant of Detectives, e-mail message to author including correspondence with Ted Engelbart, former Special Assignment Squad member, January 10, 2015.

[8]Ibid.

[9]*Milwaukee Journal*, February 20, 1985, p. 10; *Milwaukee Sentinel*, January 1, 1993, p. 5A.

[10]*Milwaukee Sentinel*, February 9, 1980, p. 1.

CHAPTER ONE

GENESIS OF ONE-PERCENT MOTORCYCLISTS

Contemporary motorcycling in the United States was born in 1901, when the first American made motorcycle was built by Oscar Hedstrom, at the request of George Hendee, in Middletown, Connecticut. The new motorbike served as a pace vehicle for high profile bicycle races. Six months later, Hendee opened a factory in Springfield, Massachusetts. In 1902, the first Indian motorbike, which had only one cylinder, was sold to a retailer. Three years later, Indian introduced a Vermillion colored bike, which became nationally known as "Indian red."[1]

As the twentieth century began, the age of the machine also emerged. Americans quickly fell in love with two technological facets: The assembly line and the combustion engine, which, when coupled together, made the apparatuses of modernity affordable for the masses. In 1903, William Harley and Arthur Davidson sold their first Harley-Davidson motorbike from the confines of a small wooden shed. Three years later, the company moved to a larger building along Chestnut Street on Milwaukee's near north side. The American motorcycle genie was now out of the proverbial bottle[2]

Nonetheless, the popularity of motorcycle riding and racing suffered a set back on June 28, 1914, when Serbian nationalist Gavrilo Princip assassinated Austrian Archduke Franz Ferdinand. Soon, the people of Europe found themselves in the throes of an ugly, large scale war. Three years later, after the United States entered the conflict, the American military supplied motorcycles to army dispatch riders. With a bit of irony, Roy Holtz, the first American solider to enter Germany — the nation where engineer Nicholas Otto invented the first four-stroke combustion engine — did so while riding a Harley-Davidson.[3]

On the home front, the motorcycle was used to make a political statement. In 1916, two sisters, Augusta and Adeline Van Buren, rode their Indian motorcycles from coast-to-coast and traversed the summit of Pike's Peak. Descendants of former President Martin Van Buren, Augusta and Adeline, ages thirty-two and twenty-seven, sought to prove that women could serve in the armed forces and, therefore, should have a right to vote. South of the U.S. border, Mexican revolutionary, Poncho Villa, flashed a smile while mounting an Indian motorcycle in a dusty Mexican town. The freedom and rugged individualism associated with motorcycling was soon equated to the American pioneering spirit.[4]

In the interwar period, interest in motorcycle racing rapidly grew. To generate public support, motorcycle riders pursued the daring and unusual. In the mid-1920s, motorcycle chariot racing was popular. Typically, two or more rider-less motorcycles would be tied together to pull a makeshift chariot, whose drivers controlled the reins of the iron horses. In 1929, the "Wall of Death" exhibition began in Great Britain, and overtime, a similar concept found its way to the United States. The wall consisted of a perpendicular cylinder about twenty feet high. To walk away in one piece, motorcycle riders had to maintain enough speed to move around the walls of the tube without tumbling to the bottom.[5]

The October 24, 1929, the stock market crash, infamously known as Black Tuesday, resulted in the ensuing Great Depression. From 1929 – 1933, real U.S. GDP fell by more than a third and stock prices declined sixty-seven percent. With unemployment at thirty-two percent, the disposable income required for leisurely activities vanished virtually overnight. In 1933, Indian produced just 1,667 motorcycles. As a result, the growing public interest associated with racing and riding motorcycles for sport took a decade-long hiatus.[6]

Similar to other twentieth century cultural phenomena, the contemporary history of the motorcycle subculture was impacted by World War II. After the Japanese attack at Pearl Harbor, the U.S. government quickly retooled the manufacturing sector to meet the demands of a wartime economy. Indian Motorcycle and the Harley-Davidson Motor Company ramped up production and produced models in support of the war effort. Indian's 750cc V-twin and Harley-Davidson's "BMW-like VA" engines expeditiously transported a small number of military personnel in the European theater. In the latter part of the war, however, the military phased out the use of the motorcycle in favor of the jeep.[7]

In the aftermath of the victory over Japan in World War II, thousands of discharged military personnel had returned home and discovered that they missed the camaraderie and the adrenaline associated with combat operations. Seeking an alternative to the mundane nine-to-five lifestyle, many veterans gravitated towards the evolving biker subculture. By 1947, scores of motorcycle clubs had formed throughout the United States. Over the July Fourth weekend, the events surrounding a gypsy tour held in a small west coast town, forever etched the image of the outlaw biker into the overall culture.[8]

Located forty miles northeast of Monterey, California, the city of Hollister's Gypsy Tour tradition began as a one-day event in 1935, but soon evolved into a three-day festival. The 1947 tour, which was sponsored by the AMA and the Salinas Ramblers Motorcycle Club, was held at Bolado Park, a racing venue on the outskirts of town. Yet it was a gathering of 2,000 bikers in the town's center that morphed into a rowdy, alcohol-fueled disturbance. Intoxicated motorcyclists became involved in fistfights, rode their bikes into taverns, disregarded traffic regulations, and held races in the street. Hollister Police Lieutenant Roy McPhail, whose seven-officer-strong police department quickly found itself overwhelmed, noted that the bikers had "taken the town." Soon, the city's police chief, Fred Earl, summoned the assistance of the California Highway Patrol. "Armed with tear gas guns," noted *San Francisco Chronicle* reporter C.J. Doughty, "the officers herded the cyclists into a block on San Benito Street" and ordered a dance band to play. About fifty remaining hooligans were then rounded up by police. "If we jailed everyone who deserved it," Earl told the press, "we'd have herded them in by the hundreds." [9]

Within a matter of weeks, the perception generated by the images of a handful of inebriated motorcyclists became a lasting reality. After the mêlée, *Life* magazine featured an article regarding the Hollister disturbances that included a staged photo of an alleged biker, Eddie Davenport, barely clinging to a handlebar of a motorcycle with a beer bottle in each hand. Playing defense, the growing motorcycle press sought to deflect attention away from its constituency by blaming profit seeking tavern owners for overserving patrons.[10]

Other media outlets sought to benefit from the controversy and exaggerated the level of disorder. The magazine *American Motorcycling* went so far as to refer to the drunken fracas as the "Hollister holocaust." The *Pasadena California Independent* further reported that "outlaw riders" had taken over and painted the small town "bright red." The mainstream press and the residents of Hollister showed little interested in delineating citizen bikers — the vast majority of those who complied with the law — from the outlaws.[11]

Some motorcycle enthusiasts did their best to counter the media narrative of the monolithic renegade-rider. In a letter to the editor of *Life*, Paul Brokaw, the editor of the magazine *Motorcyclist*, expressed disapproval of a "very obviously arranged and posed" photo of Eddie Davenport by an "unscrupulous photographer," who had branded "tens of thousands of innocent, clean-cut" bikers as undesirables. In essence, Brokaw's letter seemed to echo the comments of the Secretary of the AMA, Lin Kuchler, who publicly stated, "The disreputable cyclists were possibly one-percent of the total number of motorcyclists, only one-percent are hoodlums and troublemakers."[12]

A year to the day later, the AMA sanctioned another gypsy tour three-hundred and sixty miles south of Hollister. In a virtual repeat of events, a thousand motorcyclists packed the downtown area of Riverside, California to drink beer and watch unauthorized street races. When an Air Force officer and his wife attempted to traverse a main thoroughfare, a crowd descended upon their vehicle. After smashing out the windows, the couple was extricated from their car and punched. During the ensuing commotion, a woman riding as a passenger on her boyfriend's motorcycle, was killed when her intoxicated boyfriend lost control of his bike.[13]

"Every police and sheriff's officer this citrus-belt city could muster was called out tonight," a report in the *New York Times* noted, "to defend the town against more than 1,000 motorcyclists who caused heavy damaged last night. The following Tuesday, the *Santa Cruz Sentinel* published a photo of two members of the Boozefighters seated on their motorcycles drinking beer under the caption, "Cyclists take over town," and noted that forty-eight people had been arrested.[14]

The consumers of news, who had heard or read about the events at Hollister and Riverside, especially those who came of age during Prohibition, were likely troubled by a potentially new form of gang activity. To many Americans, gangs were explicably linked to ethnic organized crime, which undermined public order, spawned political corruption, and gave undue influence to street toughs and secret societies. The Sicilian crime families that comprise *La Cosa Nostra* had tentacles in the United States as early as 1890, but over a decade passed before immigrants with ties to the Italian syndicate were linked to retaliatory slayings. On April 14, 1903, a middle-aged woman passing the New York Mallet and Handle Works pulled back a coat that had been placed over a barrel. Inside, she discovered the body of Benedetto Madoina, whose death was caused by eighteen shallow stab wounds. Legendary detective Joseph (Giuseppe) Petronsino traced Madoina's homicide to the Morello gang, a group with strong connections to the mafia in the United States and Italy. These acts of violence, while troubling, were typically confined to ethnic neighborhoods and had little impact on the overall population.[15]

The passage of the *Prohibition Act of 1920* expanded the scope and depth of American organized crime. Making the sale and manufacturing of alcohol illegal resulted in bootlegging, which brought some of the most "vicious multi-ethnic young gang members to the fore" of the broader culture. Salvatore Lucania, better known as Charles "Lucky" Luciano, and Frank Costello, a Luciano associate, established a powerful underworld presence in New York City. Al Capone set up shop in Chicago, where members of his south side organization — disguised in police uniforms — shot and killed seven rivals in the infamous St. Valentine's Day massacre. In Detroit, the Purple Gang, a group of Jewish gangsters "with a reputation for being more ruthless than Al Capone's mob," supplied many of the city's 15,000 speakeasies with their brand of illegal booze. When Prohibition ended in 1933, organized crime lost access to its most lucrative racket. Eight years later, after Japanese airplanes attacked Pearl Harbor, many of organized crime's potential recruits found themselves members of a much different outfit — the U.S. military. The change of the law and the country's two-front war had, in effect, marginalized the American underworld.[16]

With the war over, and with thousands of veterans returning home, the specter of a new face of organized crime, such as the warring factions involved in the "Hollister holocaust" and the unruly mob at Riverside, was a matter that law enforcement and the press would naturally take seriously. Some of the notorious motorcycle clubs present at Hollister were the Pissed-Off Bastards of Bloomington, the Boozefighters, and the Market Street Commandos. All three of these clubs sported logos that could easily be construed as belonging to miscreant groups. Moreover, the trepidation of the public and the media were not necessarily unwarranted hyperbole. Less than a year later, the Pissed-Off Bastards of Bloomington were folded into the Hells Angels (HAMC), a newly-formed motorcycle club chartered in Fontana, California by Otto Friedl. In 1954, the Market Street Commandos dropped their club's patch and became the HAMC's San Francisco chapter. Led by "angry Wino Willie" Forkner at Hollister, the Boozefighters remain one of the oldest, active one-percent motorcycle clubs.[17]

With the press and politicians on the lookout for post-war foreign and domestic threats, the debauchery ascribed to a handful of drunken bikers became the impetus for a new breed of bad boys. Although *Motorcyclists* magazine attributed the actions of the Riverside mob to "fringe" riders and a group of "troublemakers," a local law enforcement report cited "one percent of irresponsible" motorcyclists as the facilitators of public disorder. From this point forward, a debate emerged concerning the evolution of the "one-percent" and "citizen" biker idioms. A Northwestern University Traffic Institute manual for investigators links the term "one-percent" to the secretary of the AMA's post-Hollister response, while Texas Tech University historian Randy McBee believes that the term "emerged first out of the controversy surrounding Riverside in 1948." The "citizen" label is, therefore, associated with the ninety-nine percent of motorcyclists who live within the confines of the law and the rules of the AMA.[18]

Seeking to cash in on the image of America's new breed of bad boys, Hollywood released *The Wild One*, a 1953 film starring Marlin Brando as motorcycle gang leader Johnny Strabler. On the streets of a small town that appeared strikingly similar to Hollister, Brando's Black Rebels Motorcycle Club clashed with their rival, the Beetles MC, a group led by a leather clad Lee Marvin. In the biker subculture, The *Wild One* arguably had a degree of influence. Some one-percent motorcycle clubs adopted their norms, mores, and attire from the film. The Black Rebels MC's patch — a skull and crossbones — is very similar to "Charlie," the Outlaws Motorcycle Club's logo. Ralph "Sonny" Barger, the former national President of the HAMC, saw Marvin's character, Chino, as a role model, and even purchased the striped shirt that the actor wore in the movie.[19]

Citing remarks made by Birney Jarvis, one of the founders of the Hells Angels' San Francisco chapter, McBee argues that *The Wild One* may have played more of a role in the formation of the outlaw subculture than Hollister and Riverside. However, William Dulaney, a professor of organizational communication at the Air Force Culture and Language Center, gives *The Wild One* little mention in an article regarding the important history of outlaw clubs. Due to the cultural aspects adopted from the film, McBee is correct to identify *The Wild One* as being somewhat influential; however, the creation of the one-percent paradigm rests firmly with the Hollister narrative.[20]

While McBee focused exclusively on the west coast motorcycle subculture, Thomas Barker, a professor of Justice Studies at Eastern Kentucky University, followed the one-percenter migration eastward. In 1935, the McCook Outlaws Motorcycle Club (OMC) was established at a tavern on Route 66, a short distance from Chicago. Barker notes that James F. Quinn's social work thesis, *Outlaw Motorcycle Clubs*, purports that the McCook Outlaws had requested to join the Hells Angels in 1946, only to have "their petition permanently tabled." This decision, Quinn surmised, has led to the long-standing hostilities between the two clubs. History, however, seems to debunk this particular claim as the HAMC was not formed until 1948.[21]

How the Outlaws evolved from this point forward is somewhat debatable. Barker indicates that the McCook Outlaws simply changed the geographical location of their name to the Chicago Outlaws and relocated to the Windy City in 1950. Danny Lyon, a member of the Outlaws from 1964-1967, and the author of a well-received pictorial of the OMC, claims that the McCook Outlaws disbanded in 1947 "when most of its surviving members became policemen in Chicago and its suburbs." Lyon believes that the club was reformed as the Chicago Outlaws in the early 1950s. Thirteen years later, the OMC did successfully petition to join the One-Percenter Brotherhood of Outlaw Clubs (OPBOC); whereby, the club became the first recognized one-percent group east of the Mississippi River. A major change occurred on a summer weekend in 1964, when hundreds of motorcycle enthusiasts gathered in Springfield, Illinois for the city's annual motor races. Three of the groups present — the Chicago-based Outlaws Motorcycle Club, and the Milwaukee and Louisville Gypsy Outlaws Motorcycle Clubs — emerged from a meeting as the newly formed Outlaws Nation. A year later, the American Outlaws Association (AOA) was established and OMC chapters began forming in the Midwest and the south. This merger, which gave the club a presence in the city of Harley-Davidson, made Milwaukee the OMC's mother chapter in Wisconsin.[22]

Though it is believed that an estimated eight-hundred to a thousand one-percent motorcycle clubs currently exist in the United States and Canada alone, this number is difficult to ascertain. The OPBOC does not make a list of its membership available for public consumption. This shadowy organization was established during a 1960 summit for California bikers at the home of Frank Sadilek, the leader of the HAMC's San Francisco chapter. The Hells Angels, and a host of other clubs, upset with the AMA for labeling outlaw bikers as the one-percent of motorcyclists who are "antisocial barbarians," decided to make a statement. From this point forward, the HAMC, and the other clubs present — Satan's Slaves, the Gypsy Jokers, Galloping Gooses, Road Rats, and the Presidents — "decided to accept the one-percent label as a tribute."[23]

As the 1950s came to a close, the "performative" and "formative" developments of outlaw biker clubs fostered a broader transmutation. Like the nation in general, the socially turbulent 1960s ushered in era of significant change for one-percent groups. The foundations laid by the Hells Angels and the McCook Outlaws would soon add first-floor and second-floor additions. Similar to the Native Americans who had crossed the Bering land bridge 12,500 years ago, the one-percent subculture would move across the North American continent from west to east.[24]

[1]Indian Motorcycle History. http://www.indianmotorcycle.com/en-us/history#1900, accessed April 27, 2016.

[2]Davidson, Willie. *100 Years of Harley-Davidson* (New York: Bulfinch Press, 2002), 8.

[3]MacMillian, Margaret. *The War that Ended Peace* (London: Profile Books, 2013), 545; Alford, Steven E. and Suzanne Ferriss, *Motorcycle* (London: Reaktion Books, Ltd., 2007), 45.

[4]Alford and Ferriss, *Motorcycle*, 118, 122.

[5]Viralnova, "It Doesn't Get Cooler than This: Motorcycle Chariot Racing. It Was A Real Thing," October 9, 2014, http://www.viralnova.com/motorcycle-chariots/ (accessed April 27, 2016); Men and Motors. "Brief History of the Wall of Death Motorcycle Stunt." August 10, 2014, https://www.youtube.com/watch?v=rH86GVfF79g (accessed April 27, 2016).

[6]Robert S. McElvaine, *The Great Depression: America, 1929 – 1941* (New York: Crown Publishing Group, 2009), 4; Indian Motorcycle History. http://www.indianmotorcycle.com/en-us/history#1900, accessed April 27, 2016.

[7]American Motorcycle Association Hall of Fame, "1941 Indian Military Model 841: The Wigwam's Desert Warfare Bike," http://www.motorcyclemuseum.org/asp/classics/bike.asp?id=72 (accessed April 28, 2016).

[8]Thomas Barker, *Outlaw Motorcycle Gangs as an Organized Crime Group* (New York: Springer Cham Heidelberg, 2014), 2.

[9]Roger D. McGrath, "Motorcycle Diaries: Learn to Ride — and to Fall — in 1950s California," *American Conservative.* December 17, 2007, 20; Randy D. McBee, *Born to Be Wild: The Rise of the American Motorcyclist* (Chapel Hill, NC: North Carolina Press, 2015), 19-21.

[10]Randy D. McBee, "Here's Hoping the 'Hound' and His Friends had a Good Time": The Hollister Gypsy Tour of 1947 and the rise of the "Outlaw" Motorcyclist," *International Journal of Motorcycle Studies*, Vol. II (Spring 2015), 1-8.

[11]McBee, *Born to Be Wild,* 21-23.

[12]Paul Brokaw, "Letter to the Editor." *Life.* July 21, 1947, p. 31; Hunter Thompson, Sonny Barger, Evil Knievel, Arlen Ness, Peter Eagan, and Brock Yates, Ed. Michael Dregni, *The Harley-Davidson Reader* (Minneapolis: MBI Publishing, 2006), 134.

[13]Tom Reynolds, *Wild Ride: How Outlaw Motorcycle Myth Conquered America* (New York: TV Book, 2000), 60

[14]*New York Times*, July 5, 1948, p. 5; *Santa Cruz Sentinel*, July 6, 1947, p. 1.

[15]John Dickie, *Cosa Nostra: A History of the Sicilian Mafia* (New York: Palgrave MacMillian, 2004), 161, 165-167.

[16]Ibid., 181-182; Robert A. Rockaway, "The Notorious Purple Gang: Detroit's All-Jewish Prohibition Era Mob," *Shofar: An Interdisciplinary Journal of Jewish Studies*, Vol. 20, Number One (Fall 2001): 113-130.

[17]McBee, *Born to Be Wild,* 27; Thomas Barker, *Biker Gangs and Organized Crime* (Mathew Bender & Company, Inc., 2007), 27, 34,

[18]*Motorcyclist*, "The City of Riverside Reports," August 1948, 36; Northwestern University Traffic Institute, "Outlaw Motorcycle Gang Investigations," unpublished manual (1995); McBee, *Born to Be Wild*, 23.

[19]McBee, *Born to Be Wild*, 46; Barker, *Biker Gangs and Organized Crime*, 33; Lee Marvin, *Point Blank (*Tucson, AZ: Schaffner Press, Inc, 2013), 90.

[20]McBee, Born to Be Wild, 48; William Dulaney, "A Brief History of "Outlaw" Motorcycle Clubs," *International Journal of Motorcycle Studie*s, Vol. 1 (November 2005), 1-11.

[21]Barker, *Biker Gangs and Organized Crime*, 79-80; James F. Quinn, "Outlaw Motorcycle Clubs" (Master's Thesis, University of Miami, 1983).

[22]Barker, *Biker Gangs and Organized* Crime, 79-80; Danny Lyon, *The Bikeriders* (New York: The MacMillian Company, 1968), viii.

[23]Northwestern University Traffic Institute, "Outlaw Motorcycle Gang Investigations," unpublished manual (1995), 2 (held by author); Barker, *Biker Gangs and Organized Crime*, 37.

[24]William Dulaney, "A Brief History of "Outlaw" Motorcycle Clubs," *International Journal of Motorcycle Studies*, Vol. 1 (November 2005), 1.

CHAPTER TWO
NORMS, CUSTOMS, AND TRADITIONS OF OUTLAW CLUBS

Similar to other fraternal organizations, outlaw motorcycle gangs (OMG) have, over the course of time, developed a set of norms and mores. Since one-percent bikers follow their own set of rules and use a unique vernacular, an elucidation of the customs and traditions that comprise the subculture is necessary to pull back the veneer and shine a proverbial light through the fortified clubhouse door. Essential topics that merit discussion include club membership, club colors and organizational bylaws, OMG-affiliated women, the social and political philosophy of outlaw bikers, the subculture's code of silence, and the internationality of prominent one-percent clubs.

In a manner consistent with other legacy organizations, outlaw motorcycle clubs maintain a recruitment process to select new members, which, from start-to-finish, can take two to five years. The one-percent affiliation ladder typically has four phases: Being a "righteous" biker; becoming a club hang around and/or friend of the club, a period that allows members to assess an individual's attributes; the prospect/probate phase, which generally lasts a year or more; and then, if successful, entrance into the club as a patch holder.[1]

The prospect, probate, or striker phase is the most laborious. Wannabe club patch holders serve club members by standing guard duty, cleaning the clubhouse, running a variety of errands, and performing other tasks, all of which "are critical in maintaining the inter-member strength, operational cohesiveness, and ultimate survival of the group." This stage is also a "testing period" to ensure that the prospect adheres to the core values of the club. The prospect/probate stage (also referred to as a "striker" in Canada) culminates in what must be a unanimous vote of the club. In some instances, a prospect may be denied entry into the club, or a would-be member's entry-level phase may be extended. In order to become a patch holder, a prospect must be a male and own a large motorcycle manufactured in Western Europe or North America. Most OMGs either directly or indirectly restrict membership to non-African-American men. Current and former law enforcement officers are prohibited from becoming members, as are individuals deemed to be "snitches."[2]

Dr. Thomas Barker associates the outlaw biker recruitment process to "the saloon society," namely the bars that motorcycle clubs use as hangouts. These taverns are usually in blue collar areas "where the boundary between the outsiders and club members comes together." It is in these types of venues where wannabe bikers transition from club hang-arounds to potential prospects. Daniel Wolf, an anthropology professor, notes that the "initiation phase" of those prospecting for outlaw motorcycle clubs has noticeably changed "in the degree and intensity" since the 1960s and early portion of the 1970s. In the formative period of the OPBOC, the time it took for a striker to become a patch holder of a one-percent club took as little as three months. During this period, clubs would typically hold a "test by fire initiation," which might consist of a physical altercation with a patch holder or ordering a prospect to swim in a dangerous river. In the 1980s, the prospect phase shifted from a test requirement to "more of the way of jovial hazing and celebration." In general, the prospect or striking phase lasts from six months to two years, but will include a period that encompasses an entire riding season.[3]

Dulaney's "quasi-covert participation" with the Forgotten Warriors Motorcycle Club illustrates that members of one-percent clubs are "constantly scouting for potential members." In many instances, club patch holders observe possible candidates "surreptitiously." Persons deemed contenders for hang-around status are normally selected from an inner circle of members' friends or relatives. The personal attributes of prospective club recruits are discussed at club meetings, commonly called "church." Members of the one-percent subculture seek righteous individuals, defined as those willing to abide with the "unwritten code of honor within the biker system," for membership status. This so-called honor system includes assisting club members by lending spare motorcycle parts and having the courage to respond to "real or perceived" threats. It is also important for would-be members to understand biker symbolization, such as pins, clothing and artifacts, as well as the culture's lexicon.[4]

An important aspect of the one-percent subculture is the reverence given to club colors. Dulaney argues that a one-percent club's colors "unify disparate meanings in a single form." Wolf notes that the patch an outlaw motorcycle club selects differentiates the members of a club "from the rest of society as a powerful and elite macho group." Although these colors are presented to each OMG member, the patches and insignias remain the property of the club, as do any rings, tattoos, or other items that display a group's logo. In one instance, after a member of the Hells Angels (HAMC) was found shot to death near I-10 at Indio, California, investigators received information that the deceased — whose HAMC back and arm tattoos were cut from his body — had embezzled from the organization. Since club colors are prized possessions, losing a set to a rival club or to the police can result in a severe beating. However, this ritualistic practice can sometimes backfire. When an OMG member is arrested, and contraband, such as a weapon, is concealed within a set of colors, investigators familiar with the group's practices can leverage the return of the colors, which could be seized as evidence, in exchange for information regarding the club's activities.[5]

The colors of most one-percent motorcycle clubs consist of a three-piece patch sewn to a cutoff denim throw over, a leather vest or another outermost garment. The upper rocker identifies the club. The club logo or patch is found in the center. The bottom rocker typically lists the member's geographical location. In Wisconsin, for example, the Outlaws Motorcycle Club makes use of two geographical rockers — Milwaukee and Wisconsin. Being the OMC's first state charter, the Milwaukee chapter's bottom rocker is geographically specific. The Kenosha, Janesville, Madison, La Crosse, Eau Claire, Green Bay, Stateline, and Waukesha chapters are relegated to the broadly-defined Wisconsin bottom rocker.[6]

Outlaw motorcycle gang prospects typically wear colors that display the top and bottom rockers minus the club's official patch. On the front of a set of colors, members usually display their club monikers (i.e. Shock, Jingles, or Madman). Other patches, such as the OMC's SS lightning bolts or the HAMC's Filthy Few, may indicate that a club member has participated in an act of violence against a rival club or that the patch holder is particularly ruthless. The following may also be found on the front of a set of colors: A 1% badge; a RIP (rest in peace) patch that pays homage to a deceased member of the club; a red wings emblem that makes others aware that the patch holder has performed an act of cunnilingus on a menstruating white woman; or a FTW (Fuck the World) insignia — a proclamation that symbolizes a member's anti-social personality.[7]

Each one-percent club has its own set of bylaws, although these rules are often somewhat similar. To the outlaw biker, these are the rubrics of the world that actually matter. When members of one-percent groups speak of something being "legal," they are referencing the laws of the club, not state or federal statutes. In 1978, the Outlaw Motorcycle Club's bylaws consisted of twenty-six rules that, in part, incorporated the following: Penalties for stealing from fellow members, a violation punishable by the loss of club membership and an "ass beating"; no "fucking around" with another member's "old lady" without the consent of the member; fines for missing national events; a rule that banned "Jap" bikes; a requirement that each member own a motorcycle with an engine size of at least 650cc; a ban on speaking to the police or reporters "for any reason"; and fines for missing meetings. Each OMG chapter employs a club enforcer — a characteristically menacing individual with a propensity for violence — whose function it is to impose punishment for rule violations and collect fines from wayward members. One set of bylaws eerily notes, "If you just say fuck this and throw down your colors in front of the clubhouse or a brother's house, anywhere!!! YOU WILL BE VISITED!!!"[8]

OMG-Affiliated Women

Although membership in an outlaw biker club is limited to non-African-American males, OMG-affiliated women fill a particular niche within the subculture as mamas or old ladies. Mamas are property of the club and, therefore, provide sexual services to the entire membership. Old ladies belong to an individual patch holder. A mama's colors, for example, may read "Property of the Outlaws," while an old lady's colors will list a specific member (i.e. Property of Big Al). A fully-patched member of a club can demand that his old lady have sex with others if, for example, the biker is in need of cash or if his "patched old lady" has failed to meet expectations.[9]

OMG women also play ritualistic roles that primarily consist of sexual gratification. Some OMGs ask that new members bring a sheep to their initiation ceremony. A sheep is an adult female who is expected to engage in sexual relations with each member during the initiation proceeding. OMG members also participate in group sex, which, in the vernacular of outlaw bikers, is referred to as "pulling a train." Some mamas or sheep volunteer to pull a train, while other women are forced into group sex because they did something to embarrass a patch holder. To facilitate this process, some OMG clubhouses set aside an area known as "the train room."[10]

These sex acts enable OMGs to ferret out male and female law enforcement infiltrators, who would — for personal, legal, and ethical reasons — likely refuse to participate. Based on his observation of the Rebels MC, Wolf views OMG "male-female relations" as a mutually accepted part of the one-percent subculture. "Male dominance and aggressiveness," Wolf explains, "are complemented by female passivity and subservience"; whereby, "the asymmetrical quality of sexual relations" in outlaw clubs "reflects the nature and distribution of power."[11]

Biker women also perform an essential economic function as money earners for outlaw clubs. Many mamas and old ladies gain employment as topless dancers. In one study, almost all the table dancers employed in three Mississippi cities were working for OMGs. Many of the dancers also make extra cash by offering sex to men at strip clubs on the side. As long as a steady stream of income is forthcoming, OMG members typically permit women affiliated with the club to determine their own levels of "nightclub participation." Although the control and sexual degradation of OMG women defies the norms of mainstream society, one-percent bikers have no shortage of female participants. Some mamas and old ladies relish the bad boy lifestyle, while others share a true love of the motorcycle subculture. Another group of OMG-affiliated women studied suffered from low self-esteem.[12]

While law enforcement warns that OMG-affiliated women are used "to hinder" criminal investigations, and sometimes seek employment with government agencies to gain access to various data bases, Wolf identifies biker women as "the major threat to the social cohesion of an outlaw motorcycle club." Marriages or relationships may undermine a one-percent prospect's belief that the club comes first. In some instances, a prospect's wife may be questioned by members of a club in an effort to ascertain if the relationship will interfere with the biker's obligations to the organization. On other occasions, tension exists when mamas seek the affection of an old lady's fully-patched member. While conflicts between OMG affiliated women are generally not taken seriously by the club, a bitter dispute may cause a jilted party to become a law enforcement informant.[13]

Social and Political Philosophy of Outlaw Clubs

Linked to outlaw bikers' conceptualization of the roles of women, the norms and mores of one-percent motorcycle clubs are an off-shoot of the subculture's social and political philosophy — a complex pro-military veteran, national socialist and, yet, male libertarian value system. To grasp the ideology of the one-percent motorcyclist, McBee believes it is important to understand "the conservative ascendency" of the Post World War II period. For example, in 1965, eighteen members of the HAMC's Oakland chapter attempted to disrupt an anti-Vietnam War protest with force. Some journalists were perplexed that the bearded, disheveled bikers — a group that certainly looked the part of an anti-establishment organization — would endeavor to harm members of the counterculture. The Hells Angels, however, perceived the protestors as weak-kneed cowards, a character trait antithetical to the masculinity of outlaw bikers.[14]

Since the late 1940s, OMGs have adopted an Aryan philosophy that has resulted in a "convergent evolution, where the bikers and white supremacist independently adopted similar symbols or customs." One-percent biker organizations and white supremacist groups also share a similar lexicon and often recruit from comparable membership pools. In many instances, the rules of one-percent clubs specifically prohibit African-Americans from becoming members. For example, while a previous Outlaws Motorcycle Club's National Constitution noted that, "All members must be white...," the bylaws of the Hells Angels state that "no niggers in the club."[15]

How one-percent clubs communicate is consistent with the shadowy nature of the subculture. Discussing a club's business with outsiders, especially as it relates to unlawful activity, is usually forbidden by organizational bylaws. The success of an OMG stems, in part, from its ability to stonewall investigations and to retaliate against those who pursue some type of action against the club and/or its members. An outlaw motorcycle club's capability to intimidate victims, witnesses, and even the police, is described by Barker as "the power of the patch." Unlike the secret societies of La Cosa Nostra, the clout wielded by an OMG emanates from its visibility; though, similar to LCN groups, one-percent motorcycle clubs understand the importance of *omerta* or silence, especially as it relates to criminal activity. Many outlaw bikers believe, although sometimes mistakenly, that the chances of law enforcement permeating a tight-knit club are grim. "We can't be infiltrated," said Sonny Barger, the former national President of the HAMC. "No cops can get inside of us, they don't have the resources, the manpower or the time to wait. We're unbeatable and untouchable."[16]

Wolf equates the one-percent culture's restrictive communication strategy to "the precision of a paramilitary organization" that only discusses business on a need-to-know basis. As such, club members turn to "each other for help" and "protect themselves with a rigid code of silence." When the code of silence is broken or when the power of the patch fails to deter individuals from coming forward, OMGs sometimes retaliate. One example is the 1977 slayings of four people in Gaston, Oregon. A year earlier, a twenty-three-year-old former prostitute, Margo Compton, testified against HAMC member Otis "Buck" Garrett, who was later convicted of operating a San Francisco brothel. After the trial, an HAMC associate hunted down the former witness. Before she was shot to death, Compton was bound and forced to watch as a nineteen-year-old friend and her six-year-old twin daughters were each shot in the head, execution style. This research will spotlight the significance of the code of silence in the one-percent subculture and will show what occurs when this particular aspect of the biker honor system is violated.[17]

Understanding the code of silence, as well as other cultural forms of outlaw biker communications, is important when contemplating the vast, internationality of one-percent clubs. By the early 1980s, several OMGs had established an overseas presence. While the politics of OMG chapters is primarily local, three of the big-four clubs — the Hells Angels, the Outlaws, and the Bandidos — are multinational organizations. Smaller one-percent clubs, such as the Mongols, Warlocks, Vagos, and Sons of Silence, are also engaged in organized crime on a global scale. As of 2010, seven American-based OMGs had a total of four hundred and eighty-four chapters outside of the United States. While the Italian crime families of *La Cosa Nostra*, the Russian mafia, and the El Salvadorian-based *Mara Salvatrucha* (MS-13) are foreign imports, OMGs are America's sole organized crime export. For example, the Outlaws Motorcycle Club (OMC) has chapters in Canada, Russia, Australia, Japan, Thailand, the Philippines, and throughout Europe. Due to the mobility of the Outlaws Motorcycle Club, the locations of their various chapters, and the national rallies members attend, this research will, on occasion, step outside the geographical scope contained within its title.[18]

Conflict between law enforcement and outlaw bikers, as well as the government's response to OMGs, is also a component of this research. Gary Keiffner, a professor of Ethics and Governance at Fiji National University, has called the tactics and methods of law enforcement as they pertain to motorcyclists "discrimination." Keiffner specifically cites the 1977 death of Roger Lyons, a member of the OMC's Milwaukee chapter, who, he purports, was beaten "to death with billie-clubs [sic] and boots" during his arrest by Milwaukee police. This book will discuss the Lyons' case in detail; however, the biker's death was probed by an aggressive district attorney in front of an inquest jury, whose findings concerning probable suspects were inconclusive. Keiffner also failed to put the existing tensions between the OMC and the Milwaukee Police Department in their proper context, which gives the impression that the Lyons' affair occurred in a vacuum. Furthermore, this research will, in part, counter Dulaney's assertion that many of the government's perceptions of outlaw motorcycle clubs are "urban legends" or "unsubstantiated absurdities," and will challenge Kieffner's premise of a broad brush of police harassment as it relates to one-percent clubs. Barker's research spotlights the evolution of outlaw biker enforcement by local, state and federal officials, which has significantly improved since the mysterious 1964 arrival of the OMC in Milwaukee.[19]

The Transformative Years

From the late-1950s through the early 1970s, outlaw motorcycle clubs gradually transformed from a collection of rogue bikers to organized criminal enterprises. During this period, the one-percent mentality quickly migrated from the west coast to America's heartland. Similar to events after World War II, some returning Vietnam-era combat veterans found themselves drawn to the biker subculture. Believing that their military service was being intentionally marginalized by anti-war protestors, these veterans took solace in the brotherhood offered by other righteous bikers.[20]

As the membership rolls changed, so did the image of outlaw clubs. Four years after the formation of the One-Percent Brotherhood of Outlaw Clubs (OPBOC), the one-percent subculture once again captured the attention of high-level government officials. In 1964, four members of the Hells Angels' (HAMC) Oakland chapter — C.H. Cross, Marvin W. Gilbert, John T. Tracy, and James T. Miles — were arrested and later charged with raping two teenaged-girls. The alleged attack occurred on a Monterey, California beach after a Labor Day weekend racing rally. The girls were subsequently examined by Dr. Earl J. Kolb, who "found no evidence of sexual assault." Due to a lack of physical evidence corroborating the allegations, Deputy District Attorney Ralph Drummond dismissed the charges. However, the ensuing media attention, as well as the declaration by Monterey's police chief, Frank Marinello, that the Hells Angels were no longer welcome in town, resulted in a political firestorm.[21]

After State Senator Fred Farr demanded an inquiry of "outlaw motorcycle clubs," California's attorney general, Thomas C. Lynch, ordered a statewide investigation. Less than a year later, the California Department of Justice released its findings. Dubbed the "Lynch Report," the attorney general's review indicated that the state was home to a thousand outlaw bikers who had participated in the crimes of robbery, car theft, forgery and narcotics trafficking. The attorney general's office also distributed a list of known outlaws to law enforcement agencies. To its credit, the Lynch Report made an effort to differentiate rogue riders from the members of the AMA, and duly noted that the individuals included in the document were "not typical of the average motorcycle rider in California." Nevertheless, William Dulaney, a critic of the government's classification of motorcycle clubs as gangs, noted that the Lynch Report "can be seen as the first large-scale bureaucratic attempt to portray motorcycle clubs as a clear and present danger to local, state, and ultimately international constituencies."[22]

While the media coverage associated with the Lynch Report caught the attention of law enforcement nationally, two other major incidents raised the criminal profile of one-percent clubs. The first episode transpired on a balmy November evening in 1967, when eighteen-year-old Christine Deese appeared at a West Palm Beach, Florida hospital emergency room. Medical personnel found the young woman's explanation for the puncture wounds to her hands dubious and contacted the police. Initially, Deese told investigators that she had fallen on a wooden plank, but soon admitted that her boyfriend, James "Spider" Owings, had inflicted the injuries as punishment. Having had refused to prostitute herself and turn over the proceeds by sundown, several members of the Outlaws Motorcycle Club drove four-inch spikes through Deese's palms and nailed the five-foot-six-inch, one-hundred and thirty-five pound woman to a tree. The shocking crime made national headlines.[23]

The second incident took place at a pubic venue and resulted in significantly more coverage in the mainstream press. On December 6, 1969, the Rolling Stones retained several members of the Hells Angels — for $500 in free beer — to provide security during the Altamont free concert. The HAMC members, some of whom appeared intoxicated, at times used pool sticks to beat back the crowd. During a set by the rock band, Jefferson Airplane, several members of the HAMC began "beating and stomping perceived troublemakers." Musician, Marty Balin, jumped from the stage in an effort to stop the attacks on the crowd but was knocked unconscious. After an hour break, the concert resumed and the members of the HAMC reappeared. A short time later, the bikers observed an eighteen-year-old African-American man, Meredith Hunter, in the company of a white woman. Some members of the HAMC jumped from the stage and began beating Hunter, who brandished a handgun. While being disarmed, Hunter was beaten and stabbed to death.[24]

McBee argues that members of the HAMC were extremely overzealous and that "the violence at Altamont left an indelible mark on the public perceptions of the counterculture," while the death of Hunter brought "the importance of race to understanding motorcycling and its relationship to the black community." Dulaney, on the other hand, minimized the conduct of the Hells Angels at Altamont by lending credence to a statement made by Sonny Barger, who claimed that Hunter had shot an HAMC member. Barger did not witness the club's confrontation with Hunter and the biker with the enigmatic gunshot wound has never materialized. Barker strongly aligns with McBee and concludes, "The true viciousness of the Hells Angels was also exposed that day at Altamont."[25]

When coupled with the Lynch Report, the two high-profile crimes, committed by different one-percent clubs on opposite ends of the country, became the impetus for the government's use of the outlaw motorcycle gang (OMG) idiom. However, an actual "working definition" of OMGs was not formalized until the 1987 International Outlaw Motorcycle Gang Investigators Association (IOMGIA) conference, which reads, in part:

> A group of individuals who have formed as an association based on the riding of large motorcycles, have developed a unique insignia of membership and are documented as engaging in one or more of the following activities shall be deemed sufficient for the group's designation as an "outlaw motorcycle gang.

The "activities," as noted above, include any actions or the threat of any action pertaining to the crimes of murder, arson, kidnapping, gambling, extortion, robbery, drug trafficking, and the broad area of "dealing in obscene matters," punishable by at least one year in prison.[26]

As motorcycle club violence made headlines in the mid-to-late 1960s, premier one-percent motorcycle groups carved the nation into geographic spheres of influence. Originally a citizen biker club, the Pagans MC (PMC) was formed by Lou Dobkins, a biochemist at the National Institute for Health, in Prince George's County, Maryland. Within the span of seven years, the PMC had evolved into a secretive one-percent club with ties to east coast La Cosa Nostra groups. Another outlaw club, the Bandidos, led by former Vietnam veteran, Donald Eugene Chambers, grew to prominence from its humble beginnings in Houston, Texas. Law enforcement sources familiar with the Bandidos believe Chambers formed the club to control the Lone Star State's drug trafficking and prostitution rackets. Together, the Hells Angels, the Outlaws, the Pagans and the Bandidos motorcycle clubs are considered "the largest and most consistently radical of all 1% clubs," and are commonly referred to as the "big four." Barker asserts that another one-percent motorcycle club, the Sons of Silence (SOS), has created a paradigm shift to a "big five." Established in Niwot, Colorado by U.S. Navy veteran Bruce Richardson in 1966, the SOS began as a citizen social club. When the SOS morphed into a "criminal gang," Richardson exited the group, which currently has chapters in thirty states.[27]

Each OMG has its own club insignia. The Outlaw Motorcycle Club's skull and pistons character is nicknamed "Charlie." The Bandidos emblem — a Hispanic man wearing a sombrero and pointing a revolver — is known as the "Fat Mexican"; The Hells Angels' crest, the "Death Head," has been trademarked by the club; while the Pagans' logo incorporates the Norse fire-giant, Surtr.[28]

As the big four clubs staked their geographical claims, competition with other motorcycle groups resulted in conflicts that were typically resolved at the local or state level. On March 6, 1971, one-hundred and fifty members of the Breed Motorcycle Club and thirty members of a fledging chapter of the Hells Angels became involved in a large scale riot at Cleveland's Motorcycle Custom and Trade Show. The confrontation started when Breed members gathered around three custom motorcycles that the Hells Angels had on display. Someone in the crowd yelled "Now!" and the fight was on. "We didn't know where to turn," said Patrolmen Thomas Burton, who was inside the convention hall when the fight broke out. "We just started clobbering everybody." Over one-hundred and fifty police officers were summoned to the scene and "tear gas was used to break up the mob." When the chaos ended, three Breed members — Bruce Emerick, Thomas Terry, and Andrew Demeter — and two members of the HAMC —Emelio Gardull and Jeffrey Coffey — had succumbed to stab wounds.[29]

Sixteen months later, an argument over a stolen motorcycle led to a highway shootout between members of the Storm Troopers and Pagans motorcycle clubs in Durham, North Carolina. Sheriff Marvin Davis told the press that members of the Storm Troopers "set up" the gun battle that occurred on I-85. A witness to the incident, Rush Paula Roebuck, told authorities that the Pagans were riding in a van, which was spotted by members of the Storm Troopers. When the van stopped, three Storm Troopers jumped from the bed of a pickup truck and opened fire. "It sounded like machine guns," said Roebuck. "Once they started shooting, they just didn't stop." Pagans' members, Lance Burger and Thomas Cruggs, both from Florida, died in the shootout that left four others wounded. Within eighteen months of the shooting, the Storm Troopers dropped their clubs' patch and became the Hells Angels' Durham chapter.[30]

In the midst of this transitional phase within the one-percent subculture, which occurred from the late-1950s through the mid-1970s, the Outlaws Motorcycle Club (OMC) established a presence in Wisconsin. As Dr. Randy McBee notes: "Much of what has been written about motorcyclists is not from academics. There is some good material that is often asking interesting questions but it doesn't approach the material in the same way that a historian would approach it." Although a handful of historians have researched the outlaw bikers, the activities of Wisconsin's only major OMG — the Outlaws Motorcycle Club — has, at least from an historical perspective, gone virtually unnoticed. From this point forward, primary sources will be used to shakeout the history of the OMC in the Badger State. [31]

[1] Barker, *Biker Gangs and Organized Crime*, 65-72.

[2] Daniel Wolf, *The Rebels: A Brotherhood of Outlaw Bikers* (Toronto: University of Toronto Press, 1991), 66, 88-89, 110; Barker, *Biker Gangs and Organized Crime*, 68.

[3] Ibid, Barker, 61, 68; Wolf, *The Rebels: A Brotherhood of Outlaw Bikers*, 111.

[4] William Lee Dulaney, "Over the Edge and Into the Abyss: The Communication of Organizational Identity in an Outlaw Motorcycle Club" (Ph.D. diss., Florida State University, 2006), 67, 69, 70-71.

[5] Ibid., 159; Wolf, *The Rebels: A Brotherhood of Outlaw Bikers*; 118; Larry Powalisz, retired Milwaukee Police Department detective, e-mail message to author, December 30, 2014.

[6] Powalisz, e-mail message to author, September 15, 2014.

[7] *Shepherd Express Metro* (Milwaukee), February 24, 2000, p. 14; Northwestern University Traffic Institute, 14-16.

[8] Wolf, *The Rebels: A Brotherhood of Outlaw Bikers*, 276-277; *Milwaukee Sentinel*, May 7, 1980, p. 5; Black Pistons Motorcycle Club, Bi-Laws/Rules, April 2004 (held by author).

[9] Columbus Hopper and Johnny Moore, "Women in Outlaw Motorcycle Gangs," *Journal of Contemporary Ethnography*, 18 (January 1990): 363-387.

[10] Ibid., 373.

[11] Northwestern University Traffic Institute, 11, Wolf, *The Rebels: A Brotherhood of Outlaw Bikers*, 137.

[12] Hopper and Moore, *Journal of Contemporary Ethnography*, 372-379.

[13] Northwestern University Traffic Institute, 12; Wolf, *The Rebels: A Brotherhood of Outlaw Bikers*, 138, 140, 156.

[14] McBee, *Born to Be Wild*, 194.

[15] "Bigots of Bikes: The Growing Links between White Supremacist Groups and Biker Gangs," *Anti-Defamation League*, September 2011 (held by author); American Outlaws Association, National Constitution, Bylaw Number One, 1981(held by author); H.A.MC. World Rules, Frisco, Rule adopted on August 3, 1986 (held by author).

[16] Barker, *Outlaw Motorcycle Gangs as an Organized Crime Group*, 45; Kerrie Droban, *Running with the Devil: The True Story of ATF's Infiltration of the Hells Angels* (Guilford, CT: The Lyons Press, 2007), inside cover.

[17] *Eugene Register*, July 22, 1994, p. 3C; Wolf, *The Rebels: A Brotherhood of Outlaw Bikers*, 9.

[18] Tom Barker, "American Based Biker Gangs: International Organized Crime," *American Journal of Criminal Justice* (January 2011), 208, 212.

[19] Dulaney, "A Brief History of "Outlaw" Motorcycle Clubs," 7; Gary L. Kieffner,

"Police and Harley Riders: Discrimination and Empowerment," *International Journal of Motorcycle Studies*, Vol. 5, Issue 1 (Spring 2009), 1; Barker, *Biker Gangs and Organized Crime*, 100-103; Gary L. Kieffner, "Riding the Borderlands: The Negotiation of Social and Cultural Boundries for Rio Grande Valley and Southwestern Motorcycling Groups" (Ph.D. diss., University of Texas – El Paso, 2009), 215.

[20]Dulaney, "A Brief History of "Outlaw" Motorcycle Clubs," 6.

[21]*The Fresno Bee Republican*, September 27, 1964, p. 19.

[22]*New York Times*, March 16, 1965, p. 15; William Dulaney, "A Brief History of "Outlaw" Motorcycle Clubs," 7.

[23]Barker, *Biker Gangs and Organized Crime*, 39; McBee, *Born to Be Wild*, 228-229; Dulaney, "A Brief History of "Outlaw" Motorcycle Clubs," 8.

[24]Barker, *Biker Gangs and Organized Crime*, 39-40; McBee, *Born to Be Wild*, 226-227.

[25]Barker, *Biker Gangs and Organized Crime*, 39; McBee, *Born to Be Wild*, 228-229; Dulaney, "A Brief History of "Outlaw" Motorcycle Clubs," 8.

[26]Northwestern University Traffic Institute, 2, 25.

[27]Dulaney, "A Brief History of "Outlaw" Motorcycle Clubs," 8; *Barker, Biker Gangs and Organized Crime*, 78-81; James F. Quinn, "Angels, Badidos, Outlaws and Pagans: An Evolution of Organized Crime Among the Big Four 1% Motorcycle Clubs," *Deviant Behavior*, Vol. 22, Issue 4 (2001): 379-390; Thomas Barker, *Outlaw Motorcycle Gangs as Organized Crime Groups*, 32.

[28]Alex Caine, *The Fat Mexican: The Bloody Rise of the Bandidos Motorcycle Club* (New York: Random House, 2009), 178; Stephen L. Mallory, *Understanding Organized Crime* (Sudbury, MA: Jones & Bartlett Learning, 2007), 158.

[29]*Milwaukee Journal*, March 8, 1971, p. 11.

[30]*Star-News* (Wilmington, NC), July 3, 1972, p. 3B; Barker, *Biker Gangs and Organized Crime*, 9.

[31]Dr. Randy D. McBee, Professor of History, Texas Tech University, e-mail message to author, June 30, 2015.

CHAPTER THREE

ARRIVAL OF THE OUTLAWS
MOTORCYCLE CLUB IN WISCONSIN

On a hot summer weekend in August 1964, hundreds of motorcycle enthusiasts gathered in Springfield, Illinois for the city's annual motor races. Three of the groups present — the Chicago-based Outlaws Motorcycle Club, and the Milwaukee and Louisville Gypsy Outlaws Motorcycle Clubs — emerged from a meeting as the newly formed Outlaws Nation. A year later, the American Outlaws Association (AOA) was established and, within a matter of months, OMC chapters were formed in the Midwest and the south.[1]

The OMC's Milwaukee chapter was founded by three brothers — James, John, and Joseph Bisenius — from nearby West Allis. "We took all the hell-raisers in Milwaukee and put them into one club, the best," said John Bisenius, who explained the club rule as, "You gotta be dirty."[2]

The Bisenius brothers made news in 1966 after James, who had just been freed on bail for a weapons offense, was arrested for kissing his brother, John, in a waiting room at the Milwaukee County Safety Building. The incident made national headlines. An article that traversed the wires of United Press International told of "cynical old policemen" shaking their heads at the decadence. "One of the [Outlaws] visitors wore an old Wehrmacht helmet. Two had gold earrings," and the bikers' belts were "fashioned from motorcycle chains, which police said could be "whipped free in an instant and used as five pound clubs." The kissing antics, said James Bisenius, were intended to make a statement. "We are fighting society and that's what we want."[3]

Enforcing the law in a manner consistent with the norms and mores of this period, Circuit Court Judge Ryan Duffy, Jr. later ruled that two brothers kissing in the office of the district attorney constituted disorderly conduct and ordered the two men to pay $100 fines.[4]

During the 1970s, the OMC's Milwaukee chapter embarked on a campaign of dominance and control over rival Wisconsin motorcycle clubs. The majority of smaller one-percent groups either fell into line or dropped their club's patch. However, one motorcycle club, the Heaven's Devils MC, refused to acquiesce to the Outlaw's demands. For the better part of a decade, the OMC's Milwaukee chapter embraced a strategy of violence and intimidation against the Heaven's Devils. By the early 1980s, these heavy-handed tactics had marginalized and/or eliminated the OMC's Wisconsin-based rivals and culminated in the deaths of nearly a dozen people. In the ruthless world of outlaw bikers, the OMC's Milwaukee chapter became known as the "Wrecking Crew."[5]

The Milwaukee Police and the OMC

Four months prior to the formation of the Outlaw Motorcycle Club's Milwaukee chapter, fifty-three-year-old Harold Breier became the Milwaukee Police Department's twelfth police chief. Breier was a gruff, rough-around-the-edges autocrat, whose tactics often drew the wrath of the city's growing African-American community. The mentality of the police chief, a man who had walked his first beat prior to the Japanese attack on Pearl Harbor, was an outgrowth of his intrepid reputation as a street officer.[6]

Considered a "crack marksmen," Breier was promoted to detective in 1946. At the time, Milwaukee factories, such as Briggs & Stratton, Allen Bradley, Allis-Chalmers, Master Lock, and Harley-Davidson, produced many of the world's iconic products; however, the highly industrialized city also had a seedy underside. In September, Police Chief John Polczyn warned the Common Council the crime was escalating and asked for an additional fourteen patrolmen and four detectives. "Auto thefts have trebled over last year," Polczyn told the city's alders, while burglaries had doubled. During this period, Milwaukee also experienced significant labor strife as unions flexed their post-war muscles, which, in several instances, resulted in police officers monitoring the picket lines.[7]

After eight years of tracking down car thieves and investigating robberies, Breier began ascending through the ranks and, by 1960, had risen to Inspector of Detectives. Although he had previously shot a suspect in the line of duty, an incident during the July Fourth weekend in 1963 lent a certain credence to Breier's law-and-order image.[8]

In late June, twenty-two-year-old Michael Weston had escaped from a Wisconsin correctional facility in Williams Bay, a rural community fifty-two miles southwest of Milwaukee. Using a false identity, Weston rented a room above the Tee Pee Inn, a neighborhood tavern near S. 1st and W. Mitchell Streets on the city's south side. Short on cash, the convict obtained a pistol from an acquaintance and soon turned the gun on Susan Milligan, a nineteen-year-old mother of two. When Weston demanded money, Milligan fled and ran into a car occupied by Theodore Adams and Susan Curro. Weston then ordered Milligan from the car at gun point, slapped the woman, and demanded ten dollars. When Adams stepped from the car and intervened, Weston shot-and-killed the nineteen-year-old Good Samaritan.[9]

Six hours later, as an estimated 250,000 people lined Milwaukee's downtown streets for the Day in Old Milwaukee Circus Parade, a detective received a call from an informant, who had observed a man matching Weston's description enter the East Sider tavern, located on the corner of N. Farwell Avenue and E. Brady Street, just two miles north of the parade route. With over fifty officers on the lookout for Weston, Breier tasked himself and Detective Sergeant Edwin Shaffer with the fugitive's apprehension. After entering the tavern, the two officers observed the wanted man, who then pointed a gun in their direction. Breier and Shaffer both opened fire. Weston survived the shooting and later confessed to three other armed robberies.[10]

Touted by the media, Breier's fearlessness became an overnight sensation. *Milwaukee Sentinel* reporter James G. Wieghart chronicled the run-in with the killer fugitive in an article titled *Capture Proves Breier's Theory*, which echoed the Detective Inspector's credo: "Don't ask an officer to do anything that you are afraid to do yourself." Less than a year later, Police Chief Howard Johnson announced his retirement and Breier was selected for the MPD's top job from a pool of sixty-three highly qualified candidates.[11]

Even after his promotion to chief of police, Breier refused to set aside his patrol officer's cap. On December 23, 1965, the police chief and Deputy Inspector Charles Jackelen were on their way to lunch when a dispatcher radioed about a possible hold-up in progress in the 1400 block of W. Fond du Lac Avenue. Just two blocks away, Breier and the deputy inspector were the first officers to arrive. "I went the front [of the building]," Breier told the press. "I saw a colored man standing to the right with a bloody butcher knife. I told him to put his hands up and come out." Instead, the suspect called the chief "a dirty name" and threw the knife at Breier, who later shot and wounded the man. When asked about his "feelings" concerning the incident, the chief replied, "I've shot three people. I still don't know how I feel."[12]

In short order, the police chief's fearless reputation became an interwoven component of the Milwaukee Police Department's institutional persona. "There was some speculation," noted retired MPD homicide lieutenant Steve Spingola, "that Chief Breier was the impetus for Clint Eastwood's Dirty Harry character. After all, they had the same first name, shared a similar rank, and both shot robbery suspects."[13]

As the nation embarked on an era of significant social and political upheaval, Breier assigned those who shared his us-against-them management style to key positions, including the Special Assignment Squad (SAS). During the mid-1960s, Milwaukee's civil rights movement had gathered momentum and began a four-year battle to wipe away the city's segregated housing practices. East of the Milwaukee River, a vocal counterculture had gained a foothold in the Brady Street neighborhood. Following the lead of FBI Director J. Edgar Hoover's Counterintelligence Program (COINTELPRO), Breier expanded the SAS. Christened the Red Squad by its critics, the Special Assignment Squad was "formed to investigate organized crime and subversive activities."[14]

In the mid-1960s, the SAS declined to classify the Outlaws as an organized crime group. Instead, the OMC was simply seen as a group of rowdy, pro-military veteran bikers that did little to challenge the city's political status quo. While the SAS maintained an archive on one-percent motorcycle clubs, the unit's primary focus was *La Cosa Nostra*, new left organizations, and the Black Panthers. As a result, the OMC was immune from any repercussions related to long-term surveillance.[15]

Although the new commander of the MPD's Special Assignment Squad, Captain Edward Reitz, did not perceive the OMC as an organized crime outfit, Breier later ordered a newly formed Tactical Enforcement Unit (TEU) to keep tabs on the club. Born as a response to the social turbulence of the 1960s, the TEU became known as the "seven-hundreds," a designation that corresponded to the units' squad numbers. In the aftermath of a large scale, north side riot, the TEU became the nation's first full-time special weapons and tactics division.[16]

While street toughs, civil rights advocates, counterculture types, and outlaw bikers, roundly denounced the special weapons and tactics squad as oppressive and heavy-handed, the TEU's reputation for crime suppression was well-known in local law enforcement circles. Rank-and-file officers were also aware that the TEU and the SAS had the backing of the chief of police. In the halls of the MPD, members of these two units were referred to as "Breier's boys." Although the police chief publicly denied that organized crime existed in Milwaukee, the TEU' was tasked with keeping tabs on the activities of the Outlaws Motorcycle Club.[17]

Miller's Charge

Over two years passed before the Outlaws Motorcycle Club's Milwaukee chapter established a permanent clubhouse. In the interim, the bikers staked their claims to a handful of neighborhood taverns. The Outlaws were particularly concerned about the TEU's street leader, Sergeant Frank Miller, who some "regarded as one of the most ruthless members of the Milwaukee Police Department." In the late 1960s and early 1970s, Sergeant Miller and the TEU diligently worked to tap down threats to public order. Regardless of a group's racial or ethnic composition, real or perceived societal malcontents where greeted with an equal dose of Miller-time enforcement actions.[18]

During the racially tumultuous summer of 1967, Miller's TEU officers escorted a group of NAACP protestors from a raucous south side open housing march to the Freedom House, a residential building at 1316 N. 15th Street. The old wooden structure served as a rallying place for Father James Groppi and the NAACP's Youth Council. After demonstrators smash the windshield of a squad car, Miller directed officers to fire tear gas canisters towards the dwelling. Miller later told the press that the occupants of a white Chevrolet had tossed a firebomb into the Freedom House and that the home subsequently burst into flames. The sergeant's critics, however, were skeptical. Just prior to the start of the fire, police officers "herded" the news media from the block. Another journalist, Stuart A. Wilk, a twenty-year-old reporter for the *Milwaukee Sentinel* who had defied the ban, was arrested for "gathering information" about the civil rights rally.[19]

Three years later, another incident on city's east side cemented the image of the TEU's street leader. Near the latter part of June 1970, administrators at St. Mary's Hospital complained that throngs of hippies, who had gathered at all hours of the night in nearby Water Tower Park, had upset "patients and staff" at the facility, which had yet to be outfitted with air conditioning. Responding to the hospital's concerns, the Common Council passed an ordinance to close the park at 10 p.m. A few weeks later, a city crew posted a "Park Closed at 10 p.m." sign, but members of the counterculture were in no mood to comply.[20]

On July 13, Milwaukee police, determined to enforce the new ordinance, waded into the park at 10:20 p.m. and began dispersing the crowd. The ensuing confrontation resulted in "six police officers and two newsmen" being injured. The occupants of the park who had stood their ground also paid a price. The damaged caused by club-wielding officers quickly filled St. Mary's emergency room. As police moved the crowd of three hundred people down Lincoln Memorial Drive, the flower children vowed to return and stake a claim to the park after hours.[21]

On the evening of July 14, reinforced by radical Yippies, the park's occupants tore down the "Park Closed" sign. This time around, the police came ready for battle. The TEU's street leader mustered his helmet-clad troops at the park's North Avenue entrance. A few seconds after ten, Miller screamed "charge" and scores of police officers chased the rabble down a steep hill towards Lake Michigan. An editorial in the *Milwaukee Sentinel* ripped the protestors for their "defiant attitude" and chided the multitude of gawkers. "If every hippie in town owned a car and drove it passed the Water Tower, there wouldn't have been that big" of a traffic jam. Another editorial, which appeared in left-of-center *Milwaukee Journal*, declared that Miller's "charge" was akin to tossing fuel on a smoldering fire.[22]

Although a high-ranking member of the MPD's command staff was present at Water Tower Park, the officers present knew that Miller was running the show. "I was standing next to the inspector on duty when Sergeant Miller decided and declared that it was time to jump off," former patrolman Randall Miller noted. "I don't remember the inspector's name but the look on his face, when he realized that he was not (and never was) in charge, was priceless."[23]

From the counterculture's perspective, Sergeant Miller was public enemy number one. A year earlier, the underground newspaper *Kaleidoscope* had printed a "Wanted" poster of Miller that figuratively charged the sergeant with the "suppression of free speech," a "conspiracy to violate the civil rights of Black People and other minority groups," and a "general inability to function as a feeling member of the Human Race." Within a week, copies of the "Wanted" poster began appearing inside anti-establishment venues.[24]

The enthusiasm exhibited by TEU officers during Miller's "charge" was likely fueled by a different issue of *Kaleidoscope*. Four months earlier, the radical newspaper had printed the names and addresses of MPD officers assigned to the TEU, the SAS, and the vice squad. On the same philosophical-page as Miller, the police chief had the sergeant's back. Miller's critics "...didn't know what the hell they were talking about," Breier later told a reporter. "They wanted law enforcement and yet they didn't want law enforcement."[25]

Sooner or later, any radical groups seeking to establish a base of operations in Milwaukee would find themselves engaged in a battle of wills with the city's tough-as-nails police chief and the high profile sergeant in-charge of the Tactical Enforcement Unit.

The Outlaws and the City Limits

Prior to the formation of the TEU, Sergeant Miller used all of the tools regularly at his disposal to keep the Outlaws Motorcycle Club in check. On January 7, 1966, the sergeant, then a member of the MPD's vice squad, paid a visit to the Seaway, a bar located in an isolated industrial area of S. Water Street. The tavern, Miller learned, had morphed into the OMC's unofficial clubhouse. As bartender Edward J. Steele was being cited for selling beer to a minor, an officer observed an obscene statue on top of a refrigerator, which was confiscated as evidence. Four days later, the Seaway's owner, thirty-six-year-old Vincent R. Kozmut, was charged with possessing obscene materials. Believing that the club was under intense surveillance by MPD, the Outlaws declined to wear their colors while riding Milwaukee.[26]

Seeking to avoid Miller's long-arm of the law, members of the OMC's Milwaukee chapter frequented venues outside city limits. During the 1966 Memorial Day weekend, fifty-five Outlaws invaded a Mukwonago racetrack. After causing property damage, the bikers left the event, visited a local gas station, and fueled their motorcycles without paying. While this incident was non-violent, a perception of the OMC as bullies on bikes emerged. With one-percent bikers increasingly in the news, Waukesha Daily Freeman reporter Bob Hull sought to enlighten the public in an article titled, *"Advice to Talking to Cyclists: It's not Wise to Mention 'Outlaws.'"*[27]

Nine months later, the OMC sought to establish a makeshift clubhouse at 2024-A N. 3rd Street. Within the span of a month, a handful of complaints made their way to the MPD's District Five station, the temporary work location of the recently transferred Frank Miller. In response, the captain of the police district asked the City of Milwaukee Health Department to inspect the dwelling. Two officers accompanied the Health Department's inspector and discovered a "girl" living at the residence, who was summarily arrested for "city ordinance violations."[28]

On New Year's Eve, the Third Street clubhouse — a "one story faded yellow bungalow" that stood behind another small home on the same lot — was the scene of a large scale disturbance, which resulted in the arrests of eleven OMC members. The following day, Milwaukee's first mysterious fire of 1967 gutted the home. Milwaukee Fire Department Battalion Commander George Boyce reported that no one was present when fire crews arrived. At about the same time, however, first responders were sent to the Port Bowl, locate at 3900 N. Port Washington Road, where members of the OMC where holding another large party.[29]

"The smoldering remains of a sofa lay in the yard near the [club] house," wrote *Milwaukee Sentinel* reporter Steve Buggs, and "several piles of rubbish and beer cans and bottles were strewn around outside." After making his way inside the fire scene, the reporter observed a few dilapidated chairs and an old table. "The walls in one room were covered with designs and slogans" and plaster had been liberated from the walls in "several places." A photograph in the *Milwaukee Sentinel* spotlighted the filthy conditions. Garbage was stacked under the kitchen sink, a rickety sign had been altered to read "Outlaws Welcome," and a swastika rested against a wall.[30]

According to Miller, the clubhouse had been "under surveillance" since the Outlaws had moved into the home in October. Neighbors, fearful of retaliation, "were reluctant to talk [to a reporter] about the Outlaws and the activities at the house." One area resident said that members of the club are at the home every night and host parties on the weekends that last into the wee hours of the morning. Over the course of the New Year's weekend, the activities of the Outlaws had generated four calls for police service.[31]

Lacking a clubhouse, the OMC's Milwaukee chapter, once again, became somewhat nomadic. Just four months after the Third Street fire, Judge Ronald Drechsler — acting on a complaint from the City of Franklin's mayor — granted a temporary restraining order that prohibited members of the Outlaws from entering taverns in the Milwaukee suburb. Then, over the Labor Day weekend, about fifty Outlaws and ten members of the Rebels MC were involved in a theft of chickens, which were subsequently slaughtered and barbecued at a Kettle Moraine State Forest campsite. As the party ebbed, several members of the Outlaws suggested that they have sexual relations with the wife of a Rebels' member and a fight resulted. The large scale brouhaha caused the Waukesha County Sheriff's Department's to deploy its multi-purpose, crowd-control vehicle for the first time.[32]

Outside the city's limits and away from Milwaukee's large police force, law enforcement agencies in suburban and rural areas lacked the necessary staffing to affect an action against a large group of outlaw bikers. In one instance, a twenty-five-year-old woman alleged that she was abducted from Milwaukee and taken to a Town of Dupont cheese factory in rural Waupaca County. During the February 3, 1968 party, investigators learned that members of the Outlaws had turned the abandoned food processing plant into a makeshift shooting range. For whatever reason, the bikers became upset with the woman and decided to lynch her. The OMC's leader, identified in the criminal complaint as Joseph Bisenius, interceded, allegedly told the woman that she "owed him a favor," and then asked her to perform an "indecent act." The woman told detectives that when she refused, she was assaulted, and then shot in the arm. The rape charge brought against Bisenius was later dropped after the complainant, who had moved to Texas, did not appear in court. In regards to the shooting, another defendant, twenty-nine-year-old Daniel J. Martin, entered a guilty plea and was sentenced to four-and-a-half years in prison.[33]

The widely publicized sexual assault allegation pulled back the veneer of the hard-partying, one-percent bikers. In response, the OMC reached out to the counterculture. In early 1968, an unnamed writer from *Kaleidoscope* interviewed members of the club. The anonymous author described the meeting as "a mind-expanding experience in itself." The writer traveled to "Pig's" (James Bisenius) apparent abode to discuss matters with the OMC's club president. The mood of the Outlaws' members present was described as "somber," due to the pending sexual assault allegations. "Comments [concerning the incident] began flying immediately," but, because of their "legal implications," the newspaper declined to print the remarks. The author, however, did mention that the Outlaws believed untraditional sexual relations with women affiliated with the club "are common knowledge, and no girl can plead ignorance."[34]

As the weather warmed and riding season began, James Bisenius' lawsuit concerning Wisconsin's helmet law was reviewed by Dane County Circuit Court Judge W.L. Jackman. The judge took issue with Bisenius' claim that a rule requiring motorcyclists to wear helmets constituted discrimination against those who ride motorcycles. "The operation of a motor vehicle on a public highway," said Jackman, "is not an unlimited constitutional right."[35]

With the helmet law giving Sergeant Miller's crew yet another reason to regulate the Outlaws, the club's weekend rides ventured into rural areas with a limited law enforcement presence. In mid-June, a hundred members of the OMC terrorized a group of Twin Cities' motorcycle enthusiasts in Wood County. After attending a rally in Wisconsin Rapids, the nine citizen bikers returned to a campground in Nekoosa only to find that members of the Outlaws' Milwaukee and Chicago chapters had started a large bonfire and set up kegs of beer. Initially, one of the citizen bikers' tents was set on fire. Then, after breaking into a car, a member of the OMC doused a sleeping bag with a flammable liquid, stared intently at the woman wrapped inside, and tossed a match onto the garment. "God must have been with me," the woman told reporter Cliff Miller, "because a lot of times, that zipper [to the sleeping bag] sticks, but it just ran down." Once outside, the woman observed members of the OMC placing objects that were ablaze on her tent. A group of Outlaws then grabbed the woman and passed her from member-to-member. In a rage, the woman's husband punched five OMC attackers. Two motorcycles owned by the couple were then seized and thrown into the bonfire. The victims complained that the police response was inadequate and ineffective.[36]

When Cultures Collide

Since their inceptions in the late 1940s, outlaw motorcycle gangs (OMGs) have adopted an Aryan philosophy. One-percent groups typically patronize low income, blue collar areas in close proximity to minority neighborhoods. As the 1968 riding season ebbed, the Outlaws Motorcycle Club's reception in the community was as unhospitable as its club's members. Besides the ominous presence of the TEU, the city's growing African-American population was encroaching on drinking establishments frequented by the renegade bikers. Although Milwaukee was one of the nation's most segregated cities, the OMC's racially divisive philosophy sometimes resulted in a clash of cultures that necessitated a police response.[37]

In the early 1960s, Milwaukee Alderwoman Vel Phillips sponsored a city ordinance to ban discriminatory housing practices. When other members of the Common Council and Mayor Henry Maier balked at the measure, the NAACP orchestrated a number of sit-ins. Three years later, Phillips and Father James Groppi — a white, Catholic priest — initiated a series of open housing marches that culminated in white neighborhoods. Groppi later formed the NAACP Youth Council Commandos. The group's leader, nineteen-year-old Dwight Benning, described the Commandos as "militant" and promised to "protect the rest of the youth council members on the picket line." In the summer of 1967, Milwaukee experienced a racially-charged riot that resulted in the deaths of four people, including one patrol officer. The disturbance stemmed, in large part, from redlining — a segregated housing practice that prohibited African-Americans from living west of the 27th Street corridor on the city's near north side. After the riot, racial tensions remained high, especially in areas located near the city's former redline.[38]

On September 29, 1968, two members of the OMC — Robert Spalda and James Harvestine — confronted a young black couple as they walked past the Peppermint Lounge, a biker hangout at 2821 W. North Avenue, a block-and-a-half west from the former red line. Eighteen-year-old James Isaac alleged that Spalda shoved him and then spit in his face. Spalda then entered the bar, returned with an ash tray, and struck Isaac with the object. Isaac told investigators that, after he was hit, Harvestine shouted, "Come on, let's get the nigger." Isaac fled on foot and then summoned the NAACP's Youth Council Commandos. Within a matter of twenty minutes, fifty Commandos arrived at the Peppermint Lounge and confronted thirty-five members of the OMC. The fracas caused nearly three dozen police officers to respond. After restoring order, Sergeant Frank Miller instructed TEU officers to escort the Outlaws from the area. Eight members of the Commandos and two Outlaws were arrested. Harvestine was later charged with disorderly conduct and Spalda with battery.[39]

In the aftermath of the racially charged incident, the OMC continued to frequent taverns on the north side and opted to open a small clubhouse near N. Hubbard Street, less than a mile from the Third Street fire. As the next decade emerged, and the development phase of the Outlaws Motorcycle Club came to close, the group's Milwaukee chapter evolved into the "Wrecking Crew," a moniker attributed to the group's ruthless endeavors. Besides competing with, and later subduing, other one-percent clubs, the OMC was on a collision course with the Milwaukee Police Department's resolute police chief.

[1]Barker, *Biker Gangs and Organized Crime,* 79-80

[2]*Milwaukee Sentinel,* May 6, 1980, p. 1; *The Daily Telegram* (Eau Claire, WI), January 10, 1966, p. 2.

[3]*The Lincoln Star* (Lincoln, NB), January 10, 1968, p. 6.

[4] *Milwaukee Sentinel,* May 6, 1980, p. 1; *The Daily Telegram* (Eau Claire, WI), January 10, 1966, p. 2; *Milwaukee Journal,* January 24, 1966, p. 2; Beverly V. Roberts, *American Bikers: The Flash Collection* (Birmingham, MI: Flash Production, LLC), 19.

[5]*Shepherd Express Metro* (Milwaukee), February 24, 2000, p. 13.

[6]Andrew Witt, *The Black Panthers in the Midwest* (New York: Taylor & Francis Group, 2007), 43; Steven Spingola, retired MPD homicide lieutenant, e-mail message to author, June 25, 2014.

[7]Gerald D. Kleczka, "In Memory Of Harold A. Breier, Former Milwaukee Chief of Police," September 11, 1998, *Capitol Words,* http://capitolwords.org/date/1998/09/11/ E1701-4_in-memory-of-harold-a-breier-former-milwaukee-chie/ (accessed May 6, 2016); *Milwaukee Journal,* August 1, 1946, Part 2, p. 1; Milwaukee Journal, September 13, 1946, Part 2, p. 1.

[8]Gerald D. Kleczka, "In Memory Of Harold A. Breier, Former Milwaukee Chief of Police," September 11, 1998, *Capitol Words,* http://capitolwords.org/date/1998/09/11/ E1701-4_in-memory-of-harold-a-breier-former-milwaukee-chie/ (accessed May 6, 2016).

[9]Steven Spingola, Best of the Spingola Files, Vol. 1 & 2 (Milwaukee: Badger Wordsmith, LLC, 2013), 72; *Milwaukee Journal,* September 13, 1946, Part 2, p. 1.

[10]Ibid, 72.

[11]*Milwaukee Sentinel,* July 5, 1964, p. 7; Steven Spingola, *Best of the Spingola Files, Vol. 1 & 2,* 72.

[12]*Milwaukee Sentinel,* December 24, 1965, pp. 1 and 3.

[13]Spingola, email to author, June 26, 2014.

[14]Patrick Jones, *The Selma of the North* (Cambridge: Harvard University Press, 2009), 97; *Milwaukee Journal,* July 8, 1968, Part 2, p. 1; Richard Gid Powers, *Secrecy and Power: The Life of J. Edgar Hoover* (New York: Free Press, 1987), 8; *Milwaukee Journal,* April 17, 1964, p. 4; Snyder, "Chief for Life: Harold Breier and His Era.," 30.

[15]Spingola, e-mail message to author, January 7, 2015; Charles Berard, Milwaukee Police Department Lieutenant, e-mail message to author, January 12, 2015; Witt, *The Black Panthers in the Midwest,* 54.

[16]Maralyn A, Wellauer-Lenius, *Milwaukee Police Department* (Chicago: Arcadia Publishing, 2008), 12.

[17]Powalisz, e-mail message to author, January 7, 2015; Spingola, e-mail message to author, February 9, 2015; Ibid., 15 June, 2014; *Milwaukee Sentinel,* October 13, 1975, p. 5.

[18]Berard, e-mail message to author, January 12, 2015; Witt, *The Black Panthers in the Midwest*, 44.

[19]*Milwaukee Sentinel*, August 31, 1967, pp. 1, 8, and 12.

[20]*Milwaukee Sentinel*, July 14, 1970, p. 1.

[21]*Milwaukee Sentinel*, July 14, 1970, p. 1; Mark Goff, "The East Side Erupted in Violence 45 Years Ago," *OnMilwaukee.com*, May 5, 2015, http://onmilwaukee.com/buzz/articles/1970watertowerpark.html (accessed May 20, 2015).

[22]Ibid., *Milwaukee Sentinel*, July 15, 1970, pp. 1 and 12.

[23]Randall Miller, *Facebook* post, May 21, 2016, https://www.facebook.com/steve.spingola/posts/1374254379256611?comment_id=1374309032584479&reply_comment_id=137 (held by author).

[24]*Kaleidoscope*, Volume 2, Number 5 and 6 (31), January 17, 1969, UWM Libraries Digital Collections and Initiatives, http://collections.lib.uwm.edu/cdm/compoundobject/collection/kal/id/2280/show/2249/rec/19 (accessed May 23, 2016).

[25]*Kaleidoscope*, Volume 2, Number 5 and 6 (31), January 17, 1969, UWM Libraries Digital Collections and Initiatives, http://collections.lib.uwm.edu/cdm/compoundobject/collection/kal/id/2280/show/2249/rec/19 (accessed May 23, 2016); *Kaleidoscope*, Volume 3, Number 2 (54), March 20,1970, UWM Libraries Digital Collections and Initiatives, http://collections.lib.uwm.edu/cdm/compoundobject/collection/kal/id/2226/show/2225/rec/3 (accessed May 23, 2016); *Milwaukee Sentinel*, August 26, 1994, p. 5A.

[26]*Milwaukee Journal*, January 11, 1966, p. 1; *Milwaukee Sentinel*, May 6, 1980, Part 1, p. 13.

[27]*Waukesha Daily Freeman*, May 1, 1966, p. 1; Ibid., June 7, 1966, p. 1.

[28]*Milwaukee Sentinel*, January 3, 1967, Part 1, p. 9.

[29]*Milwaukee Sentinel*, January 3, 1967, Part 1, p. 5.

[30]Ibid.

[31]Ibid.

[32]*Eau Claire Leader*, April 2, 1967, p. 1; *Waukesha Freeman*, September 5, 1967, p. 1.

[33]*State of Wisconsin vs. Joseph Michael Bisenius*, Criminal Complaint, Waupaca County, WI, February 6, 1968 (held by author); *Eau Claire Leader*, February 6, 1968, p. 2; *Milwaukee Journal*, August 11, 1968, p. 11; Ibid., February 20, 1968, p. 9.

[34]*Kaleidoscope*, Volume 1, Number 8, February 16, 1968, UWM Libraries Digital Collections and Initiatives, http://collections.lib.uwm.edu/cdm/compoundobject/collection/kal/id/1308/rec/20 (accessed May 24, 2016).

[35]*Manitowoc Herald-Times*, May 15, 1968, p. 10.

[36]*Appleton Post Crescent*, June 18, 1968, p. 4.

[37]Randy D. McBee, "A Potential Common Front": Hunter Thompson, the Hell's Angels, and Race in 1960s America," *International Journal of Motorcycle Studies*, Vol. I (July 2005), 1-3; Lloyd Barbee Papers, Racial Isolation in Milwaukee Public Schools, 1967, Box 96, Folder 7, University of Wisconsin – Milwaukee Libraries, Milwaukee, WI.

[38]Thompson, *The History of Wisconsin,* 378; Jones, *The Selma of the North,* 111; *Milwaukee Sentinel*, October 6, 1966, p. 5.; *Milwaukee Journal*, August 1, 1967, p. 1.

[39]*Milwaukee Journal*, September 30, 1968, Part 2, p. 1.

CHAPTER FOUR

OUTLAWS, INDIANS, AND ORGANIZED CRIME

The National Organized Crime Planning Council defines organized crime as "…those self-perpetuating, structured, and disciplined associations of individuals, or groups, combined together for the purpose of obtaining monetary or commercial gains or profits, whereby or in part by illegal means while protecting their activities through a pattern of graft or corruption." In the early 1970s, outlaw motorcycle gang investigators noticed that several one-percent clubs had made the transition from ruffian tormentors to deadly eradicators. This shift in status was a byproduct of the subculture's involvement in organized criminal activity.[1]

In Wisconsin, members of the Outlaws Motorcycle Club operated stolen vehicle rings, trafficked drugs, and sold stolen guns. The OMC's Milwaukee chapter also sought to expand the group's geographical reach in an effort to dissuade rival clubs from challenging their hegemony in the Badger State. In some instances, if a motorcycle club targeted for an OMC takeover agreed to drop their patch (i.e. disband their organization), a select number of the former members might gain entry into the Outlaws. When certain clubs resisted a hostile takeover, the OMC resorted to heavy-handed tactics, such as the stabbing death of nineteen-year-old John A. Werner.[2]

In the late 1960s, the Untouchables Motorcycle Club had just over a hundred members, but the club's new president, Garry E. Horneck, ridded the group of "all the leakers" and reduced the roster to just thirty-five members. The Untouchables MC also maintained a large clubhouse near Highway 67 in Sheboygan County near the Sheboygan-Manitowoc County lines.[3]

On March 1, 1970, members of the OMC attended a party hosted by the Untouchables. An Outlaws' prospect, Werner sustained a life-threatening stab wound after an altercation at the party. In an effort to circumvent a police response, medical assistance was not summoned. Instead, Werner was conveyed to a local hospital by Cheryl Pellowski, the girlfriend of the Untouchables' President, Garry Horneck, and Robert Hueckstaedt, of Milwaukee. A few hours later, Werner was pronounced dead and the Sheboygan County Sheriff's Department launched a homicide investigation. Potential witnesses — fearful of possible OMC reprisals — were less than forthcoming.[4]

Within the span of a few weeks, the Untouchables MC had dropped its patch and became the OMC's Sheboygan chapter, a move that enabled the Wrecking Crew to keep tabs on potential state's witnesses. In the short-term, the Outlaws' campaign of orchestrated stonewalling proved effective. Within a few years, though, the wall of silence began to fissure when a resentful spouse threatened to contact law enforcement.[5]

As the investigation into Werner's death grinded to a halt, Victoria Horneck, the wife of the Outlaws' new Sheboygan Chapter President, learned than Werner had been conveyed to the hospital by a female acquaintance of Garry Horneck. As the couple's relationship began to falter, Garry became fearful that his wife would offer details concerning a forged payroll check and Werner's death to investigators.[6]

On July 1, 1972, the Sheboygan County Sheriff's Department received a call that a boot was observed in what appeared to be a shallow grave in a wooded area of a farm three-miles northeast of Elkhart Lake, Wisconsin. When deputies arrived, they carefully dug around the site and located the body of twenty-five-year-old Victoria Horneck. A preliminary autopsy showed that Victoria had died of multiple gunshot wounds.[7]

Based on a tip from an Outlaws' associate Robert A. Hoganson, Detective Leroy Nenning told a judge that a black 1959 Cadillac, owned by Richard Losing, had transported three shovels to excavate the grave and the gloves worn while transporting the body; that Hoganson was present when Victoria Horneck was shot; and that the murder and the concealment of the corpse occurred between June 28 and July 1, 1972, in the Town of Rhine. Upon executing a search warrant at Horneck's Sheboygan home, located at 2212-B N. 15th Street, detectives recovered a .22 caliber revolver, a box of .22 caliber ammunition, five unfired .25 caliber cartridges, and a bloody pillow case. Another Sheboygan search warrant, executed at 703-A Jefferson Avenue, revealed the three shovels used to dig the shallow grave. The shovels had been "borrowed" from Lucille Gottschalk by Losing, and then returned the "day after the murder was committed."[8]

The Sheboygan County District Attorney's office later convened a John Doe probe — a Wisconsin legal process similar to a federal grand jury. Testifying at the secret hearing, Hoganson told Judge John Bolgert that, on June 28, Garry Horneck lured his wife to a Town of Rhine farm. "When I knock her down," Horneck instructed Hoganson, "that will be your signal to shoot her." After being forced to the ground, Hoganson fired rounds from a pistol but did not strike the woman. As Victoria begged for her life, she back peddled into a wooded area by followed by her husband. A few moments later, Garry Horneck fired four or five gunshots, emerged from the woods, and told Hoganson to "get everything out of her pockets, and any money you can keep." Horneck then told Hoganson to find Losing, and then convey his wife's body to the prospective grave site.[9]

Charged with his wife's murder, the case against Horneck proceeded to trial. Three months later, a jury handed down a guilty verdict and a judge sentenced the biker to life in prison. Frustrated by a lack of any success with his appeals, Horneck contemplated his options.[10]

As the investigation into Sheboygan chapter inched forward, the OMC sought to consolidate and/or eliminate other one-percent clubs in southeastern Wisconsin. In the shadowy world of outlaw motorcycle gangs, a club's colors might signify an allegiance with a member of the big-four. For example, since the OMC's patch colors are black and white, motorcycle clubs, whether they are citizen bikers or one-percent groups, may wear black and white patches to illustrate their *de facto* support for the Outlaws. Since the patch colors of the Hells Angels (HAMC) are red and white, the OMC is generally suspicious of clubs that sport red and white colors, even if they are unaffiliated with the HAMC. In the 1970s, the Milwaukee-based Heaven's Devils MC was one such group.[11]

With the exception of the Heaven's Devils, the OMC's campaign of intimidation had worked well. By the middle of 1974, the Saints and the Savage Seven motorcycle clubs had disbanded. Still, if just one group refused to drop their patch, other clubs might also resist; as a result, the OMC upped the ante. On April 26, 1974, two members of the Outlaws committed a home invasion armed robbery at 2571 N. 37th Street, a residence frequented by members of the Heaven's Devils. After gaining entry into an apartment, Peter E. Olson and Thomas J. "Bugger" Roehl, along with an unidentified white female, robbed Heaven's Devils members Jack Guehrer, Scott Girga, and Thomas Ponchik, of their club colors at gunpoint. A small amount of cash was also taken from Michael Vermilyea, the club's president. One of the actual written rules of most one-percent organizations' is a refusal to contact and/or cooperate with law enforcement. Vermilyea, however, instructed the Heaven's Devils to report the incident to the MPD. With Olson and Roehl charged with five counts of party to the crime of armed robbery, and the code of silence shattered, the retaliation began in earnest.[12]

In the wee hours of July 22, 1974, a shotgun blast blew out the windows of Heaven's Devils' member John Otto's residence. Then, on July 26, five incidents, which occurred almost simultaneously, left little doubt that the OMC was on the offensive. As Michael Vermilyea watched television in a living room chair at his parents' ranch-style home, a shotgun blast shattered the front picture widow. As Vermilyea took his mother to the floor, a second round tore into a nearby wall. A few miles away, fire was set to the home of Heaven's Devils' member William Boch. Scott Girga, whose club colors were taken during the April robbery, had his residence hit by a Molotov cocktail. The front windows of another dwelling, owned by Heaven's Devils' member David Wall, were blown out by a shotgun blast. The home of yet another member was struck by a volley of gunfire before a five-gallon gasoline bomb was tossed inside. Fortunately, the explosive's wick was inadvertently extinguished in the process. Two days later, Assistant District Attorney Stephen Jacobs asked Judge Robert Cannon to expedite the trails of Olson and Roehl, and told the Court, "I don't want to bring in dead bodies as witnesses."[13]

The case against the two Outlaws was heard in mid-September. After a two-day trial, a Milwaukee County jury found Olson and Roehl guilty of two counts of armed robbery. Both men were sentenced to seven years in prison, although Roehl, who had previously been charged with firing gunshots into the home of an elderly Wauwatosa couple, was ordered to serve his time consecutively to any prison sentences previously imposed. While the convictions of the two bikers proved that law enforcement could punch a hole through the one-percent wall of silence, the war between the OMC and the Heaven's Devils was just getting started.[14]

In the aftermath of the convictions, the OMC's purported enforcer, twenty-nine-year-old John W. Bushman, and a club hang-around, Joseph Stoll, were federally indicted in the Eastern District of Wisconsin for firearms trafficking. The plot to procure and distribute the stolen guns began with the theft of a 1974 Chevrolet Camaro.

The sporty vehicle was the pride and joy of the Morley-Murphy Company's warehouse foreman, who had parked the car in a corner of the employee lot when he arrived one morning. After his crew of workers had left for the day, the foreman's car was nowhere to be found. Though the police took a stolen auto report and insurance would cover the loss, a set of spare keys to the warehouse, which the foreman had kept inside the car, weighed heavy on his mind. Should he report the missing set of keys, an expensive replacement of the facility's locks would stain the man's otherwise exemplary personnel jacket. Under the impression the auto thief would unlikely put two-and-two together, the foreman decided to forgo disclosing the matter to company officials.[15]

As Morley-Murphy's luck would have it, the foreman's hunch was dead wrong. The Camaro had been boosted by Billy Wadsworth, a man who had spent his formative years in the Illinois School for Troubled Children. By his early twenties, Wadsworth had become so prolific at stealing cars that a local television station in Chicago ran a segment that dubbed him "Billy the Kid, gone in sixty seconds." The moniker stuck and, for those on both sides of the law, America's fastest auto thief became universally known as "Billy the Kid."[16]

Wadsworth delivered the foreman's blue Camero to a Waukesha County farm owned by Clifford Machan. The property's large barn served as chop-shop that was operated by Bushman. A few nights later, Wadsworth returned to the Morley-Murphy warehouse and was pleased to learn that keys for the door and the alarm remained unchanged. After resetting the alarm, Wadsworth waited in a nearby alley for several minutes. When the police did not respond, the thief realized that the warehouse manager had failed to report the missing set of keys.[17]

The following evening, Billy the Kid boosted a van from the rear of a closed business. After picking up Bushman — also known as "Flapper," a tongue-in-cheek reference to his surely disposition — Wadsworth backed the van to the warehouse's overhead door and the two men quickly went to work. Within a span of fifteen minutes, over two hundred guns were loaded into the van. The firearms were then taken to a Milwaukee body shop owned by an OMC associate and secured in a large storage container.[18]

A few days after the burglary, Bushman returned to the body shop with an associate from his chop-shop, Joe Stoll. Bushman retrieved a rifle and a revolver from the stash of stolen guns and the two men traveled to Libertyville, Illinois, where the firearms were transferred to two members of the Outlaws Motorcycle Clubs' Chicago chapter. With a federal case hanging over his head, one of the Outlaws was working as an informant for the Bureau of Alcohol, Tobacco and Firearms (ATF). As Bushman and Stoll returned to Wisconsin, they failed to spot the small aircraft that hovered above them. A few months later, the U.S. Attorney's office in the Eastern District of Wisconsin had obtained indictments for Flapper and his accomplice.[19]

Bushman was arrested and freed on bail, but investigators were unable to find Stoll, who was hiding on Machan's farm with his girlfriend, twenty-year-old LuAnn Irby, a striptease dancer from International Falls, Minnesota. Irby had recently landed a gig at the Cheetah Club, a seedy north side strip joint near N. 35th Street and W. Villard Avenue. While delivering yet another stolen vehicle to the chop-shop, Wadsworth entered a garage and observed Bushman, Stoll, and Irby. A cardboard box on a nearby table was packed with spent welding rods and TNT, taken from an old "powder box" near a quarry that Bushman and Wadsworth had burglarized a few months earlier. Bushman told Wadsworth that he planned on making "a little present for the Heaven's Devils."[20]

Game Changer

Like other boys his age, fifteen-year-old Larry Anstett earned a few dollars delivering morning newspapers prior to attending classes at Wilber Wright Junior High School. On November 5, 1974, just after six a.m., Anstett tossed the Tuesday edition of the *Milwaukee Sentinel* onto his customers' stoops in the 3200 block of N. 83rd Street, a neatly kept blue collar neighborhood on Milwaukee's northwest side. On the roof of a nearby Oldsmobile, the paperboy spotted a square package "wrapped like Christmas gift." Anstett approached the vehicle and reached for the bundle, which immediately detonated. The bomb's high-powered explosive charge sent shrapnel spiraling through the teenager's neck and torso. Anstett's face was seared beyond recognition, his right eye was jettisoned from its socket, and his hands blown away at the wrists. The teenager's violent demise was instantaneous.[21]

Having observed the package while returning home after dropping his wife off for work, Calvin Taylor thought that vehicle's owner probably placed the bundle on the roof of the car and forgot to retrieve the gift. Taylor briefly contemplated taking the package to the door of Vermilyea home, but, according to his son, "... something told him to leave it alone." About ten minutes later, the paperboy decided otherwise.[22]

Had Anstett completed his route at the usual time things may have concluded differently. "I saw him [Anstett] just as I was finishing my route," said fellow paperboy Lou Colello. "I asked him why he was later than usual, but he just shrugged his shoulders." A close friend of Anstett's, Phil Sierlecki, heard about the explosion while monitoring police calls on a radio. "I didn't know if it was Larry or Lou Colello," said Sierlecki, "because they both have routes in that area. Then, later one of my teachers told me."[23]

Now a retired Milwaukee Police Department detective, Roger Hinterthuer was a thirty-year-old plainclothes police officer on the date of the bombing. Searching for potential witnesses, Hinterthuer and his squad partner, Bill Matson, canvassed a row of ranch-style homes one-block east of the detonation site. After speaking with a woman, Hinterthuer saw something strange resting on a bush hedge near the front of the home. Matson stepped off the porch to get a better look and determined the object to be one of the paperboy's fingers.[24]

A few hours after the blast, Wadsworth drove another stolen car to the Sussex farm chop-shop, where he observed Bushman and Stoll seated inside a pickup truck. Bushman told Wadsworth that the attack on the Heaven's Devils had "went south" and that "a newspaper kid" was killed. In mid-November, Wadsworth returned to the farm and asked to speak with Stoll. "Joe's gone and he ain't comin' back," said Bushman. Wadsworth was under the impression that Stoll and his girlfriend, LuAnn Irby, had gone underground.[25]

Since the Oldsmobile was owned by Michael Vermilyea, investigators attributed the bomb's placement to the ongoing feud between the Outlaws and the Heaven's Devils. Detectives quickly assembled a list of three dozen potential suspects and began "picking up everyone they could for questioning." In all, the MPD arrested fifty-four members of the OMC and distributed a brochure with the arrestees' mugshots to area law enforcement agencies. An attorney representing the Outlaws told the *Associated Press* that the club "absolutely, categorically, to a man, denies having anything to do with it." While the victim's family grieved, the *Milwaukee Sentinel* established a $5,000 reward fund. "The world isn't safe for little children anymore," said the paperboy's stunned father, Ralph Anstett. "It isn't safe."[26]

As the investigation proceeded, a forensic examination of the explosive device indicated that the high-powered charge was initiated by a six-volt dry cell battery; that the bomb was triggered by a "trembler switch," which then dispatched circular pieces of metal shrapnel; and that the Anstett's body has sustained two hundred wounds.[27]

For over a year-and-a-half, MPD detectives worked the Anstett case before the inquiry turned cold. The investigation remained in the hands of the detective bureau and was not passed to the SAS, even though law enforcement officials had learned that some OMC members were involved in organized crime. The decision regarding which unit would probe the bomb blast was important. The MPD's detective bureau reacted to serious crimes after they occurred and then thoroughly reconnoitered felonies. The SAS used proactive strategies, such as surveillance and vehicle stops, to link members of a group to other crimes, which sometimes gave the unit's detectives the needed leverage to develop informants. Moreover, due to Harold Breier's insistence that every detective was equally capable of investigating any crime, the MPD had yet to establish a full-time homicide squad. Similar to the Werner investigation, individuals with information in the Anstett case refused to step forward out of fear that the Outlaws would retaliate. Meanwhile, two potential witnesses, Joe Stoll and LuAnn Irby, had seemingly vanished.[28]

Regardless of the investigation's status, the murder of the innocent paperboy was a game changer. In the aftermath of the raucous housing marches and the 1967 riot, Milwaukee's moment in the national spotlight was once again dubious. Larry Anstett's senseless death served as a wake-up call for the MPD command staff and the city's press corps. In the public sphere, the perception of the Outlaws Motorcycle Club — from that of a group of rowdy, non-conformists to a gang of narcissistic hoodlums — seemingly changed overnight. Now retired, Milwaukee County District Attorney E. Michael McCann related that the paperboy's homicide was one of the most difficult cases ever investigated during his thirty-eight-year tenure.[29]

The Indian Connection

The American Indian political movement was initially established inside a Stillwater, Minnesota prison in 1962. The movement's founders, Clyde Bellecourt and Eddie Benton Banai, sought to build a "red civil rights" organization. The group failed to get much traction until 1968, when George Mitchell and convicted felon Dennis Banks joined its ranks and changed the name from the

Concerned Indian Americans (CIA) — an acronym problematic with the counterculture — to the American Indian Movement (AIM).[30]

By the early 1970s, AIM had established chapters in several cities, including Milwaukee. On August 14, 1971, over a dozen members of the group took control of the shuttered U.S. Coast Guard Station near McKinley Marina and Lake Michigan. AIM representatives told the press that the provisions of the 1868 Treaty of Ft. Laramie enabled the occupiers to reclaim property abandoned by the federal government. A portion of the seized U.S. Coast Guard Station housed an Indian Community School, which offered the "takeover the legitimacy it would not otherwise have enjoyed."[31]

In mid-October 1972, several Indian caravans departed Seattle, San Francisco, and Los Angeles enroute to St. Paul, Minnesota, where AIM members would stage for a march on Washington, D.C. AIM labeled the national event the "Trail of Broken Treaties." On its way to the nation's capital, the caravan spent a few days at the U.S. Coast Guard Station in Milwaukee. During the visit, the director of the Milwaukee Indian Community School, Dorothy Ogrodowski, complained that AIM members "broke down doors and windows" and "stole some of our children's drums." Harriet Beilke, the secretary at the school, told a reporter that "hundreds of those AIM Indians came in here and destroyed a lot of our things," and further lamented that "they just walked right in here and said, 'Okay, who's going to Washington with us?' and when we wouldn't go, or let the children go, they just sort of camped out for a while." The conduct of AIM members in Milwaukee was sign of things to come. After arriving in the nation's federal district, the protestors took over the Bureau of Indian Affairs building.[32]

On trip back from Washington, AIM member Leonard Peltier stopped in Milwaukee. During the early morning hours of November 22, 1972, Peltier had a run-in with off-duty Milwaukee police officers Ronald Hlavinka and James Eccel. The incident occurred at the Texas restaurant on the city's south side. Hlavinka alleged that Peltier pointed a Beretta pistol at his midsection and attempted to fire the weapon. A scuffle ensued and the officers wrestled the gun away from Peltier, who was subdued and arrested. Eccel later admitted kicking Peltier "about four or five times" while the handcuffed prisoner was lying on the floor of a prisoner transport van. Charged with attempted murder, Peltier was a freed on bond and fled the state.[33]

Within a span of a few years, the leadership of AIM grew increasingly militant. On February 27, 1973, a handful of radical Indians, along with others from the American Indian Movement, entered and subsequently took over Wounded Knee, a small village on the Pine Ridge Indian Reservation in South Dakota. When first responders from the Bureau of Indian Affairs arrived, the agents were greeted with gunfire. During the seventy-day standoff, two Indians involved with the takeover were killed and two police officers suffered serious injuries. After the siege at Wounded Knee ended, AIM's radicalized leaders sought to acquire more firepower.[34]

In the spring of 1975, AIM leaders began stockpiling an arsenal of dynamite, hand grenades, and a variety of firearms on a private strip of land near the village of Oglala, South Dakota. Though the FBI had successfully cultivated informants, an apparent intelligence gap prevented agents from gleaning information concerning certain radicalized members of AIM, which had gathered near a group of dwellings on a hill known as the Tent City.[35]

The earlier apprehensions of seven AIM members near Hot Springs, South Dakota should have tipped-off the FBI that large caches of weapons were flowing to the Pine Ridge Reservation. On March 1, 1975, a van registered to the American Indian Council on Alcoholism, located at 2452 W. Vliet Street, in Milwaukee, was stopped by deputies from the Fall River County Sheriff's Department for a failure to display license plates. Upon approaching the vehicle, the deputies observed "some materials" that were contraband, secured the scene, and obtained a search warrant. Inside the van investigators found a fully automatic machine gun and explosives. Three of the seven people arrested included Herbert Powless, an AIM leader from Milwaukee, who played a prominent role in the U.S. Coast Guard Station takeover, and Mary Chief Eagle and Madonna Slow Bear, both from Ogala, South Dakota, where the Tent City was located. At the time of the stop, Powless was free on bond pending charges of conspiring to transport unlawful firearms to Wounded Knee in 1973.[36]

With the FBI unaware of his presence, fugitive Leonard Peltier, wanted for the attempted homicide in Milwaukee, had made his way to Ogala's Tent City. Investigators had stopped by the Jumping Bull compound on June 25, 1975, and Peltier, armed with an AR-15 semi-automatic rifle, was prepared to stand his ground if and when the agents made another visit. Shortly before noon the following day, gunshots were fired at FBI Agents Ron Williams and Jack Coler from an area near the Jumping Bull compound. "There are Indians on the rise," Williams radioed, "and if we don't get help quickly, we'll be dead men." After a period of about ten minutes, neither agent answered the radio. Later, when rounds from a 30/30 rifle were fired at responding officers, a BIA agent shot-and-killed Joe "Killsright" Stuntz.[37]

Investigators later located the decomposing corpses of Williams and Coler face down near Coler's vehicle. "Both men had suffered gun blasts to the face at point-blank range," wrote Joseph Trimbach, who responded to the incident from his FBI command in Memphis, Tennessee. "They had been executed, their heads literally blown apart by a high powered weapon." The attackers had also ransacked Coler's car and removed a .308 rifle and the agent's FBI jacket.[38]

Peltier fled to the Rosebud Reservation and later to Canada, but investigators caught a break on September 10, 1975, when a car exploded on a busy turnpike ten miles north of Wellington, Kansas. Inside the vehicle — formerly occupied, in part, by Robert Robideau, Norman Charles, Michael Anderson, and Darlene Nichols — investigators discovered ten guns, including some automatic rifles and ten hand grenades. An AR-15 rifle recovered from the car was forensically linked to the FBI agents' murders. Coler's .308 rifle was also recovered. ATF traces later linked two of the recovered firearms to the Morley-Murphy burglary in Milwaukee.[39]

Convicted of running stolen guns to fellow members of the Outlaws Motorcycle Club in Illinois, John Bushman was serving a four-year prison term when federal agents questioned him about the weapons recovered from the heavily damaged car on the Kansas Turnpike. The former enforcer for the OMC's Milwaukee chapter told investigators that he had "no idea" how the guns taken from the warehouse found their way to members of AIM and had nothing else to say to investigators.[40]

Retired Milwaukee Police Department Detective Roger Hinterthuer had a hunch that the firearms taken in the Morley-Murphy burglary were possibly transferred after Clifford Machan and Bushman stopped at the home of Machan's parents in South Dakota in the mid-1970s. Machan's mother, Majorie, later told the detective that her son and Bushman "went to see Cliff's Indian friends. I don't think they even stayed the night." Hinterthuer later learned that, during stint in 1972 and 1973, Machan had served time in a Pierre, South Dakota prison with AIM leader Russell Means.[41]

Yet, since AIM had an active chapter in Milwaukee, the initial meeting with Machan's "Indian friends" may have been a simple negotiation. It is possible that a go-between in Milwaukee — a member of a Wisconsin-based Indian tribe and a longtime associate of the Outlaws — may have facilitated the transfer of the firearms locally. After all, the body shop that initially housed the stolen guns was less than a mile from N. 25th and W. Vliet Streets.

By the mid-1970s, the cast of characters associated with the Outlaws Motorcycle Club spotlighted the group's transformation from hell raisers to racketeers. Sometimes, though, the activities of greedy criminals register on law enforcement's radar screen. The chop-shops operated by OMC crews had, in part, decreased the metro Milwaukee stolen vehicle recovering rate by five percent. The annual addition of five hundred vanishing vehicles caught the attention of the insurance industry and their cabal of lobbyists in Washington. Soon, the FBI's Milwaukee office received an infusion of federal money to assemble as task force comprised, in part, of MPD auto squad detectives.[42]

[1] Howard Jeffrey Papers, Bureau of Alcohol, Tobacco and Firearms, Intelligence Report, 1969-1994, Box 489, Folder 1, RD 44711, 230/62/03/02 RG 60, United States National Archives, College Park, MD.

[2] *Fond du Lac Commonwealth Reporter*, March 3, 1970, p. 13.

[3] Garry Horneck, interview with Wisconsin Department of Criminal Investigation Special Agents Louis Tomaselli and Wendell Harker, October 28, 1976 (held by author).

[4] *Milwaukee Sentinel*, October 27, 1977, Part 2, p. 11; *Sheboygan Press*, December 3, 1976, p. 3.

[5] *Sheboygan Press*, April 6, 1970, p. 23.

[6] *State of Wisconsin v. Garry Horneck*, Summation of Information from a John Doe Hearing, signed by District Attorney Lance B. Jones, Sheboygan County, WI, October 6, 1972 (held by author).

[7] *Manitowoc Herald-Times*, July 3, 1972, p. 1.

[8] *State of Wisconsin v. Garry Horneck*. Affidavit in Support of a Search Warrant, authorized by Judge John Bolgert, Sheboygan County, September 29, 1972 (held by author).

[9] *State of Wisconsin v. Garry Horneck*, Summation of Information from a John Doe Hearing, signed by District Attorney Lance B. Jones, Sheboygan County, WI, October 6, 1972 (held by author); *Milwaukee Journal,* October 20 1972, Part 2, p. 2.

[10] *The Daily Tribune* (Wisconsin Rapids), October 21, 1972, p. 7.

[11] *Milwaukee Journal*, August 11, 1974, p. 1.

12   *State of Wisconsin v. Peter Edward Olson and Thomas John Roehl,* Criminal Complaint, Milwaukee County, signed April 30, 1974 (held by author); *Milwaukee Journal,* August 11, 1974, p. 6.

[13] Ibid., August 11, 1974, p. 1; *Milwaukee Sentinel,* July 27, 1974, p. 5.

[14] *Milwaukee Journal*, February 17, 1972, Part 2, p. 11; *Thomas J. Roehl v. Wisconsin. Wisconsin Supreme Court*, Case No. 75-718-C-7 (held by author).

[15] Roger Hinterthuer, *Justice Delayed is Justice Denied* (Bloomington, IN: iUniverse, 2015), 14.

[16] Ibid., 5.

[17] Ibid., 16.

[18] Ibid., 17.

[19] Ibid., 21; Kurt Chandler, "Justice Denied," *Milwaukee Magazine*, March 2001, 39.

[20] Ibid.; Hinterthuer, *Justice Delayed is Justice Denied*, 23; *Milwaukee Journal*, October 3, 1974, Part 2, p. 1.

[21]*Milwaukee Journal*, November 5, 1974, p. 1; *Milwaukee Sentinel*, May 6, 1980, p. 7; *La Crosse Tribune*, November 6, 1974, p. 24. Chandler, "Justice Denied," 38.

[22]*La Crosse Tribune*, November 6, 1974, p. 24.

[23]Ibid.

[24]Hinterthuer, *Justice Delayed is Justice Denied*, 27.

[25]Chandler, "Justice Denied," 39.

[26]*Milwaukee Sentinel*, December 17, 1979, p. 5; Ibid., November 6, 1974, p. 5; Ibid., March 4, 1975, p.5; *Fond Du Lac Commonwealth Reporter*, November 13, 1974, p. 8; *Milwaukee Sentinel*, December 17, 1979, p. 5.

[27]Hinterthuer, *Justice Delayed is Justice Denied*, 27.

[28]Spingola, e-mail message to author, January 7, 2015; *Milwaukee Sentinel*, May 6, 1980, p. 13; Spingola, e-mail message to author, January 17, 2015; Chandler, "Justice Denied," 40

[29]*Florence Morning News* (Florence, SC), November 6, 1974, Part B, p. 5; Chandler, "Justice Denied," 38.

[30]DonnaRae Paquette, "AIM: The History," *Windspeaker*, Vol. 1, July 1998, 10.

[31]Susan Applegate Krouse, "What Came Out of the Takeovers: Women's Activism and the Indian Community School in Milwaukee," *American Indian Quarterly*, Vol. 27, No. 3 and 4, Summer & Fall, 2003, 535 – 536.

[32]*The Gallup Independent* (Gallup, NM), October 19, 1972, p. 1; *Milwaukee Sentinel*, November 17, 1972, p. 5; *New York Times*, November 7, 1972, p. 73.

[33]*Milwaukee Journal*, January 23, 1978, Part 2, p. 4.

[34]Joseph H. Trimbach, and John M. Trimbach, *American Indian Mafia* (Denver: Outskirts Press, Inc., 2008), 73.

[35]Joseph H. Trimbach, and John M. Trimbach, *American Indian Mafia*, 327.

[36]*Milwaukee Sentinel*, March 5, 1975, p. 1.

[37]Joseph H. Trimbach, and John M. Trimbach, *American Indian Mafia*, 330, 345.

[38]Joseph H. Trimbach, and John M. Trimbach, *American Indian Mafia*, 333.

[39]*United States v. Leonard Peltier*, Decision of the U.S. Court of Appeals (8th Cir.), 585 F.2d 314, September 14, 1978; *The Atchison Daily Globe* (Atchison, KS), September, 11, 1975, p. 1; Hinterthuer, *Justice Delayed is Justice Denied*, 22.

[40]Hinterthuer, *Justice Delayed is Justice Denied*, 33.

[41]Ibid., 122-123.

[42]Ibid., 46.

CHAPTER FIVE

ENEMIES LIST

T
he intense law enforcement scrutiny that followed the bombing death of Larry Anstett did little to diminish the battle of wills between the Outlaws Motorcycle Club and the Heaven's Devils. Unlike the legendary feud between the Hatfields and McCoys, however, there was no tit-for-tat as the Outlaws became the principal aggressor. Throughout the 1970s, bad things mysteriously occurred to individuals, organizations, and motorcycle clubs who dared challenge the OMC. Law enforcement officials further hinted that two open criminal investigations — a fire set to a dwelling that served as an office for an alternative newspaper and the shooting death of a bartender — may have links to the club.

In the early morning hours of February 22, 1975, an arson fire severely damaged the offices of the *Bugle American*, an alternative newspaper located at 2779 N. Bremen Street, in Milwaukee's Riverwest neighborhood. The blaze began when a fuel can exploded just outside the front door of the two-story, stick built dwelling. Although a half-dozen people were asleep on the second-floor, only one minor injury was reported. The newspaper's twenty-nine year-old managing editor, Michael Jacobi, his wife, and their one-year-old infant were awoken by a "loud sound" and exited the building before the front of the structure burst into flames.[1]

Aware of the suspicious fires at the NAACP's Freedom House, the Outlaws Motorcycle Club's Third Street clubhouse, and the underground newspaper *Kaleidoscope*, the counterculture suspected Sergeant Frank Miller or the Milwaukee Police Department's Special Assignment Squad. Three years later, however, Milwaukee County District Attorney E. Michael McCann told the press that Peter E. Olson, a former member of the Outlaws, had provided information concerning the *Bugle American* fire. A former investigator theorized that an argument between the hippies at the leftist newspaper and the misogynist Outlaws, who frequented a tavern just four blocks from the *Bugle American's* offices, may have heightened tensions between the groups.[2]

Just one month later, a possible act of retaliation claimed the life of a thirty-six-year-old Waukesha County bartender. On March 14, 1975, at about 1:30 a.m., Margaret Schlieper closed the Black Caesar tavern on Highway SS in the Town of Pewaukee. The pub was a popular meeting spot for members of the Heaven's Devils. In need of a ride to her Sussex home, Schlieper slid into the car of Heaven's Devils member Thomas "Rainbow" Rein. Recognizing that Rein and two other club members had been overserved, the now off-duty bartender and mother of four, retrieved the keys and started the car. After exiting the dark parking lot, Schlieper drove east on a rural two-lane highway towards Goerke's corners, in the Town of Brookfield. A few minutes later, a set of headlights quickly approached the car from behind. The vehicle, described as "a green 1966 or 1967 station wagon," pulled into the lane for westbound traffic to pass. A sudden loud bang was quickly followed by a burst of shattering glass from the driver's side window. Slumped against the front passenger's side window, Rein awoke as his vehicle careened into a ditch and flipped onto its side.[3]

Three of the car's occupants survived the crash, but Schlieper, who was struck in the left side of her face with a birdshot load from a 12 gauge shotgun, died at the scene. The blast that took her life caused extensive brain damage and a severe skull fracture. Searching for a motive, investigators were unsure which occupant was the intended target — the owner of the car, Rein, who had just testified against the Outlaws, or Schlieper, who was the midst of a messy divorce, and whose husband operated a custom motorcycle shop with one-percent biker customers.[4]

Combing the Black Caesar's parking lot, investigators located a pile of cigarette butts in a corner of the lot behind a tree. A theory emerge that the perpetrator had been in the lot for some time watching and waiting for either Rein or Schlieper to leave the tavern. "We don't have anything concrete, I'm sorry to say," said Waukesha County Sheriff Edward O'Conner, whose typically sleepy jurisdiction, to the west of Milwaukee County, had experienced its seventh murder in eleven weeks. After the shooting, MPD Detective Roger Hinterthuer ascertained that a member of the Outlaws had owned a green station wagon when the homicide occurred.[5]

While the chop-shop at Clifford Machan's Sussex farm, and the shooting that emanated from the Black Caesar in rural Waukesha County, exemplified the one-percent subculture's growing influence in the metro Milwaukee area, a 1975 Memorial Day incident in a rural county near the center of the state underscored the expansive reach of the Outlaws Motorcycle Club in Wisconsin.

After making the ninety-five mile trek to Green Lake, a small town in a county with less than 18,000 residents, three OMC members tangled with two patrons at Spike's tavern. The Outlaws then left the bar and returned with nine other members, who had made camp between Princeton and Neshkoro. During the ensuing brawl, the door to the tavern was torn from his hinges, a pool table was turned on its side, and "flying barstools" shattered windows. A crushed neon sign started a small fire, which was quickly extinguished. When deputies arrived, twenty-four-year-old James "D.D." Demitriou, a member of the Outlaws' Milwaukee chapter, and an associate Roy Mitchell, of Beloit, were taken into custody. Two other individuals, nineteen-year-old Thomas Stobbe, of Berlin, and John Bosak, of Green Lake, were hospitalized after being hit by fists and pool sticks "wielded by the bikers."[6]

The Outlaws "just smashed up everything in the place," said Spike Breivogel, the tavern owner's father, "and it only took them about three minutes." Authorities later learned of a plot to spring the two arrestees. In short order, law enforcement established roadblocks "to prevent cyclists from entering Green Lake." A confrontation between law enforcement and a group of responding Outlaws "ended peacefully on Princeton Road" and the disgruntled bikers left town. Two days later, Demitriou and Mitchell were charged with aggravated battery and freed on $2,500 bail.[7]

Clubhouse Connections

Prior to the 1975 riding season, the OMC's Milwaukee chapter opened a new clubhouse at 1139 W. Bruce Street, at the site of a former tavern in an industrialized area on the near south side. The building housed a first-floor bar and a small second story apartment. A vending machine, which dispensed beer and other beverages, was located near the clubhouse entrance. On the main floor, the Outlaws kept a human skeleton in a casket. A sign later posted above the bar infamously proclaimed, "Nobody knows how many niggers the Outlaws have killed." During an investigation at the clubhouse, one investigator further observed "an operable guillotine with blood spots on it." The centrally located clubhouse made the OMC a more cohesive outfit, but the location also became a focal point for the Milwaukee Police Department. Over the course of the next three-and-a-half years, investigators alleged that the club had formulated plot and committed crimes within the confines of the rickety building.[8]

One such conspiracy literally took aim at the Outlaws' rivals. On August 24, 1975, Heaven's Devils' members Jory Fraker and Gregory Nauertz were riding their motorcycles southbound on U.S. Highway 141 in Milwaukee County. As the riders passed under the County Line Road overpass, a member of the OMC, Scott W. Mattes, released a sixty-six pound piece of concrete from the bridge above. When the object slammed into the roadway, Fraker heard a loud thud, observed Nauertz's bike collide with a concrete chunk, and watched as the out-of-control motorcycle slid onto the road's gravel shoulder. Although the crash had occurred at a speed of fifty-five miles per hour, Nauertz suffered only abrasions to his right knee and a swollen ankle. Nauertz's passenger, Dawn Wimmer, also sustained non-life threatening injuries.[9]

A witness to the incident, Fredrick P. Stratton, Jr., the future CEO of the Briggs & Stratton Corporation, observed Mattes flee the overpass and enter a red van, which was waiting on N. Port Washington Road. Driven by Joseph Sorce, Jr., the van quickly left the area. When police attempted to stop the vehicle on County Line and North Upper River Roads, State Trooper Gregory Boening observed a brown paper bag, which housed a .38 caliber revolver, "being thrown from the passenger's side window." After the recent acts of violence orchestrated by members of OMC, the Milwaukee County Sheriff's Witness Protection Unit provided Nauertz and Wimmer with a twenty-four hour security detail. Mattes and Source were subsequently convicted of attempted murder and received significant prison sentences.[10]

Once again, members of the Heaven's Devils cooperated with a criminal investigation and, therefore, defied the subculture's rule to never collaborate with law enforcement. After a fight or an act of biker-on-biker violence, the one-percent code of silence typically kicked in. "That was the way I lived. I preached it," said the former President of the Hells Angels' Minnesota chapter, Pat Matter, who also enforced the norms and mores of the righteous one-percenter.[11]

In another instance, a plan to conceal a homicide was hatched at the Bruce Street clubhouse. On December 7, 1975, at about 1:30 a.m., Kathleen Ann Hanrahan was the passenger in a car driven by her husband, Charles Radtke as they traveled home from a Christmas party. As the couple's car moved southbound on U.S. Highway 141 (currently I-43), just north of the Milwaukee County Courthouse Annex, a black over light colored automobile suddenly cut in front of them. After passing the black over light colored car, the vehicle began tailgating the couple. At the National Avenue off-ramp, Radtke exited I-94 and pulled over to let the vehicle pass; however, the suspicious car suddenly stopped behind the couple. Hanrahan looked on as her husband stepped from the driver's side door and approached the black over light colored vehicle. A few seconds later, Hanrahan heard a loud pop and watched as the car sped away southbound on the National Avenue off-ramp. Hanrahan ran to Radtke's side and found her husband lying in "a pool of blood, with what appeared to be a gunshot wound to the head."[12]

After being dispatched to the scene, Patrolman Ken Jacobs conducted a cursory examination of Radtke, who had sustained a gunshot wound just below his right eye. The round had traveled through Radtke's brain and exited from the rear of his skull. Jacobs conveyed the pulseless, non-breathing shooting victim to Milwaukee County General Hospital where Radtke was declared dead on arrival.[13]

Detectives from the Milwaukee Police Department arrived and conducted an extensive investigation. Investigators suspected a member of the Outlaws Motorcycle Club. Several months later, a hold-up man was arrested by the Milwaukee County Sheriff's Department for armed robbery. In exchange for leniency, Allen Martini agreed to provide information concerning the homicide of

Radtke. At a secretive John Doe hearing, Martini told a court that, in the early morning hours of December 7, 1975, he was present at the Outlaws' Bruce Street Clubhouse. Martini observed a panicked OMC member, Patrick J. Zinuticz, enter the building with a .22 caliber revolver in his hand. Zinuticz then stated, "I just shot somebody on the freeway." Martini walked outside the clubhouse and saw a black over white Buick with blood on the driver's side rear door. Zinuticz then wiped away the blood with a rag. At "the direction of Harry Nelson," the purported enforcer for the OMC's Milwaukee chapter, Martini drove the Buick from the scene and was present when the car was concealed inside Nelson's garage.[14]

Initially charged with first degree murder, Zinuticz's attorney, Alan Eisenberg, negotiated an amended plea to homicide by negligent use of a firearm with Assistant Milwaukee County District Attorney Jon Reddin. The deal further permitted Zinuticz to enter an Alford-type plea, which enabled the defendant to assert his innocence. At a February 28, 1978 hearing, Judge Harold B. Jackson, Jr. sentenced Zinuticz to just a year in the county jail for the talking of a human life, even though the suspect and his alleged co-conspirators had sought to conceal and destroy evidence.[15]

As the MPD ratcheted-up the pressure, and with Bruce Street clubhouse under continuous scrutiny, the Outlaws began visiting taverns in the working-class suburb of South Milwaukee. On April 25, 1976, approximately twenty-five OMC members and/ or associates committed $1,500 worth of damage at the Nearly Normal tavern during an argument over the pool table. Then, on June 5, Jerry Ermi, the owner of Lucifer's bar, was told that some members of the OMC had stolen the establishment's electric roaster. On June 9, the owner of the Branding Iron tavern, Virginia Phillips, declined to serve a group of Outlaws and referred to the bikers as "animals." At about four a.m., three men were observed running from Phillips' closed tavern after a door at the rear of the building, which had been doused with gasoline, burst into flames. Asleep in an apartment above the bar, a mother and her six-month old infant perished in the ensuing fire.[16]

The two deaths, as well as the Outlaws' apparent takeover of the South Milwaukee taverns, riled local residents, who chided the village's police chief, Henry Tylicki, over his department's tepid response. "From what I hear, people have no respect for South Milwaukee cops," bar-owner Ermi warned, "and will take the law into their own hands." Several local residents told a reporter that they would form a vigilante group to protect themselves. "I can match any guns that they've [the Outlaws MC] got," said one unidentified man. Tough talk aside, the OMG code of silence once again prevented law enforcement from bringing those responsible for the arson-related deaths to justice.[17]

Having stonewalled and obstructed law enforcement in the Werner and Anstett homicides, as well as the South Milwaukee arson deaths, some members of the OMC threw caution to the wind. On March 2, 1977, off-duty Milwaukee Police Officer Michael Bartlett became involved in "an exchange of insults" at a tavern near S. 5th and W. Rogers Streets, a gritty area on the city's near south side. After leaving the pub, Bartlett drove a few blocks, stopped for a red traffic light, and then observed three men exit a van that had pulled behind him. The men then extracted the off-duty officer from his car. On his way to the ground, Bartlett was punched in the face before the men stomped on the off-duty officer's head. When Bartlett shouted that he was a Milwaukee police officer and displayed his law enforcement credentials, one of the men shouted, "We don't care!"[18]

After concealing the van's license plate with a hub cap, the assailants attempted to leave the area. The badly beaten Bartlett reentered his car, followed the suspects, and later forced the van off road at S. 3rd Street and W. Lincoln Avenue, a block west of the MPD's Second District station. Having heard the ruckus, the district's Station and Security officer, James Menger, responded and observed blood stains on the boots of twenty-four-year-old James "D.D." Demitriou. During the assault, Bartlett suffered a broken nose and a fractured jaw. The other occupants of the van, OMC associates Mark W. Venus and Alan W. Venus, were also arrested and subsequently charged with the attack.[19]

Aware of the Outlaws Motorcycle Club's propensity for violence, Police Chief Harold Breier assigned an officer to monitor Bartlett's home, located in a quiet, residential neighborhood less than a mile from the city's major airport. On March 6, at about 1:30 a.m., an unidentified man fired two gunshots at twenty-three-year-old Police Officer Susan Ortel, who was seated in a squad car outside Bartlett's home. The first round lodged in the squad car's door. The second bullet just missed the officer and shattered the passenger's side window. Ortel returned fire, pursued the shooter on foot, and then observed a car flee the area. The brazen attack put law enforcement on high alert. "Information has been received that a group known as the Outlaws are planning on blowing up a police station," a teletype sent by Muskego Police Lieutenant Earl Zabel warned. "The date and time of which is unknown. The information comes from an unreliable source but one that would have access to such information."[20]

With the beating of the off-duty officer and the assassination attempt of Ortel etched into the minds of law enforcement, the charges against the Venus cousins and Demitriou were later dismissed. The impudence of the two attacks left a bad taste in the mouths of rank-and-file Milwaukee police officers. With tensions between the officers of the Milwaukee Police Department and the Outlaws Motorcycle Club at an all-time high, one could only imagine what might occur if and when these two groups suddenly clashed.

Grudge Match

Six months later, the predictable confrontation between officers from the Milwaukee Police Department and the Outlaws came to fruition. On September 30, 1977, Milwaukee policer officers, including members of the TEU, responded to a report of a large fight at the Bus Stop, an exotic dance club located at 5012 W. Capitol Drive. Witnesses said that Roger Lyons and two other members of the OMC, Michael Goodman and Harry Ross, were involved in a wrestling match with three customers. The scuffle lasted about a minute. When officers arrived on the scene, they struggled with Lyons while taking the burly biker into custody.[21]

A police transport wagon later conveyed Lyons to the MPD's Seventh District station, where Officer Charles McGaver observed that the handcuffed arrestee was unresponsive and had a weak pulse. "Lyons looked like he was dazed," McGaver explained. "His complexion was pale and his eyes half open. I saw blood on his face. I felt for a pulse and it was a weak one." When asked by District Attorney E. Michael McCann if it was possible that he was "under pressure from other officers because you would report that you saw one of them strike a prisoner," McGaver, who was present when Lyons was arrested, replied, "Possibly, yes." Lyons was then conveyed to County General Hospital where he "was pronounced dead at 11:38 p.m.," as a result of an injury to his head.[22]

Skeptical of the MPD's version of events, McCann ordered an inquest. Jerome Dudzik, the leader of the labor union representing rank-and-file Milwaukee police officers, questioned the district attorney's objectivity and asked Governor Martin Schreiber to appoint a special prosecutor. "He [McCann] has impugned the character of not only the officers involved in the incident," Dudzik said, "but also all Milwaukee police officers, except for a few that he publicly stated were supervisory officers whom he could trust to do the investigation." Schreiber refused to get involved and the inquest proceedings moved forward.[23]

During the hearing, McCann aggressively questioned police witnesses. Sergeant Dean Collins testified that he was at the Bus Stop tavern in the immediate aftermath of the fight. While he observed Officer Victor Venus deliver baton blows to Lyons' legs as the biker was on the floor, Collins "was satisfied that no officer acted improperly." A TEU officer, James Koleus, was questioned concerning an inconsistency between his official report and a statement that he made to detectives. "I don't know why I would omit that [overhearing Goodman say that he observed Lyon's fall in the prisoner transport van]. I put that in my report."[24]

The credibility of the inquest's citizen witnesses, as well as their inconsistent testimony, proved problematic. A dancer at the club, nineteen-year-old Andrea Jackson, testified that the actual fight was over when the police arrived. Jackson further stated that one officer, whom she described as being "tall, with a mustache, dark hair, slim," wearing "a raincoat," glasses and a quasi-gold badge, struck Lyons in the head with a nightstick. Jackson's description fit that of Collins, although others testified that the sergeant — an officer with a stellar reputation, who later became a Catholic deacon — never drew his baton. Another witness, Robert Hackbarth, told the Court that that he saw police officers with batons take swipes at Lyons, although he did not observe any of the swings connect. According to Hackbarth, Lyons looked as if he was "half drugged, half carried" as he was escorted out of the tavern by police. Likely the least credible witness in the eyes of the inquest jury was Michael Goodman, a member of the OMC's Chicago chapter. Goodman testified that the police simply "threw" Lyons into the transport van and that, after he rolled his fellow club member over, Goodman observed Lyons' "bloody" face. "They just beat the hell out of him."[25]

Less than a month-and-a-half after the altercation, the inquest jury returned its verdict: Lyons had died as a result of an unjustifiable homicide by reckless conduct committed by a person or persons yet to be determined. District Attorney E. Michael McCann gave two explanations for the jury's verdict: First, if patrons involved in the fight with Lyons caused his death, they did not act in self-defense; and, second, if Lyons was killed by police, officers used unreasonable force.[26] "Perhaps the only certainty resulting from the Lyons inquest," a Milwaukee Sentinel editorial noted, "is that relations between the district attorney and the Police Department are more strained than ever." The morning newspaper's assessment of the Lyons' affair had missed the mark. From the MPD's and the OMC's points of view, there was blood in the water. Caught in the middle, the Milwaukee County District Attorney's office had acted as an ex post facto referee for the no-holds barred grudge match.[27]

[1]*Milwaukee Journal*, February 22, 1975, p. 1.

[2]David Armstrong, *A Trumpet to Arms: Alternative Media in America* (Los Angeles: J.P. Tarcher, Inc., 1981), 148-149; *Milwaukee Journal*, December 5, 1968, p. Part 2, p. 1; *Milwaukee Sentinel*, July 27, 1978, p. 5; Powalisz, e-mail message to author, September 28, 2014.

[3]*Waukesha Daily Freeman*, March 15, 1975, p. 1; Roger Hinterthuer, *Justice Delayed is Justice Denied* (Bloomington, IN: i-Universe, 2015), 34-35.

[4]Ibid., 35; *Waukesha Daily Freeman*, March 15, 1975, p. 1.

[5]Ibid., Hinterthuer, *Justice Delayed is Justice Denied*, 35.

[6]*Fond du Lac Commonwealth Reporter*, May 28, 1975, p. 21; *The Capital Times*, May 27, 1975, p. 8.

[7]Ibid.; *Fond du Lac Commonwealth Reporter*, May 28, 1975, p. 21.

[8]*Milwaukee Sentinel*, April 3, 1980, p. 5; *Milwaukee Sentinel,* May 10, 1980, p. 10.

[9]*State of Wisconsin v. Scott W. Mattes and Joseph A. Source, Jr*, Criminal Complaint, Milwaukee County, signed August 25, 1975 (held by author).

[10]*Milwaukee Sentinel*, May 8, 1980, p 5; *State of Wisconsin v. Scott W. Mattes and Joseph A. Sorce, Jr.*, 1975CF5052A and 1975CF5952B (held by author).

[11]Kristy Belacamio, "Former Hells Angel and Cop Who Chased Him Share Their Unlikely Friendship," Pioneer Press, July 26, 2014, http://www.twincities. com/2014/07/26/former-hells-angel-and-cop-who-chased-him-share-their-unlikely-friendship/ (accessed July 19, 2016).

[12]*State of Wisconsin v. Patrick Joseph Zinuticz*, Criminal Complaint, Case No. I-8783, Milwaukee County, December 2, 1976 (held by author).

[13]Ibid.

[14]Ibid; *Waukesha Daily Freeman*, December 3, 1976, p. 1.

[15]*State of Wisconsin v. Patrick Joseph Zinuticz*, Court Case notations, Case No. I-8783, Milwaukee County, December 2, 1976 (held by author).

[16]*Milwaukee Journal*, June 29, 1976, p 1; Ibid., June 29, 1976, p. 5; Ibid., June 30, 1976, p. 1.

[17]Ibid., June 29, 1976, p. 1; Ibid., June 29, 1976, p. 5.

[18]Jack Lemke, retired MPD Intelligence Unit detective, e-mail message to the author, February 13, 2015; *State of Wisconsin v. James Louis Demitriou, Mark Walter Venus, and Alan Wayne Venus*, Criminal Complaint, Milwaukee County, signed March 2, 1977 (held by author).

[19]Ibid., Lemke, e-mail message to the author, November 16, 2014.

[20]*Milwaukee Journal*, March 7, 1977, p. 1.

[21]*Milwaukee Journal*, November 2, 1977, Part 2, p. 4

[22]*Milwaukee Sentinel*, November 5, 1977, p. 1; *Milwaukee Journal*, November 2, 1977, Part 2, p. 4; *Milwaukee Sentinel*, November 10, 1977, p. 5; Ibid., November 10, 1977, p. 11; Ibid., October 18, 1977, p. 12.

[23]*Milwaukee Journal*, October 26, 1977, Part 2, p. 11.

[24]*Milwaukee Sentinel*, November 8, 1977, Part 2, p. 1; Ibid., November 10, 1977, p. 5.

[25]*Milwaukee Sentinel*, November 5, 1977, p. 1; *Milwaukee Journal Sentinel,* February 4, 2002, p. 2B; *Milwaukee Sentinel*, November 3, 1977, p. 5; Ibid., November 3, 1977, p. 5.

[26]*Milwaukee Journal*, November 12, 1977, p. 10.

[27]*Milwaukee Journal*, November 12, 1977, p. 10; *Milwaukee Sentinel*, November 16, 1977, p. 12.

CHAPTER SIX

TESTIFIERS

It took almost six years for law enforcement to catch a break in the John Werner homicide investigation. In 1976, convicted murderer Garry Horneck, the former leader of the Outlaw Motorcycle Club's Sheboygan affiliate, contacted Louis Tomaselli, a special agent with the Wisconsin Department of Criminal Investigation (DCI). After agreeing to turn state's witness, Horneck was interviewed at the state prison in Waupun, where the convict told Tomaselli that the Outlaws were responsible for the death of *Milwaukee Sentinel* paperboy Larry Anstett. Incarcerated at the time of the bombing, Horneck's information was based solely on discussions with OMC associates; however, the former President of the Untouchables Motorcycle Club was present when Werner was murdered and was willing to offer a detailed account events.[1]

During an October interview with Tomaselli and Agent Wendell Harker, Horneck explained that the March 1, 1970 party was arranged in conjunction with James Bisenius, the President of the Outlaws Motorcycle Club's Milwaukee chapter. The party started just after dark. About sixty members of the Outlaws and fifteen members or associates of the Untouchables were initially present. An OMC associate — a former member who was previously booted from the club — agreed to fight Werner to earn back his patch.[2]

After Werner was pushed into a circle of bikers, the former OMC member and Werner began to grapple. Within the span of a few minutes, it was clear that Werner had "got the best" of his competitor. After being hit in the back of the head with a rake thrown by an Outlaw, Werner was ordered to walk to a nearby river and "clean up." As he staggered to the river, Horneck observed "J.B." throw a wine bottle that struck the wounded biker in the back of his head. Werner then fell to ground, slowly recovered, and made his way to the river.[3]

After returning to the Untouchables' clubhouse, the Outlaws' club enforcer ordered Cheryl Pellowski, a female acquaintance of

Horneck's, to attend to Werner's injuries. As Pellowski washed away the blood from Werner's face, Horneck heard one of the bikers shout, "Kill the fucker." Werner was then laid on a table and stripped of his club colors. According the Horneck, Bisenius told Pellowski to convey Werner to the hospital to get "sewed up." Two members of the Outlaws then carried Werner from the clubhouse.[4]

Once outside, Horneck observed a knife being passed from one Outlaw, Peter Olson, to another, Craig Hopper, who then stabbed Werner in the belly. The puncture wound produced a "poof" sound and a small about of blood oozed from the wound. Werner was then loaded into the rear of a station wagon. A member of the Outlaws then told Pellowski, "Cunt, take him to the hospital and tell them that you found him at the train depot."[5]

Horneck further told Tomaselli that members of the Outlaws' Milwaukee chapter planned to have Werner killed in Sheboygan County to "bring additional stress on the Untouchables" to become an OMC charter. Earlier in the day and prior to the stabbing, members of the Outlaws had gotten the Werner's stepbrother intoxicated so that he could "not interfere while they were setting up plans to kill" Werner. Horneck "believed the reason Werner was murdered was that he had testified against one of the Outlaws' leaders "Joseph Bisenius in some assault and rape charges that were pending against" him. According to Horneck, John Bushman, William Held, and James Bisenius — all members of the OMC's Milwaukee chapter — were also present "at the party when Werner was killed."[6]

Two months later, after an offer of use immunity was extended by the United States Attorney's office in the Eastern District of Wisconsin, U.S. Internal Revenue Special Agent Wayne Saubert and DCI Special Agent Ronald Feurer interviewed James "Pig" Bisenius, who was President of the Outlaws Motorcycle Club's Milwaukee chapter from "its inception in 1966 until March 1972."[7]

Bisenius told the agents that the Outlaws had met at a tavern in Milwaukee prior to traveling to the Untouchables' party. A short time later, James "Sniveler" Pfieffer, an OMC member familiar with the Sheboygan area, led a caravan of six to ten cars to the clubhouse near Highway 67. Some of the OMC members present were William Held and John Bisenius.[8]

During the fight with an associate of the club, Werner received a cut to his forehead. When Cheryl Pellowski was unable to stop the bleeding, Bisenius suggested that "someone" should take Werner to the hospital. When Pellowski asked for advice to explain Werner's injuries, Bisenius claimed that a member of the Untouchables replied, "Say you found him by the [railroad] tracks." The former club president of the Outlaws further told investigators that, when the stabbing occurred, he conveniently had his "back to the clubhouse." Bisenius further denied ever hearing that Werner had "given any information to the police regarding" his brother's 1968 sexual assault charges.[9]

After comparing statements from the two witnesses, investigators realized that the James Bisenius had acquired an acute case of selective memory. Though Horneck's summation of events provided critical details and names, Bisenus could not recall any information that would incriminate himself or other Outlaws.[10]

Based on the information provided by Horneck and another informant, Peter Olson, the Sheboygan County District Attorney's office charged Craig V. Hopper with Werner's murder. Previously convicted of battery, battery to a police officer, and injury by conduct regardless of life, Hopper entered a plea of not guilty and the case went to trial in October of 1977.[11]

Under oath at the trial, Olson testified that Werner sustained injures in a fight with another OMC prospect and needed medical attention. "When Werner [also known as Pagan] was leaving, Hopper asked me for a gun," said Olson, under oath. "I didn't have one. He [Hopper] asked me what I had. I told him 'a knife.' He asked me for it and I gave it to him." Olson further explained, "I thought Hopper was going to cut-off his ear, because of Hopper's reputation. What else would he need the knife for?" Olson firmly told the Court, "There is no question that Hopper stabbed the guy."[12]

Hopper's defense counsel, Alan Eisenberg, was a controversial figure. In 1970, the Wisconsin Supreme Court upheld a discipline ruling from the state bar that Eisenberg and his father, Sydney, had "by concerted action" engaged in behavior "of such aggravated nature as to cause Judge [John] Krueger great mental suffering and anguish." On August 28, 1968, after Krueger was allegedly told by Eisenberg that private detectives had followed him, and that the judge would "be off the bench in 60 to 90 days," Krueger entered a Milwaukee County Courthouse washroom, placed the barrel of a revolver in his mouth, and committed suicide.[13]

At a minimum, Eisenberg was a difficult person to deal with. "Judge Fiorenza has advised me to inform you," wrote Deputy Clerk of Courts Jane Schetter, in a letter to the attorney during the litigation of Hopper's case, "that if you ever slam the telephone down on him in any further telephone conversations again, you will have to answer to the Court for such conduct."[14]

Eisenberg's demeanor was not the only issue that materialized. During the trial, Olson alleged that Hopper's defense counsel had sought to suborn perjury. "Eisenberg told me that I was to say that Pagan was having relations with (another club member's) wife." Other witnesses muddied the waters with contradiction. Garry Horneck also told the Court that he had observed Hopper stab Werner, but gave conflicting estimates concerning his distance from the event. Testifying for the defense, six fellow bikers stated that they did not see Hopper in the vicinity of the stabbing. Jurors deliberated for seven hours before returning a verdict of not guilty. Although the judge who oversaw the trial publicly stated that he had no issues with Hopper's acquittal, Tomaselli, who had surreptitiously taped Olson's jailhouse conversation with Eisenberg, and District Attorney L. Edward Stengel suspected witness tampering.[15]

As investigators probed allegations of Eisenberg's professional misconduct, the press caught wind of another matter that stemmed from the Werner homicide. Two local reporters — Ken Mueller, of the *Sheboygan Press*, and Cliff Ellinger, of WKTS radio— published a series of reports that revealed the cushy treatment Sheboygan and Manitowoc County officials had afforded the state's key witness, Garry Horneck. "A former member of the Milwaukee Outlaws, convicted of murdering his pregnant wife," a dispatch from the Associated Press noted, "spent 15 months of the last two years in the Sheboygan and Manitowoc County jails — with time off for another marriage and a honeymoon."[16]

Besides providing Horneck with furloughs and congenial visits at the jail, the convicted felon also spent a weekend at the Door

County vacation home of a Manitowoc County jailer. Booked into the jail under the alias "Luke Turney," Horneck was provided with two cells, one of which was used to operate a leather craft business. He was further permitted to sunbathe on the jail's rooftop and sell belts, wallets, and holsters to county employees. After the not guilty verdict in the Werner case, however, Horneck was quietly returned to the state prison in Waupun. The cordialities extended to the former President of the Untouchables Motorcycle Club by prosecutor Lance B. Jones underlined a critical point missed by the press: Just how difficult it was for district attorneys to find witnesses — no matter how creditable — who were willing to risk testifying against members of the Outlaws.[17]

Six months after the verdict, a Washington County judge convened a John Doe hearing to investigate the allegations of misconduct that stemmed from Hopper's trial. The secret hearing was originally requested by Hopper to scrutinize the special privileges jailors had extended to Horneck, but Eisenberg's jailhouse conversation with Olson was also examined. When the probe concluded, the only persons charged were Eisenberg's private investigator, Robert S. Penny, and Joseph M. Stelzer, a Manitowoc County jailer, although a copy of the tape was sent to the Wisconsin Bar Association's Board of Professional Responsibility.[18]

Clubhouse Derailment

Under the microscope for his suspected involvement in the N. 83rd Street bombing, John Bushman continued to manage the day-to-day operations of the chop-shop. When the need arose, Flapper attended various OMC functions. On May 30, 1978, a twenty-nine-year-old exotic dancer accompanied two Outlaws to the group's clubhouse at 1139 W. Bruce Street. Once there, the woman went to a vending machine, retrieved a bottle of beer, and was suddenly approached by OMC member Joseph "Junkyard" Koller. The visitor was then thrown over Koller's shoulder and carried up a ladder to a loft.[19]

Once in the loft, the woman was thrown onto a mattress, which rested on a wooden floor. Koller began removing the woman's "jump suit" and quickly rolled the woman onto her stomach. The victim then observed two other men — one of whom was John W. Bushman — enter the loft. Koller and the other men then removed the woman's panties. When the woman screamed for help, Koller punched her in the face and ordered her to keep quiet. As Bushman and the other man held the woman's legs apart, Kollar inserted his penis into her vagina. A short time later, Koller moved to the front of the woman, forcibly grabbed her head, and, according to the criminal complaint, "placed his penis in her mouth while she was in the kneeling position." At the same time, the other men placed their fingers and "penises into her vagina." After once again being forced to her stomach, Koller and another man held her legs apart as Bushman "had intercourse" with the woman. When Bushman finished, a man, known only to the victim as "Zee," also had intercourse with her while Koller held one of the victim's legs apart and repeatedly punched the woman.[20]

After Koller, Bushman, and another unidentified man left the loft, the woman climbed down from the club's apparent train room in search of her clothing. She was then hoisted onto the clubhouse bar and told to dance. While on the bar, Koller inserted a beer bottle into the woman's vagina. Bushman placed a knife on the bar before glancing menacingly at the knife and the woman. The President of the OMC's Milwaukee chapter, Richard "Doc" Moody, reportedly told the other bikers, 'Come on, that's enough. Let her go. She's too afraid to do or say anything.'[21]

A few days later, the woman reported the assault to the police. When leaving the clubhouse, the victim told investigators that she was clad in her jump suit, but she was unable to retrieve her panties. On June 3, officers from the Milwaukee Police Department executed a search warrant at the Outlaws' clubhouse. Upon entering the building, Officer Raymond Stanczyk saw panties matching the description of victims on a clock behind the bar.[22]

Koller and Bushman were subsequently charged with sexual assault and were released on bail. Although the MPD had yet to implicate Bushman in the paperboy's murder, the former OMC enforcer had become his own worst enemy.

The year 1978 was not a good one for John Bushman. The day after MPD officers had executed the search warrant at the Outlaws' clubhouse, seven teams of investigators served an unrelated search warrant at Clifford Machan's farm. Within a matter of minutes, six of the seven teams had located probable stolen vehicles. An eighth team was assigned to locate Bushman and a Buick the biker had recently driven. After arriving at Bushman's residence, the Outlaws' former enforcer was nowhere to be found, and his wife refused to offer any details.[23]

Inside an unlocked barn, FBI agents and MPD detectives located dozens of major automobile parts. Welders and cutting torches, used to chop vehicles into pieces, were also found concealed in the large outbuilding. During the search, Machan returned to the farm and hinted that he may cooperate. As the search concluded, Detective Roger Hinterthuer climbed a ladder to inspect the barn's loft. Weaving his way past a piles of small car parts, the detective observed "a box containing two objects, each about the size of a bar of soap." A label on the box read, "DANGER — TETRONITROTOLUENE — HIGH EXPLOSVE." The first piece of physical evidence directly linking the chop-shop to the bombing death of Larry Anstett was now in hands of law enforcement.[24]

Feeling the proverbial noose tightening around his neck, and with his live-in girlfriend in tears, Machan hinted that he would be willing to provide information, but wanted to consult with his attorney. On June 28, the farm's owner appeared in the Milwaukee County District Attorney's office. During a meeting with Assistant District Attorney Jon Reddin, Machan's attorney told those present that "Cliff knows about the [Anstett] bomb and he knows about the guns [recovered from the Indians after the explosion on the Kansas Turnpike]." Machan and his attorney then agreed to return to the DA's office on July 2 to provide a statement.[25]

For the prosecutor and the detectives, who had spent nearly four years chasing down leads concerning the paperboy's gruesome murder, the atmosphere on the morning of July 2 was "electric." An hour-and-half after the scheduled meeting time, Machan had yet to appear. The detectives who had patiently waited to interview the South Dakota native believed something was awry. Fearing the worst, Hinterthuer and FBI Special Agent Charlie Brown drove to Machan's farm. When the two arrived they spoke with Machan's live-in girlfriend, who explained that, the day prior, she had answered a telephone call from Bushman. After passing the receiver to her boyfriend, she overheard Cliff agree to a rendezvous "with someone." Within a matter of minutes, an excited Machan drove off in his new truck and had yet to return.[26]

With farm's owner in the wind, the Milwaukee County District Attorney's office asked a judge issue a warrant for his arrest. In hindsight, the failure to place Machan and his live-in girlfriend in a safe house was a glaring blunder. After all, law enforcement was certainly aware of the OMC's willingness to intimidate victims and witnesses. The Milwaukee County Sheriff's Department had previously provided witness protection services to the Heaven's Devils victimized by the sixty-six pound concrete drop, and Police Chief Harold Breier had an officer monitor the residence of Michael Bartlett after his altercation with the Outlaws. In each instance, these measures shielded concerned parties from retaliatory acts. Since investigators had visited Bushman's home, seized the TNT, and released Machan from police custody absent criminal charges, it would not take long for the Outlaws' former enforcer to smell a rat.

Another Crew

Similar to *La Cosa Nostra*, members of the Outlaws Motorcycle Club operated in crews. John Bushman was, in essence, an organizational *capo*, and the only member of the club directly involved with the Sussex farm chop-shop. Other OMC cliques also operated chop-shops, trafficked drugs, and illicitly procured Harley-Davidson motorcycles.

On October 19, 1978, at about 12:15 a.m., Milwaukee native Marshall Gradingan returned home from one of the last seasonal rides on his Harley-Davidson. Though he did not notice, two members of the Outlaws Motorcycle Club had followed him. Gradingan then opened the overhead door to the detached garage behind is home, at 1912 W. Howard Avenue, and padlocked the bike to a car door. One hour later, Gradingan awoke to a "snapping noise" that emanated from the garage. From a window, he focused the beam from a flashlight towards the garage, saw the overhead door moving upwards, and watched as two men fled on foot.[27]

Gradingan ran to the garage, where he saw that a padlock had been cut from the side service door, and the car door — chained to the Harley-Davidson — had been opened. He then entered the car and drove through the neighborhood searching for suspects. Seeing nothing unusual, Gradingan returned home, parked the car in the garage, and secured the overhead door. He then concealed himself in the backyard and watched as two men approached the garage. Gradingan cautiously approached the alley and shined a flashlight on the two men, who were standing adjacent to the overhead door of the garage. The would-be thieves, later identified as Alan "The Watchmaker" Venus and Clifford "Mighty Mouse" Nowak, each had pipe wrenches and began walking eastbound in the alley. After following the two men for a short distance, Nowak turned towards Gradingan, raised a wrench, and shouted, "Get out of here or I'm going to kill you." After screaming for help, Gradingan looked on as Venus and Nowak fled eastbound and entered a light gray van parked in the 3800 block of S. 19th Street. After obtaining the van's license plate, he contacted the police.[28]

Undeterred, Venus and Nowak soon followed another biker home. After lying in wait for about an hour, the two Outlaws procured a Harley-Davidson by forcibly entering a detached garage near S. 25th Street and W. Layton Avenue. Having heard a series of odd sounds, Scott Olson glanced out a window of his home and watched as Venus pushed a motorcycle south on 26th Street towards a parked van. When Venus struggled to "wheel the motorcycle up a plank" and into the rear of the van, Nowak exited the vehicle and helped push the bike inside. The van then quietly left the area. Believing that the motorcycle may belong to a neighbor, Olson telephoned Roger Frycienski, who resided at 2501 W. Layton Avenue. When Frycienski inspected his garage, he observed that a door had been forcibly entered, and his Harley-Davidson was missing.[29]

When police were summoned, the officers recalled the earlier burglary attempt at the garage on Howard Avenue. Both crimes involved a similar vehicle and two white male suspects. Although the license plate obtained by Gradingan came back as stolen, detectives later found the Ford van parked behind Venus' Quincy Avenue residence. The following afternonn, Milwaukee County Assistant District Attorney Richard Klinkowitz charged the five-foot-eight, ninety-eight pound Nowak and the Outlaws' suspected bomb maker, Venus, with one count of armed burglary and second count of burglary. Both men were later freed on bail pending future court proceedings.[30]

By the mid-1970s, several crews within the Outlaws Motorcycle Club's Milwaukee chapter had engaged predicate acts of racketeering. While the OMC's Sheboygan chapter disbanded after Garry Horneck's arrest for his wife's murder, the club's influence in the metro Milwaukee suburbs and southeastern Wisconsin continued to grow. The Outlaws, however, had yet to vanquish their number one local nemesis: The Heaven's Devils.

[1]*Milwaukee Sentinel*, October 27, 1977, Part 2, p. 11; *Milwaukee Journal*, April 29, 1988, p. 9A.

[2]Garry Horneck, interview by Wisconsin Department of Criminal Investigation Agents Louis Tomaselli and Wendell Harker, October 26, 1976 (held by author).

[3]Ibid.

[4]Ibid.

[5]Ibid.

[6]Wisconsin Department of Criminal Investigation Agent Ron Feurer, Case Activity Report, Larry Anstett homicide, March 17, 1980.

[7]James Bisenius, interview with DCI Special Agent Ronald Feurer, Homicide of John Anthony Werner, Case No. SA-230, December 17, 1976 (held by author).

[8]Ibid.

[9]Ibid.

[10]Susan Adams, "How to Tell When Someone is Lying," *Forbes Magazine*, August 13, 2012, http://www.forbes.com/sites/susanadams/2012/08/13/how-to-tell-when-someone-is-lying/#3a9a12b439f7 (accessed June 16, 2016).

[11]*State of Wisconsin v. Craig Vaughn Hopper*. Criminal Complaint, Sheboygan County, December 2, 1976 (held by author); FBI Rap Sheet of Craig Vaughn Hopper, Record Number 70 751 H, 9, December 1976.

[12]*Milwaukee Sentinel,* October 28, 1977, Part 2, p. 12.

[13]*Wisconsin v. Eisenberg, Wisconsin Supreme Court,* 48 Wis. 2d 364 (1970); *Milwaukee Journal*, August 29, 1968, p. 1; *Milwaukee Sentinel*, July 24, 1969, p.5.

[14]*Wisconsin v. Eisenberg*, Wisconsin Supreme Court, 48 Wis. 2d 364 (1970); *State of Wisconsin v. Craig Vaughn Hopper*, Letter from Jane A. Schetter, Deputy Clerk of Courts, Sheboygan County, to Atty. Alan Eisenberg, July 21, 1977 (held by author).

[15]*Milwaukee Sentinel*, October 28, 1977, Part 2, p. 12; *Milwaukee Journal*, October 31, 1977, Part 2, p. 5; *Waukesha Daily Freeman*, October 31, 1977, p. 3; Ibid., May 25, 1978, p. 1; *Milwaukee Journal*, October 31, 1977, Part 2, p. 1.; Ibid., May 25, 1978, p. 1.

[16]*Wisconsin State Journal*, February 25, 1978, Sec. 4, p. 2.

[17]Ibid.

[18]*Milwaukee Journal*, April 27, 1978, Part 2, p. 1; Ibid., October 13, 1978, Part 2, p. 4; *Milwaukee Sentinel*, March 13, 1978, p. 9.

[19]Kurt Chandler, "Justice Denied," *Milwaukee* Magazine, March 2001, 39; Powalisz, e-mail message to the author, January 12, 2015; *Milwaukee Sentinel*, April 3, 1980, p. 5.

[20]*Milwaukee Sentinel*, April 3, 1980, p. 5; *State of Wisconsin v. Joseph Roger Kollar and John Wayne Bushman*, Criminal Complaint, Case #J-2990, June 5, 1978.

[21]Ibid.; *Milwaukee Sentinel*, April 3, 1980, p. 5.

[22]*State of Wisconsin v. Joseph Roger Kollar and John Wayne Bushman*, Criminal Complaint, Case #J-2990, June 5, 1978.

[23]Roger Hunterthuer, *Justice Delayed is Justice Denied* (Bloomington, IN: iUniverse, 2015), 96-97.

[24]Ibid., 99.

[25]Ibid., 106.

[26]Ibid., 106; Chandler, "Justice Denied," 40.

[27]*State of Wisconsin v. Alan Wayne Venus and Clifford Nowak*, Criminal Complaint, Milwaukee County, October 20, 1978.

[28]Ibid.

[29]Ibid.

[30]*Milwaukee Sentinel*, January 25, 1980, p. 7; *State of Wisconsin v. Alan Wayne Venus and Clifford Nowak*, Criminal Complaint, Milwaukee County, October 20, 1978.

CHAPTER SEVEN

FAILING JUSTICE

B y the late 1970s, several members of the Outlaws Motorcycle Club began frequenting a four-block stretch of taverns in the blue collar suburb of West Allis. While retired detective Larry Powalisz described this area as a "red light district," local residence referred to neighborhood as "the strip." Members of the club, said thirty-nine year MPD veteran Lieutenant Charles Berard, typically patronized bars with "a lot of street people — when I say street people I mean guys that ran on the streets" and where the "girls were hardcore. That's the type of environment the Outlaws love coming to." And "the strip," which has since been bulldozed and redeveloped, offered the club access to a variety of individuals who dabbled in the underground economy.[1]

Similar to the earlier incidents in South Milwaukee, once the Outlaws settled in, it did not take long for trouble to follow. During the early evening of December 28, 1978, the West Allis Fire Department received a call from Dottie Ellis, the bartender at Marlo's Windup, a tavern at 6418 W. Greenfield Avenue. When police arrived, they found a nineteen-year-old African-American man incapacitated from a single stab wound to his abdomen. The victim had a faint pulse. Paramedics rushed the man to Milwaukee County General Hospital and he was pronounced dead at 9:30 p.m.[2]

Ellis told police that she had heard "a loud thump at the front door of the tavern" and believed that someone may have been pounding at the door. She then went outside and observed a black male lying on the sidewalk. Believing that the man was intoxicated, Ellis notified the Fire Department.[3]

Another witness, Arthur A. Albright, left the M & R bar, heard a loud thud and soon observed a man lying on the sidewalk. Albright then crossed Greenfield Avenue and "picked the man up and asked him what was going on." When Albright observed blood on the fallen man's jacket, he ran inside of Marlo's Windup to ask for help and was told that Ellis had already summoned assistance.[4]

The deceased victim, nineteen-year-old Vaughn Cox, did not carry identification and was later identified through fingerprints. Investigators initially believed that the murder was linked to an earlier car accident, but the man who had fled the accident scene was not Cox. Family and friends told officers that Cox had a gay lover that he had met at the Phoenix, a bar on S. Second Street in Milwaukee. After sifting through several leads, Detectives Ruthstz and Erdmann interviewed a West Allis man who said that Cox and he had "engaged in fellatio on each other" three weeks earlier, but that he had not seen the victim since.[5]

Two months later, West Allis police caught a break. A man in custody for auto theft told a corrections officer that he had information relevant to the Greenfield Avenue homicide. On the night Cox was stabbed, the informant related, he was shooting pool at the Play Pen — a strip club two doors east of Marlo's Windup — when a member of the Outlaws Motorcycle Club, named "Gilbert," entered and had a seat at the bar next to his friend "Ron." Upon seeing a black male approach the bar, Gilbert called the man a "nigger" and an argument ensued. After a dancer intervened, Gilbert and the black male, later identified as Cox, took seats at opposite sides of the bar. Fifteen minutes later, Cox stood up and left the tavern. Gilbert and another man then followed the man outside. A few days later, "Ron" told the informant that Gilbert had asked a friend for a knife, ran up to the victim, and stabbed the man in his side.[6]

Detectives further leanred that twenty-three-year-old James Sinden had spoken with Ronald Gerger, who was present on December 28, at the Play Pen with Gilbert "Fidel" Aspuro and John T. Marefke. According to Gerger, when Cox entered the bar, Aspuro called him "a nigger." Cox then shouted, 'You don't call me a nigger,' and Aspuro replied that Cox was 'messing with the wrong people.' Aspuro then asked Marefke for a knife and the three men followed Cox outside the bar. Aspuro then told Gerger and Marefke to get in a car and leave because he "had just stabbed the guy."[7]

West Allis police also spoke with a woman who had witnessed a prior confrontation between Aspuro and another black patron. A divorced mother of four and part-time go-go dancer at the Play Pen,

"Tattoo Terry" arrived for work on an evening in December when Aspuro entered the tavern. When an African-American man placed his coat over a bar stool, she heard Aspuro shout, "No black nigger is going to come into the bar and take my stool." The black man then stood up and replied, "Hey, it's cool, man," and moved to the other side of the bar. When "Tattoo Terry" retrieved a stool for the man, the dancer told investigators that Aspuro remarked, "I see you're a nigger lover and he is going to get his…and so will you." At bar time, Aspuro left alone; however, after hearing about the Cox homicide, the go-go dancer thought that the Outlaw may have committed the stabbing because "he is getting nuts and hates black people." The dancer further asked West Allis detectives if Aspuro was a member of the Outlaws Motorcycle Club and remarked, "If he is, I can kiss my ass goodbye."[8]

As investigators began making progress in the Cox homicide, Alan Venus — free on bond for the pending burglary charges — traveled to Louisville, Kentucky with thirty-four-year-old Outlaws' associate, Michael Petri. From a Ramada Inn hotel room, Venus and Petri hatched a plan to pass phony U.S. currency at local businesses.[9]

On March 22 and 23, 1979, Venus and Petri passed counterfeit $20 bills at a Burger King restaurant, two Outlook Inn taverns, and the Tim Tam Bar. A witness to one of the transactions jotted down the license plate number of the suspects' vehicle. At 2:10 a.m., an officer on patrol spotted the counterfeiters on Old Shepherdsville Road. A search of the vehicle revealed $2,000 in bogus $20 bills and paperwork that identified a particular room at the Ramada Inn. Investigators then obtained a warrant to search the hotel room and discovered ink, cast stamps, and an additional $48,000 of counterfeit $20 bills printed on low-grade paper.[10]

The following Monday, the case was handed to the U.S. Secret Service. Within a week, the U.S. Attorney's office had indicted Venus and Petri for possessing a forgery device and the possession of forged instruments. After entering a guilty plea, Venus was sent to a federal prison in Oxford, Wisconsin.[11]

Also free on bond for the south side burglaries, Clifford Nowak was implicated in the beating of a man at a South Milwaukee tavern. Just before midnight on May 9, 1979, Nowak, along with recently patched Outlaws' member Edward "Shock" Anastas, James "Dumper" Kowalski, and Anthony Lawnicki, visited Frenchy's bar to confront a man about a previous bet. About a year earlier, Carey Celske had made a wager with Anastas concerning which man was tough enough to become a member of the OMC. If one man succeeded and the other failed, the loser would surrender their Harley-Davidson to the new member of the club.[12]

When Anastas asked the loser of the bet to step outside, Celske agreed, but only if Anastas did so *mano a mano*, but the three men who had accompanied Anastas quickly followed. When Celske's friend, Peter Griffin, stepped from the tavern, Anastas "charged" Griffin and knocked him to the ground. According to the criminal complaint, Nowak, Kowalski, and Lawnicki then struck Griffin in the head over a dozen times. The four men then punched Celske in the face and fled in a truck.[13]

Though the entire incident occurred in "approximately twenty seconds," Griffin sustained an injury to his head and was "bleeding extensively" from a stab wound to the left side of his chest. He was rushed to Trinity Memorial Hospital in an ambulance and survived the attack. A few days later, the Milwaukee County District Attorney's office charged Anastas and Nowak with being parties to the crimes of endangering safety by conduct regardless of life and battery.[14]

With Eisenberg's assistance, the Outlaws had, for the most part, gamed the Milwaukee County court system. Anastas was released on bond, as was Nowak, who was already out on bail for the south side burglaries. Clearly, several members of the Milwaukee County judiciary seemed disinterested in addressing the club's criminal gang activities. As a result, several Outlaws charged with serious crimes were quickly returned to the community with lenient bail conditions. As the 1979 riding season began in earnest, judicial leniency would further impact events.

Five years after the shooting war started, the OMC had yet to vanquish the resilient Heaven's Devils MC. On July 18, 1979, prosecutors in Ozaukee County secured the convictions of OMC members Michael Drobac and Charles Willis in the shooting of Heaven's Devils' member Russell Maylock. The incident stemmed from a confrontation between the two motorcycle clubs at a large party hosted by the Ozaukee Guzzlers at a Town of Trenton farm. About four-hundred people were present when members of the Outlaws arrived. Just ten minutes later, after seeing the Heaven's Devils present, a witness said Drobac told Willis to "shoot first, ask questions later." Concerned about a possible self-defense claim, Ozaukee County District Attorney Fred Fink agreed to accept plea deals from the two defendants, both of whom remained free on a $10,000 bond.[15]

Due to their willingness to cooperate with law enforcement, the Heaven's Devils, once again, became moving targets. On December 16, 1979, at about 1:35 a.m., six members of the Outlaws, including Drobac and Nowak, crashed the Heaven's Devils' Christmas party at The Knew Boot, a saloon in the Village of West Milwaukee. A witness said that a member of the OMC nudged a Heaven's Devils' drink and the disturbance began. The Heaven's Devils removed all but two of their rivals from the premise before one of the remaining Outlaws produced a handgun and sprayed the barroom with gunfire. Standing just feet away, John Janke, known to his fellow Heaven's Devils members as "Ox," was shot in the head and died at the scene. Other errant rounds struck patrons unaffiliated with either motorcycle club. Two employees of the *Milwaukee Sentinel*, Assistant Picture Editor Paul Rieger and a general assignment reporter, John Tracy, at the tavern with twenty-three other members of the newspaper's staff, were also shot. Rieger was hit in the abdomen, while Tracy sustained a life threatening head wound. Transported to St. Luke's Hospital, Tracy remained conscious long enough to provide details to detectives. A subdural hematoma caused his brain to swell and the reporter slipped into a coma. The bullet that struck Tracy had lodged in the rear of his brain and an instrument was inserted to monitor the swelling.[16]

A group of investigators from various law enforcement agencies began to piece together the sketchy details in an effort to identify the shooter. One witness told investigators that Gilbert Aspuro had approached Heaven's Devils member Allen Kurtz, "placed a gun against his neck, and fired a shot." In the incident's aftermath, Susan Lundgren told detectives that Aspuro arrived at her home, about sixty miles north of Milwaukee, and viewed news accounts of the shooting. After seeing the suspects' descriptions, Aspuro trimmed his hair and shaved his beard. The widespread confusion that followed the shooting, coupled with alcohol consumption and fearful witnesses, hampered the inquiry. To compel witness testimony, the Milwaukee County District Attorney's office petitioned a court to conduct a John Doe hearing.[17]

As the investigation proceeded, Paul Rieger fully recovered from the gunshot wound to his abdomen, but John Tracy did not fare as well. Initially, doctors believed that the reporter would die. Tracy ultimately survived, although his quality of life was forever diminished. After leaving the hospital, the former reporter had difficultly focusing and his body frequently seized. To alert those around him to his health issues, Tracy wore a necklace that warned passersby, "John Tracy, brain injury; possible seizure; unable to talk 15-20 minutes in duration; I will be alright; med: Dilantin."[18]

The brazen spray-and-pray-type shooting inside a crowded tavern was indicative of the one-percent subculture's mindset. "These people [one-percent bikers] will go all over the place," said Berard. "They will go into bars, they will go into public venues, and they don't care. So what it [outlaw motorcycle gang violence] is doing is affecting the entire urban environment."[19]

The shootings of fellow journalists at the Knew Boot caused the press to take a closer look at the leniency of the Milwaukee County court system. On December 10, 1979, Nowak was convicted for his involvement in the south side Harley-Davidson burglaries and sentenced, in part, to a whopping thirty-days in jail. At the hearing, Nowak's attorney, Alan Eisenberg, asked Judge Robert Landry to stay the jail sentence until January 9 so the Outlaw could visit his sister in Florida for the holidays. Yet, instead of traveling to the Sunshine State, Nowak was over a thousand miles north and present during the incident at the Knew Boot saloon.[20]

In a January 25, 1980 article, *Milwaukee Sentinel* reporter John Fauber called Landry's judgement into question. Although the judge took note of Nowak's affiliation with the Outlaws, and the defendant's use of the Outlaws' clubhouse as his legal residence, Landry granted Eisenberg's request to postpone the execution of the skimpy jail stay. While Nowak and Venus each faced a maximum prison exposure of thirty-years, the reporter noted, "...the armed burglary charged was reduced to burglary" while "the second burglary charge was read into the record and dismissed." In the interim, Nowak's co-conspirator, Alan Venus, who had been arrested and convicted in federal court for the Louisville counterfeiting case, was sentenced by Landry to five-years in prison "made concurrent with the five-year federal term."[21]

As the 1980s emerged, members of the Outlaws Motorcycle Club had, for the most part, made a mockery of the criminal justice system. Larry Anstett's killer was still at-large. Joe Stoll, LuAnn Irby and Clifford Machan had gone missing. The man who stabbed Vaughn Cox to death remained free. Other victims of OMG violence, such as John Tracy, struggled mightily to simply lead productive lives. The mother and her infant — the two innocent parties killed in the South Milwaukee arson fire — figuratively cried out from their graves. When prosecutors did obtain felony convictions, plea deals, as well as modest bail conditions and lenient sentences, it did little to deter the Outlaws from engaging in criminal activity. Behind the scenes, though, a small cadre of investigators doggedly pursued leads in an effort to speak for those no longer with a voice.

[1]Powalisz, e-mail message to the author, January 7, 2015; Charles Berard, interview with author, October 17, 2015; West Allis Police Department, Supplement report, Case #A69-558.

[2]Ibid., *Milwaukee Journal*, December 29, 1978.

[3]West Allis Police Department, Police report of Officer Kriz, Case #A69-558.

[4]Ibid.

[5]Ibid.

[6]West Allis Police Department, Police report of Detective Polakowski, February 28, 1979.

[7]West Allis Police Department, Police report of Detectives Schalk and Polakowski, March 27, 1979.

[8]West Allis Police Department, Report of Detective Buday, March 22, 1979.

[9]*The Courier-Journal* (Louisville, KY), March 25, 1979, p. B10.

[10]Ibid.

[11]*Wisconsin State Journal*, December 19, 1982, p. 1.

[12]*Milwaukee Sentinel*, January 27, 1981, p. 5; *State of Wisconsin v. Edward Anastas, Clifford M. Nowak, and James M. Kowalski*, Criminal Complaint, Milwaukee County, Case No. J-7113, June 14, 1979; *Milwaukee Sentinel*, February 6, 1981, p. 5.

[13]Ibid.

[14]Ibid.

[15]*Milwaukee Sentinel*, July 19, 1979, p. 6.

[16]*Milwaukee Sentinel*, December 17, 1979, p. 1; Steven Spingola, *Best of the Spingola Files, Vol. 1 & 2*, 38; *Milwaukee Journal*, December 24, 1979, Part 2, p. 4.

[17]Steven Spingola, *Best of the Spingola Files, Vol. 1 & 2*, p. 38.

[18]*Milwaukee Sentinel*, November 28, 1980, p. 1.

[19]Charles Berard, interview with author, October 17, 2015.

[20]*Milwaukee Sentinel*, January 25, 1980, p. 1.

[21]Ibid., p. 7.

CHAPTER EIGHT

UNCLE AL STAYS BUSY

If members of the Outlaws Motorcycle Club under criminal investigation paid in cash, attorney Alan Eisenberg could have purchased a new Mercedes-Benz at the end of 1980. With several cases in the pipeline, officials from various law enforcement agencies diligently worked to punch a hole through the OMC's wall of silence.

On a chilly day in February, Milwaukee County investigator Terry M. Molthen met with a confidential informant at a location on the city's east side. The informant related that, on the morning of the 1974 bombing death of Larry Anstett, two members of the Outlaws Motorcycle Club appeared at his place of employment. One of the members of the club, who was also present at the Sheboygan party when Anthony Werner was murdered, told the informant that he had just "pointed out the home" of Heaven's Devils President Michael Vermilyea and that "other persons had placed a bomb" on the roof of Vermilyea's car.[1]

The informant further told Molthen that the Outlaws' member, who had pointed out Vermilyea's house, was "very high on some drugs" and appeared "very excited" about the "whole proceedings that were about to take place." At about 5:15 a.m., the two members of the OMC left the informant's place of employment. Less than an hour later, Anstett "picked up the package and was blown away."[2]

A few weeks later, the informant stopped by Mike's Club 65, a tavern at N. 65th Street and W. Silver Spring Drive, and spoke with the same Outlaws' member who was upset because the "Sentinel boy should not have picked up the package." The club member also said that he regretted "being involved" in the bomb plot and "wished he had gone straight home after the taverns closed" instead of getting "high on speed."[3]

The informant's statement was a critical piece of evidence. For years, investigators believed that probable co-conspirators and/

or witnesses — namely Stoll, Irby, and Machan — were dead. Yet, to earn convictions in the Anstett case, a prosecutor, fearing a credibility issue, would likely ask the informant to capture another admission on tape. Doing so, however, would be next to impossible, as the OMC was suspicious of individuals facing criminal charges. The likeliest path to obtain the cooperation of the bomber's co-conspirator was building a serious criminal case against the man — a task that, for whatever reason, had yet to materialize.

In another open case related to the paperboy's homicide, MPD detectives received information that an Outlaws' member from Ohio had killed Joe Stoll and LuAnn Irby during a party at a home on N. Richards Street. According to the informant, after being shot to death, Stoll and Irby were buried beneath the dwelling's basement floor. Police were told that the bodies were exhumed a month or two later and placed in fifty-five gallon drums that were partially filled with concrete. The barrels were then conveyed to a south side Milwaukee marina, placed on a boat, and deposited in Lake Michigan. When police later searched the residence, cadaver dogs identified an area in the basement where the bodies may have been buried.[4]

In an effort to leverage other informants, Milwaukee County District Attorney E. Michael McCann told a judge that he hoped to obtain information from three OMC associates charged with forgery. McCann described the Outlaws as "an organized, violent, criminal conspiracy" and linked the club to the homicides of Anstett and the South Milwaukee arson victims. One individual told state agents that a high-ranking member of the Outlaws had transported "substantial quantities of heroin and cocaine" between Detroit and Milwaukee by boat, which, again, linked the club to the south side marina.[5]

Then, on March 8, a well-armed entry team breached the front door of the Outlaws' dilapidated Bruce Street clubhouse. Detectives from the Milwaukee County Sheriff's Department recovered a 12-gauge sawed-off shotgun, nine other firearms, and a leather jacket with a set of Heaven's Devils' colors, from a second floor apartment. Another search warrant was simultaneously executed at 4112-B W. Orchard Street, a residence occupied by James "D.D." Demitriou. An affidavit supporting the searches linked Demitriou and Eric J. Lenger, who was present at the clubhouse, to "a state income tax form concerning a 1973 Lincoln automobile."[6]

The search also had implications for Donald "Jingles" Foshney, the former president of the OMC's Milwaukee chapter, who, detectives believed, had control over a clubhouse apartment that housed the firearms. On probation for a Kenosha County burglary, Foshney was prohibited from associating with the Outlaws absent his agent's approval and was jailed pending a Department of Corrections investigation.[7]

Amidst the flurry of OMC related activity, jury selection began for the clubhouse sexual assault allegation. Prior to the start of proceedings, Assistant District Attorney Michael Malmstadt publicly admitted that John Bushman and Joseph "Junkyard" Koller could be acquitted. Potential jurors, the prosecutor theorized, may frown upon the woman's sexual proclivities. Complicating matters, the victim told detectives that, in the aftermath of the assault, she had spent the night at the home of an Outlaws' member. In the morning, after the man's wife had left for work, she engaged in consensual intercourse with the club member.[8]

Trembling and crying on the witness stand, the twenty-nine-year-old woman testified that she was "gang raped, beaten, and forced to dance nude on a bar." Judge Robert Landry granted a number of recesses to allow the victim to collect herself. When the judge provided the victim with a glass of water, Eisenberg — believing that Landry had "displayed favoritism" — demanded a mistrial. When the judge denied the agitated attorney's motion, Eisenberg asked Landry to "admonish" the witness and instruct her to "not demonstrate for members of the jury." Landry again denied the attorney's request.[9]

Eisenberg also asked the Court for the woman's new address. After the attack, the victim had been placed in witness protection and relocated out of state. The attorney claimed that the information was needed to ascertain the cost of witness protection. The thinly veiled ploy was again rejected by the judge. Outside the presence of the jury, Eisenberg further attacked the victim's creditability. "The defense contends that the woman is the most animalistic, maniacal, degenerate perverted woman that the state has ever put on the stand in a court of law."[10]

After hearing testimony, a Milwaukee County jury deliberated for eight hours before returning a guilty verdict. Two months later, Koller was sentenced to a fourteen-year prison term, while Bushman, who remained free on bail while awaiting sentencing, would later receive a seven-year sentence. Malmstadt's roll-of-the-dice had paid off. Although the MPD had yet to implicate Bushman in the paperboy's murder, the former OMC enforcer had become his own nemesis.[11]

Two months after the jury convicted Bushman and Koller, word leaked about another Outlaws Motorcycle Club inquiry — the ongoing, six-month-old John Doe probe of the shootings at the Knew Boot saloon. Although investigators had made some progress, officials still faced legal obstacles. Pending the outcome of a ruling concerning legal counsel, the Wisconsin Court of Appeals had issued an opinion that witnesses represented by Eisenberg could not be compelled to testify by Milwaukee County Circuit Court Judge Victor Manian. Nevertheless, the OMC was beginning to feel the effects of relentless law enforcement pressure.[12]

Pushing a War Hero's Buttons

As President Lyndon Johnson dramatically escalated U.S. military involvement in Southeast Asia in the mid-1960s, thousands of young men from well-heeled families used various methods to dodge the military draft. During the same period, Oak Creek, Wisconsin native, Gary Wetzel. volunteered to serve. One of nine children, Wetzel — like many Vietnam veterans — was a product of a blue collar family.[13]

During his first tour, Wetzel was a member of an ordnance unit. He reenlisted for three years to become a helicopter gunner. On January 8, 1968, as Wetzel's unit conducted a search of enemy positions near Ap Dang An, the helicopter he occupied was hit by a rocket-propelled grenade. After a rough landing, Wetzel learned that the chopper's commander was severely wounded. When Wetzel and another crew member attempted to move the injured pilot outside the aircraft, a grenade severed the gunner's left arm at the elbow. As the same Viet Cong guerrilla readied another grenade, Wetzel reached for a Thompson machine gun and "zippered him up." After leaving the downed helicopter, and with the wounded pilot in tow, Wetzel caught a glimpse of six enemy combatants attempting to procure the chopper's

M-60 machine gun. With only one arm, Wetzel pulled the Thompson's trigger "and eliminated" the enemy.[14]

Surrounded, Wetzel sought to shoot an escape route through the enemy line. After tucking the remainder of his left arm in the belt of his pants, Wetzel ran towards the downed helicopter, made his way to the M-60s gun well, opened fire, and destroyed the communist guerrillas' automatic weapons capabilities. The badly wounded helicopter gunner then crawled through the mud and pulled several incapacitated soldiers to a medic station.[15]

Wetzel lost most of his left arm and spent six months in a military hospital. He was discharged from the Army in June 1968 and, five months later, was awarded the Congressional Medal of Honor by President Johnson. When Wetzel and his then fiancée, nineteen-year-old Bonnie Cline, returned to Wisconsin, they were greeted by members of the American Legion and ROTC cadets. By anyone's standards, Gary Wetzel was an individual with intestinal fortitude.[16]

Upon being discharged from the army, Wetzel, like thousands of other military veterans, gravitated towards the biker subculture. If one sought to push the war hero's buttons, calling Wetzel a coward would probably do the trick. On July 18, 1980, that is precisely what Outlaws Motorcycle Club member William "Veggie" Bollis proceeded to do.

After Bollis and Wetzel had a beer at the Red Robin Tap, the two men walked down the street to Wetzel's Cudahy home, located at 3944 E. Layton Avenue. A few minutes later, an argument ensued and Bollis began calling Wetzel names. During a brief scuffle, the six-foot-two-inch, two hundred and ten pound Bollis sustained a "deep cut to his forehead from a hook" that served as a prosthesis for Wetzel's amputated left arm. Bollis then "implied" that Wetzel was a "coward for refusing to assist the OMC member during an earlier fight at the Southwoods" restaurant. At Wetzel's insistence, Bollis left the house, but then, through an open window, shouted that the Medal of Honor winner was a "coward."[17]

Wetzel then retrieved two magazines of .45 caliber ammo and a Thompson semi-automatic rifle. With his antagonist still yelling through the window, Wetzel decided to scare Bollis by firing three rounds over his head.[18]

With twenty-five feet separating the Wetzel residence to the east, Eugene Witkowiak heard an argument and peered from his front porch to investigate. Witkowiak then reentered his home and went to a bathroom to hear what was transpiring. With the lights extinguished, the curious neighbor opened the window to eavesdrop. His wife, Nancy, had also entered the bathroom and the couple "crouched down so they could get a look through the window opening." After Bollis shouted, "C'mon, give me a round," Witkowiak heard several gunshots. As the couple ducked for cover, the rounds fired by Wetzel entered their bathroom and plaster fell from the walls. The Witkowiaks then crawled from the bathroom and telephoned the police.[19]

Detective Eugene Holubowicz arrested the Medal of Honor recipient, and Wetzel was charged with a felony count of endangering safety by conduct regardless of life. Since Wetzel had received counseling, the Milwaukee County District Attorney's office reduced the charge to a misdemeanor count of reckless use of a weapon in exchange for a guilty plea.[20]

About a month-and-a-half after his altercation with Wetzel, Bollis became the focus of another law enforcement action. The Outlaw, along with Mary and Kenneth Juneau, had stopped at Callahan's Bar No. 1 in Tomah, a small city one hundred and seventy-miles northwest of Milwaukee. Just after 11 p.m., a large fight, involving fifty people, broke out and quickly spread into the street. Sergeant James Woodworth, of the Tomah Police Department, told the *Milwaukee Sentinel* that several people suffered injuries in a brawl between the Tomah Tramps Motorcycle Club and a "Milwaukee-based group" of one-percent motorcyclists. Tomah police arrested Bollis and the Juneaus for disorderly conduct.[21]

Public Enemy

In the summer of 1980, David Hoover, a public affairs officer for the U.S. Drug Enforcement Agency (DEA), described the Outlaws Motorcycle Club as a "highly sophisticated, well organized" criminal organization. Hoover discussed the activities of the club with the press after the DEA released a report that described the OMC as "the gang, through its Milwaukee chapter, [that] literally controlled the entire methamphetamine distribution market in Wisconsin." The report further identified the Outlaws Motorcycle Club, and a handful of other motorcycle groups, as dangerous criminal enterprises.[22]

"These gangs are organized crime groups," said another DEA spokesman, Bill Deac. "They are nationwide, they deal in illicit drugs, they do it for profit, and they definitely are a problem." The DEA report further noted that the OMC is "the strongest club in the eastern half of the United States" and put the nationwide membership of the group at five thousand.[23]

Initially, the forty-five page DEA report was leaked to the press by Rep. Bob Walker (R-PA), the chairman of a House of Representatives' committee that held hearings on the activities of one-percent motorcycle clubs. Walker hoped that the document's release would build support for a federally coordinated clampdown on outlaw motorcycle gangs. The congressman further told the media that members of one-percent motorcycle clubs are involved "in political intimidation, political infiltration and most of the types of things associated with traditional organized crime."[24]

Events in Milwaukee accentuated Walker's remarks. On June 9, 1980, the Wisconsin Court of Appeals vacated an earlier order temporarily halting a John Doe proceeding regarding the shootings at the Knew Boot saloon. As a result, prosecutors focused their attention on a handful of Outlaws' members. Two months later, twenty-year-old Susan Yokofich, of Cudahy, entered a guilty plea to the charge of harboring her boyfriend, Edward "Shock" *Anastas*, after the incident at Frenchy's tavern. Assistant District Attorney William Sosnay told a judge that, while police searched for the biker, Yokofich looked for an apartment for the couple and bought groceries for the fugitive. After being arrested in May 1980, detectives also questioned Anastas about the shootings at the Knew Boot saloon.[25]

Just two weeks later, the Milwaukee County District Attorney's office charged a member of the OMC's Milwaukee chapter, Gilbert Aspuro, and an Outlaws' associate, John Thomas Marefke, with the homicide of Vaughn Cox. During a preliminary hearing, Ronald Gerger, who had known Aspuro and Marefke for several years, told the Court that Aspuro directed a racial epithet at Cox. When the

African-American man responded by asking, "What did you say?" Aspuro then shouted, "You heard me, nigger, take a hike." Aspuro, who had obtained a knife from Marefke, then "slammed the knife into his stomach," at which time "the black man buckled over."[26]

Prior to offering testimony at a John Doe hearing, a key eyewitness to the stabbing was placed in a witness protection program after Aspuro allegedly warned the man that he would be found dead if he told anyone about the incident. *Milwaukee Sentinel* reporter John Fauber also noted that investigators believed Marefke and Aspuro were both present during the shootings at the Knew Boot. Having previously chided courtroom officials for granting low bail for serious crimes, the reporter again noted that a circuit court judge had set bond for the Cox homicide at just $20,000.[27]

Still, the negative press coverage failed to dent the psyche of Milwaukee County's complacent judiciary, and members of the Outlaws Motorcycle Club continued to supply the journalist with enough material to make his case. On November 28, Anastas was charged with a felony count of recklessly endangering safety and another felony count of criminal damage to property after a May 9 altercation with Paul Olson at the Middle Earth tavern on S. Kinnickinnic Avenue. Witnesses said that the Outlaw entered the tavern, punched Olson, discharged four gunshots into a nearby jukebox, and then fled the pub. The owner of the tavern did not know Olson by name, but described him as six-foot-three-inch white male, about twenty-six-years-of-age, weighing about two hundred and twenty-five pounds, and having shoulder-length blond hair.[28]

The search for the jukebox killer resulted in other criminal charges. The following morning, Milwaukee police officer Eugene Grabowski, who had responded to the initial complaint of gunshots at the Middle Earth tavern, was alerted by South Milwaukee Police Sergeant Eric Slamka that Anastas was at a village bar with other Outlaws. After a brief meet, Slamka, along with several heavily armed MPD officers, simultaneously entered the tavern. Grabowski saw a man, who matched the description of Olson provided by the Middle Earth's owner, quickly "stand up, look away from Grabowski, and move his hand to the area near his waist." The officer frisked the man, later identified as Douglas P. Mattes, and recovered a .38 caliber pistol in his pocket. Mattes was later charged in federal court with being a felon in possession of a firearm.[29]

As 1980 came to a close, the legal fees generated by members of the Outlaws Motorcycle Club had bolstered the coffers of Alan Eisenberg's small law firm. With trials and investigations still pending, the defense attorney sought to fend off an increasingly aggressive law enforcement response.

[1]County of Milwaukee, Inter-Office Communication 2342, Confidential Informant, interview with Robert M. Molthen, Subject: Larry Anstett Homicide Bombing, February 28, 1980 (held by author).

[2]Ibid.

[3]Ibid.

[4]Charles Berard, Interview with author, March 16, 2015; Charles Berard, interview by author, October 17, 2015.

[5]*Milwaukee Sentinel*, June 28, 1978, p. 5; Wisconsin Department of Justice, Department of Criminal Investigation, Case Activity Report of Ronald Feurer, March 17, 1980 (held by author).

[6]*Milwaukee Journal*, March 12, 1980, Part 2, p. 5;

[7]*Milwaukee Journal*, March 14, 1980, Part 2, p. 2.

[8]*Milwaukee Journal*, April 14, 1980, Part 2, p. 2.

[9]*Milwaukee Sentinel*, April 3, 1980, p. 5.

[10]Ibid.

[11]*Milwaukee Journal*, June 13, 1980, Part 2, p. 7; *Milwaukee Sentinel*, April 3, 1980, p. 5.

[12]*Milwaukee Sentinel*, June 10, 1980, p. 8.

[13]Gary Wetzel, Medal of Honor, Vietnam. Medal of Honor Oral Histories, September 27, 2011, https://www.youtube.com/watch?v=e2fyReohlKM (accessed June 27, 2016).

[14]Ibid.

[15]Ibid.

[16]*Janesville Daily Gazette*, November 22, 1968, p. 5.

[17]State of Wisconsin v. Gary George Wetzel, Criminal Complaint, Milwaukee County, Case #J-7996, June 20, 1980.

[18]Ibid.

[19]Ibid.

[20]*Milwaukee Journal,* August 27, 1980, Accent, p. 4.

[21]*Milwaukee Sentinel*, September 2, 1980, p. 11.

[22]*Kenosha News*, July 25, 1980, p. 13.

[23]Ibid.

[24]Ibid.

[25]*Milwaukee Sentinel*, June 10, 1980, p. 8; *Milwaukee Sentinel*, August 15, 1980, Part 2, p. 14.

[26]*Milwaukee Sentinel*, October 10, 1980, p. 5.

[27]Ibid.

[28]*State of Wisconsin v. Edward J. Anastas,* Criminal Complaint, Milwaukee County, Case #1980CF009173, November 28, 1980.

[29]*United States v. Douglas Paul Mattes*, Decision of the U.S. Court of Appeals (7th Cir.), Case #81-2998, August 30, 1982.

CHAPTER NINE

DOWN BUT NOT OUT

The early 1980s ushered in a changing of the guard within Milwaukee's biker community. Some one-percenters went to prison, while others — similar to the old solider of Douglas MacArthur fame — faded away. A handful of the younger bikers made the news and some became victims.

In March 1981, the fifteen-month John Doe inquiry into the shootings at the Knew Boot saloon concluded with the arrests of Gilbert Aspuro and thirty-year-old Regan Murray for first-degree murder. After waiving a preliminary hearing, the case was set for trial. In early November, Assistant District Attorney William Sosnay asked Judge Michael Barron to dismiss the charges against Aspuro after a polygraph exam suggested that he did not fire shots at the tavern. Murray entered a guilty plea to a lesser charge of manslaughter and was sentenced to a twenty-two year prison term.[1]

The second year of the new decade literally started with a bang. Having out maneuvered the sixty-six pound piece of concrete dropped from the freeway overpass, former Heaven's Devil Jory Fraker was unable to dodge a bullet. On January 8, 1981, Fraker was shooting pool with Raymond Hill, the owner of Hill's Tap, located at 5319 W. Center Street. When an "Outlaws associate" entered the bar, Fraker put down his pool stick and walked over to Ronald Gerard, who was standing near a vending machine. The two bikers exchanged words and Fraker grabbed Gerard around the neck. After breaking free, Gerard shouted, "I didn't come down here for this crap," and left the tavern followed by Fraker.[2]

Less than a minute later, Fraker reentered the tavern and, once again, began shooting pool. A few moments later, Gerard propped open the tavern's front door, pointed a shotgun at Fraker, and shouted, "You ain't going to mess with me now, you motherfucker." As Fraker charged towards the door with a pool stick, Gerard fired a blast from the shotgun, and Fraker collapsed to the floor.[3]

A short distance from the tavern, Milwaukee Police Officer Al Holifield watched as Gerard ran from the tavern and placed a long object inside a car, parked just to the west of Hill's Tap. Holifield and his partner then approached the suspicious man. A few seconds later, the officers heard a dispatcher report that a shooting had just occurred at Hill's Tap and then noticed the shotgun on the seat of Gerard's vehicle.[4]

Medical personnel transported Fraker to St. Joseph's Hospital, where he was admitted at 1:02 a.m. and pronounced dead. At the morgue, Fraker's body was identified by his sister, Jody Ann Guehrer. An autopsy revealed that Fraker died from internal hemorrhaging that stemmed from the gunshot blast.[5]

The *Associated Press* reported that Gerard was "associated with the Outlaws Motorcycle Club," and hinted that Fraker's murder may be related to the group's long-simmering feud with the Heaven's Devils. As the investigation progressed, however, it appeared that personal animosity between the two men was the underlying factor. Gerard later entered a guilty plea to second-degree murder and was sentenced to a fifteen-year prison term.[6]

Three weeks after the Fraker slaying, jury selection began in Judge Robert Landry's court for the trial of Clifford Nowak and Edward Anastas, the two Outlaws implicated in the stabbing and beatings at Frenchy's tavern.

Testifying for the state, thirty-one-year-old Corey Celske told the Court that he had met Anastas at a summer party in Wind Lake, Wisconsin, in 1979. The two men became involved in an argument over who was "toughest," and made a bet about joining the Outlaws Motorcycle Club. If either man failed to make the cut, the loser would surrender his Harley-Davidson to the winner.[7]

In May, Anastas — wearing a fresh set of Outlaws' club colors — appeared at Frenchy's tavern to collect on the bet, but Celske no longer owned a motorcycle. After agreeing to settle the dispute outside, three other OMC associates followed the pair from the bar and Celske realized "what a sucker I was to go out there."[8]

When Celske's friend, Peter Griffin, stepped from the tavern to check on the situation, Anastas, Nowak, and two other men, kicked and punched Griffin twenty-five to thirty times before stabbing him. "I was telling them to stop," said Celske. "They stopped and they came after me."[9]

At the conclusion of the week-long trial, a jury found Anastas and Nowak guilty. Six weeks later, Landry sentenced the Outlaws to three-year prison terms. The convictions took two of the club's younger members out of circulation for the riding season.[10]

A trial with larger implications began in late February. Gilbert Aspuro and John T. Marefke faced first-degree murder charges in the stabbing death of Vaughn Cox. Realizing that the racial slurs hurled by Aspuro were problematic, Eisenberg managed the *voir dire* process so well that an all-white jury was impaneled. Since the state's key witness, Ronald Gerger, knew both defendants and testified that he was certain that Aspuro stabbed Cox, Eisenberg made a self-defense claim. During cross examination, the attorney got Gerger to admit that, although Aspuro hurled insults, it was Cox who approached the defendants.[11]

Testifying in own defense, Marefke told the jury that he offered the knife to Aspuro because he feared that Cox, who was approaching, was going to "hurt someone." The state countered that West Allis police did not find a weapon on Cox's body, and, after the stabbing, neither defendant summoned medical assistance or called the police. Marefke's testimony also contradicted a previous statement. On March 22, 1979, the co-defendant told Detectives Schalk and Polakowski that he was not at the Play Pen when Cox was stabbed. Instead, he recalled only the earlier incident when Aspuro threatened a black man who had put his jacket over a bar stool.[12]

During closing arguments, Eisenburg told the jury that some of the testimony used to prosecute Aspuro and Marefke was "puke." It was Cox, the attorney argued, who appeared belligerent "and somebody coming out of nowhere." The attorney also played to the jury's racial fears. "Is there a woman out there who doesn't fear somebody coming out of nowhere in the dark of the night." In an effort to minimize the damage caused by Aspuro's racial slurs, Eisenburg lamented: "This isn't the old West. If Mr. Cox is called a nigger, Mr. Cox could have turned the other cheek. Mr.

Cox could have walked away. Mr. Cox is not justified in forcing a confrontation."[13]

On February 26, after two days of deliberations, the jury returned a not guilty verdict. In a later interview, Eisenberg "became upset" when discussing several points in the Cox case. When asked how he could defend Ernest Lacy — an African-American man who died in police custody — and a racist member of the Outlaws. Eisenberg replied that those charged with crimes do not "hire me to be his philosopher. If people hired me to be their philosopher that would be different." Instead, the attorney viewed himself as the legal system's equivalent to Don Quixote.[14]

As was the case with the 1968 incident outside the Peppermint Lounge, Cox was a black man who just happened to be in an area visited by the Outlaws. The use of derogatory language and the subsequent stabbing of Cox sent a message to African-Americans: Think twice before visiting "the strip." Nevertheless, with Eisenberg as the Outlaw Motorcycle Club's go-to defense attorney, several of the club's members had avoided significant prison sentences.

Enforcers

In the summer of 1981, allegations surfaced in federal court that a Wisconsin native was a hitman for the Outlaws Motorcycle Club. In a Canadian Broadcasting Corporation documentary, former Outlaws' member William Edson identified himself and David Michael Marshall, of Kenosha, Wisconsin, as belonging to an OMC "death squad."[15]

On May 19, 1981, following a jury trial, Marshall was found guilty of two violations of the *National Firearms Control Act*: Being a prohibited person in possession of a firearm and unlawfully possessing a firearm during interstate commerce. Though Marshall had prior convictions in Wisconsin, he had never faced serious charges until his federal indictment. Just prior to sentencing, Assistant U.S. Attorney Lawrence Anderson told Judge John W. Reynolds that officials had received information from Canadian authorities that Marshall had performed "several contract killings for the Outlaws."[16]

On February 20, 1978, Detective Sergeant Terry L. Hall, of the Ontario Provincial Police, sent a teletype to North American law enforcement agencies indicating that Outlaws' member, Robert Cote, had been shot-and-killed by members of the Hells Angels. Hall further alleged that Marshall was sent to Canada "to avenge Cote's death." Initially, Marshall denied the allegation, but later told Hall that he was "an enforcer for the Outlaws and stated that he had killed before."[17]

Four days after Cote's murder, investigators executed a search warrant at the OMC's Montreal clubhouse. Officers arrested Marshall, as well as forty other persons present, and recovered a sawed-off rifle and thirteen other firearms. Canadian officials then deported the Kenosha resident as "an undesirable alien." In an effort to verify the information provided by Canadian authorities, the U.S. Attorney's office touched base with a law enforcement source in Illinois, who confirmed that Marshall was the "national enforcer for the Outlaws."[18]

A presentencing report told the Court that Marshall had a known mean streak. In 1965, the U.S. Marine Corps issued Marshall a bad conduct discharge due to his "negativistic, hostile, and belligerent" attitude. Having invoked his Fifth Amendment right against self-incrimination during the sentencing proceeding, Marshall declined an opportunity to rebut the government's allegations. Calling the convicted biker "a dangerous person" with a "propensity toward violent behavior," Reynolds handed down two five-year prison sentences to be served concurrently.[19]

Similar to the circumstances surrounding another OMC enforcer, John W. Bushman, the Canadian government lacked the necessary proof to make homicide allegations stick. Instead, investigators cobbled together a string of smaller criminal cases in an effort to disrupt the Outlaws Motorcycle Club.

"The biker world evolves in about a ten-year cycle," said Milwaukee Police Department Lieutenant Charles Berard. "What happens is the main membership of the bikers will end up going out for a period of time for committing crimes." These jail terms typically range from three to ten years. In the interim, outlaw motorcycle clubs go on a "recruiting spree" in an effort to get "young guys to come in." For the next five years, the younger members are groomed to "be good Outlaws." As the club seeks to regroup, a lull in criminal activity sometimes occurs. From 1982 through the mid-1980s, a brief, temporary respite — part of the evolving ten-year cycle — occurred in Milwaukee.[20]

During the last half of the 1980s, this lull enabled the Sinners Motorcycle Club's Milwaukee chapter to retool its ranks. The Sinners' new president, Charlie Goldsmith, was a force to be reckoned with. *Milwaukee Journal* sports reporter Bob Berghaus took notice of the six-foot-seven, two-hundred and seventy pound South Division High School wrestler in 1976, as the undefeated Goldsmith dominated the state public school's heavyweight championship division. Ten years later, Goldsmith had added fifty pounds of muscle and had won two Wisconsin tough man competitions. Together, with Sinners' vice president, Patrick "Whitey" Robinson, Goldsmith refused to kowtow to the edicts of the OMC's Milwaukee chapter.[21]

The tensions between the two one-percent clubs culminated outside the Sinners' Michigan Street clubhouse. One evening, the Outlaws set up a meeting with Goldsmith. During the supposed summit, six members of the OMC threatened and then pistol-whipped the Sinners' president. The Outlaws told Goldsmith that the Sinners would have to close their clubhouse or be killed. Ten days later, Goldsmith — fearing that the Outlaws would target his wife and children — moved to San Francisco.[22]

Having challenged the Outlaws, the president and the vice president of the Sinners MC had developed a reputation. When Robinson became a member of the Hells Angels' Illinois Nomads chapter, he sponsored Goldsmith, who began prospecting for the HAMC's San Francisco chapter.[23]

By 1987, the Outlaws Motorcycle Club had replenished its ranks. Some of the group's veteran members had served their prison sentences and returned to the club. Besides continuously monitoring rival groups, the OMC was keenly aware that prosecutors would use the threat of lengthy prison sentences as leverage to cultivate informants. In an effort to insulate its membership, the Outlaws kept tabs on individuals susceptible to the pressures of the criminal justice system. On August 14, 1987, Lieutenant Daniel Wozeniarski alerted the media that the New Berlin Police Department had received information that the bodies of Joe Stoll and Lou Ann Irby may be buried in Lions Park. This unusual announcement, which was made prior to the actual search, was likely done to elicit a reaction from persons under surveillance. The OMC, however, suspected someone willing to trade information in exchange for leniency, such as longtime Outlaws' member Michael Drobac,[24]

Just prior to Wozeniarski's announcement, DEA agents had arrested Drobac. A month later, the U.S. Attorney's office in the Eastern District of Wisconsin indicted Drobac and Kirk Bintzler, of Franklin , with possessing about a half-kilo of cocaine with intent to deliver. Drobac's primary racket was co-managing a north side Milwaukee chop-shop. Looking to increase his earnings, however, the biker — known as "Rerun" for having to repeat his probationary period with the club — began selling cocaine from the confines of a local tavern. After his parents posted bond, Drobac was released and given a January court date.[25]

Twice convicted for serious felonies, Drobac was looking at serving a substantial amount of prison time — possibly as much as twenty-years. Federal agents hoped that he would offer information pertaining to the activities of the Outlaws in exchange for sentencing considerations. Drobac, however, refused to cooperate and told investigators that he was not about to "rat on the Outlaws because he wouldn't live long if he did"[26]

On December 10, 1987, Washington County sheriff's deputies were summoned to the Drobac family's farmhouse on Western Avenue, in the unincorporated town of Kirchhayn, by Michael's mother, Donna. Once inside, deputies observed Drobac shot-to-death on the kitchen floor. Drobac's thirty-four-year-old wife, Sandra, was shot and died face down in her bed. The couple's ten-year-old son, Brock, was killed vis-à-vis a gunshot to the head. Investigators found no indications that the farmhouse had been forcibly entered. A forensic examination of the bodies indicated that two different caliber handguns were used in the shootings. Pages of police reports from the Bureau of Alcohol, Tobacco and Firearms (ATF) and other law enforcement agencies, as well as letters from Drobac's attorney, were spread over the kitchen table. A handful of other documents, stained with blood, were found on the floor.[27]

The Washington County Sheriff's office and Drobac's mother suspected John Bushman, the OMC's former enforcer. A resident of Florida, police placed Bushman in Wisconsin on the date of the slayings. Investigators theorized that, after arriving at the Drobacs' farmhouse unannounced, members of the Outlaws likely accused Michael Drobac of turning state's witness. In an effort to prove otherwise, Drobac retrieved the police reports and spread them across the kitchen table. Physical evidence also pointed to another member of the OMC. Thirty-five-year-old Terry Haegele, also known as "Four Foot," used crutches to compensate for a badly deformed clubbed foot. Some of the documents found on the Drobacs' kitchen floor contained a bloody "crutch print."[28]

Two competing, although somewhat similar, theories emerged regarding the motive for the murders. MPD Detective Roger Hinterthuer believed Bushman was worried that Drobac "would trade information on the Machan murder to get his charges reduced." Berard took a broader view. "There was a lot of turmoil over what was going on at the time with the Outlaws," in the late-1980s. The MPD's Criminal Intelligence Division was working in concert with other state and federal agencies, including the U.S. Internal Revenue Service, and "some members were concerned that they might be indicted." By killing the Drobacs, the OMC sought "to clean up all their loose ends," said Berard. "They considered Rerun to be a loose end. They couldn't be sure, because of Brock and Sandy that he was going to keep the company line and keep quiet."[29]

When word about the farmhouse crime scene leaked, the Outlaws realized there was yet another loose end. The distinctive bloody crutch prints made Four Foot an easy mark for prosecutors. Three weeks later, Racine County Sheriff's deputies were summoned to the home of the OMC's Milwaukee chapter enforcer, who told first responders that he had observed Haegele snoring on the couch. After the snoring ceased, the man believed Four Foot was "not breathing" and summoned medical assistance. Haegele could not be revived and was pronounced dead at the scene. An autopsy attributed the sudden death to a "multiple illicit drug overdose." A

Wisconsin Regional Crime Lab toxicology test detected cocaine, codeine, tranquilizers, and methadone in Haegele's blood.[30]

Having linked Haegele to the farmhouse murders, investigators suspected foul play. Informants told detectives that Four Foot was likely murdered. Shortly after his death, police located Haegele's car at the home of another member of the Outlaws "whom police have been trying to find for questioning since the slayings of the Drobac family." Another source told Berard that Four Foot was killed "because they found out that we [the police] knew there was a crutch print." Since Haegele suffered from trypanophobia, the three needle marks documented in the autopsy report became red-flags.[31]

The Drobac family murders and Haegele's death had a chilling effect on two veteran MPD investigators. During the late 1980s, Steve Spingola was a recently promoted detective with a go-getter's reputation. One evening, a veteran violent crimes lieutenant pulled Spingola aside. Should he ever be found dead, the lieutenant confided, members of the Outlaws should be considered prime suspects. The lieutenant related that Michael Drobac had once knocked on the door of his home at three a.m. When the then off-duty detective answered, Drobac claimed that he was simply lost and needed directions. The lieutenant believed Drobac's visit sent a message that the Outlaws knew where his family lived. Another detective also approached Spingola and explained that some members of the OMC had noticeably conducted surveillance of detectives and their families during a picnic at Humboldt Park.[32]

While several southeastern Wisconsin law enforcement agencies dedicated a plethora of resources to the Drobac and Haegele cases, a lack of witnesses brought the investigations to a predicable standstill. To make a case against John Bushman and the Outlaws, detectives needed informants.

[1]*Milwaukee Sentinel*, November 7, 1981, p. 1.

[2]*State of Wisconsin v. Ronald Joseph Gerard*, Criminal complaint, Milwaukee County, Case #J-9396, January 8, 1981.

[3]Ibid.

[4]Ibid.

[5]Ibid.

[6]*Wisconsin State Journal*, January 10, 1981, Part 4, p. 2; *Wisconsin State Journal*, December 19, 1981, Part 4, p. 2.

[7]*Milwaukee Sentinel*, January 27, 1981, p. 5.

[8]Ibid.

[9]Ibid.

[10]*Milwaukee Journal,* March 13, 1981, p 7.

[11]*Milwaukee Journal*, February 27, 1981, Part 2, p. 4.

[12]Ibid.; West Allis Police Department, Reports of Detectives Schalk and Polakowski, Case #A69-558, March 22, 1979.

[13]*Milwaukee Journal*, July 22, 1981, p. 2.

[14]Ibid., p. 1.

[15]*Kenosha News*, July 24, 1981, p. 1.

[16]Ibid.

[17]*United States v. David Michael Marshall*, 519 F. Supp. 751; 1981 U.S. Eastern District of Wisconsin, August 4, 1981.

[18]Ibid.

[19]Ibid.

[20]Charles Berard, interview with author, May 5, 2015.

[21]*Milwaukee Journal*, March 3, 1976, Part 2, p. 9; Berard, interview with author, November 17, 2015.

[22]Ibid.

[23]Ibid.

[24]*Wisconsin State Journal*, August 15, 1987, Sec. 2, p. 2.

[25]*Milwaukee Sentinel*, January 6, 1988, p. 4.

[26]Roger Hinterthuer, *Justice Delayed is Justice Denied* (Bloomington, IN: iUniverse, 2015), 148.

[27]Kurt Chandler, "Justice Denied," *Milwaukee Magazine*, March 2001, 40; Berard, interview with author, October 17, 2015; Hinterthuer, *Justice Delayed is Justice Denied*, 150.

[28]Ibid., 150; Chandler, "Justice Denied," 40; Berard, interview with author, October 17, 2015.

[29]Ibid.; Chandler, "Justice Denied," 40.

[30]*Milwaukee Journal*, February 9, 1988, p. 3B; *Milwaukee Sentinel*, January 5, 1988, p. 1.

[31]Ibid.; Berard, interview with author, November 17, 2015.

[32]Steven Spingola, retired Milwaukee Police Department Lieutenant of Detectives, e-mail message to author, November 5, 2015.

CHAPTER TEN

BOXES AND BONES

In the aftermath of the sexual assault involving John Bushman and Joseph Koller, the Outlaw Motorcycle Club's Bruce Street clubhouse was condemned by the City of Milwaukee. The group later relocated to a small building near S. 36th Street and W. National Avenue. Six years later, AOA (American Outlaws Association) Milwaukee, LLC — the business arm of the club's Milwaukee chapter — procured the rights to a spacious building located on a dead end at 1839 S. 2nd Street.

As the Internal Revenue Service investigation gained traction, it took just a year for law enforcement to execute a search warrant at the club's new location. On September 15, 1988, a task force comprised of sixty local, state, and federal officers descended on the clubhouse. Unable to breach the fortified door, officers from the MPD's Tactical Enforcement Unit used a blow torch to remove the hinges. Once inside, two menacing German shepherds greeted the entry team and were dispatched with shotgun blasts. The search for evidence of predicate acts was part of a federal grand jury investigation into the activities of the club. Three vans later transported boxes of documents and firearms from the scene. The *Milwaukee Sentinel* reported that a federal grand jury had heard testimony concerning the club's activities "in an effort to indict the Outlaws under the *Racketeering Influenced Corrupt Organizations Act* [RICO]."[1]

A predicate act, as defined by the 1970 *RICO Act*, is a misdeed that establishes a pattern of illegal activity or unlawful debt collection related to any enterprise "that affects interstate or foreign commerce." United States Code Chapter Eighteen, sections 1961-1968, defines racketeering as any violation of state laws pertaining to murder, robbery, or extortion, which are punishable by a year in prison, as well as more than one-hundred violations of federal statutes that involve mail fraud, extortion, the unlawful trafficking of narcotics, interstate theft, counterfeiting, certain immigration offenses, and terrorism. A pattern of criminality occurs when "any combination of two or more of these state or federal crimes are committed within a statutory prescribed time period."[2]

The "brainchild" of Attorney General Robert F. Kennedy and his staff of attorneys at the U.S. Department of Justice, the *RICO Act* targeted *La Cosa Nostra*, a syndicate of five Italian-American crime families. After the law was enacted, nearly a decade passed before a district-level United States attorney targeted a group of outlaw bikers with the sweeping statutes. On June 13, 1979, eleven members of the Hells Angels Motorcycle Club were indicted for racketeering. Two years later, after juries were unable to reach a verdict in two separate trials, the government dropped the charges.[3]

Now, a southeastern Wisconsin investigative task force had the OMC's Milwaukee chapter in the *RICO Act's* crosshairs. A law enforcement source further told a reporter that four people, upset with the execution of the Drobac family, had come forward with information. In one form or another, these potential testifiers had since been placed in witness protection programs. In conjunction with the racketeering investigation, officers searched for information that would prove that the Outlaws organization had received "a cut" of criminal proceeds. Another source told the newspaper that members of the Outlaws work in small crews "and they utilize non-members as much as possible to do the risky stuff."[4]

As the earlier DEA report noted, the Outlaws had significant links to drug trafficking. Since club members involved in the sale of narcotics often conducted transactions with persons unaffiliated with the club, the OMC's capacity to threaten informants was limited. One example was a Northshore metro Milwaukee cocaine ring's connection to Joseph "Junkyard" Koller — out on parole for the clubhouse sexual assault.

In the late 1980s, a veterinarian in the upscale suburb of Mequon, Shia Ben-Hur, devised a scheme to import cocaine. A contact in Columbia would surgically pack female dogs with large quantities of the drug and then ship the animals to Ben-Hur's Port Washington Road office. In order to move the dogs through customs, co-conspirators placed stickers on transport cages to alert handlers that the animals were ill and in heat. When drug enforcement canines hit on the drug-laced dogs, agents brushed aside the alerts. Once the cargo arrived, Ben-Hur would surgically remove and distribute the cocaine.[5]

FBI agents caught wind of the operation and arrested Ben-Hur. The veterinarian later told investigators that he had dealt cocaine to Koller on twenty-one separate occasions. Facing a possible twenty-five-year sentence, Ben-Hur agreed to participate in a controlled sale of five hundred and twelve grams of cocaine to Koller.[6]

With FBI agents conducting surveillance of the veterinarian's clinic, Koller drove his car into the parking lot, exited, and met Ben-Hur near another vehicle. Agents watched as Ben-Hur removed a sizeable plastic bag of cocaine and handed the sack to Koller, who walked towards his vehicle. Agents then closed in and arrested Koller, who denied knowing that the substance was cocaine. Instead, the biker asserted that he "just assumed it was flea powder" to treat his Doberman pinscher. The off-the-cuff alibi proved feeble. Investigators reported that Koller's only pooch had been killed during the execution of a prior search warrant. Prosecutors were also skeptical. Due to the number of visits to Ben-Hur's office, Koller would have procured over seven pounds of "flea powder," enough to treat a dozen animals. A hardcore member of the Outlaws, Koller refused to cooperate with the government and was sentenced to twenty-seven years in federal prison.[7]

As the investigation into Ben-Hur progressed, federal officials sought to follow the trail of the veterinarian's cocaine. On July 14, 1988, Aryln Ackley, the chairman of the Mole Lake band of Chippewa Indians, was charged with three counts of delivering cocaine to an undercover Oneida County drug agent. Investigators later alleged that Koller had provided some of the cocaine that he received from Ben-Hur to Ackley, which, again, spotlighted the Outlaws Indian connections. Ackley later entered a guilty plea and was sentenced to a five-year prison term.[8]

Box of Bones

It took nearly ten years, but investigators finally put the

squeeze to an Outlaws' associate with information regarding the disappearance of Clifford Machan, the former owner of the Sussex farm chop-shop operated by John Bushman. On December 5, 1988, two MPD auto squad detectives, Pete Simet and Dick Weibel, observed a pick-up truck that matched the description of a recently stolen Toyota. When Simet activated the unmarked squad's red light, the pick-up truck fled. A short time later, the driver — Willie Cresca — bailed out of the car but was quickly apprehended by responding officers. The Toyota actually belonged to Cresca, who bolted because of an outstanding probation violation.[9]

Cresca was a close associate of Michael "Rerun" Drobac, who had operated a chop-shop near N. 35th and W. Vliet Streets. Known as "Slant Eyes," Cresca was not considered a suspect in the Drobac family murders. While being interviewed by Simet and Hinterthuer, Cresca disclosed that Brock Drobac was actually his son. When Hinterthuer asked Cresca if he could provide details about the slayings, Cresca replied, "Yeah, it was that fucking Flapper, but I can't prove it. I can't get him for those murders, but I sure as hell can get him for another one cause I was there."[10]

During the four-hour interview with Cresca, investigators learned that, in the summer of 1978, Machan had been lured to a family farm in Waukesha County by Bushman. Cresca told police that Drobac then ordered him to the farm. When he arrived, Drobac handed Cresca the keys to Machan's truck and was told to drive the vehicle to a chop-shop on Milwaukee's north side. After returning to the farm with a different vehicle, Cresca observed Machan, whose face had been crushed, lying next to a freshly dug grave, dead from a shotgun blast to the stomach.[11]

The following day, the three MPD detectives visited the Waukesha County Sheriff's office. A group of investigators then spent the next two days locating the Letko family farm. A day later, armed with a search warrant, a small crew began digging beneath a metal shed.[12]

The morning of December 8 was seasonally cold and the nine investigators gathered in front of a propane heater. With the assistance of a backhoe from the City of Waukesha's Public Works Department, the ground inside the shed was carefully excavated.

The first bone was unearthed an hour after the dig began. After the Waukesha County Medical Examiner determined that the arm bone was indeed human, the digging continued until a full skeleton appeared.[13]

Law enforcement finally believed that they had the goods on Bushman, but cracks in the case began to surface. Since DNA testing was in its infancy, forensic pathologists were unable to identify the deceased as Machan. Moreover, Waukesha County District Attorney Paul Bucher believed that the credibility of Cresca — a career criminal with a long rap sheet — would not withstand a rigorous cross examination.[14]

In his book, *Justice Delayed is Justice Denied,* retired MPD Detective Roger Hinterthuer thoroughly documented the ensuing tensions between the Waukesha County District Attorney's office and officials from Milwaukee. Though the medical examiner believed, with a degree of medical certainty, that the remains unearthed at the Letko farm were those of Clifford Machan, Bucher continued to vacillate. Still, believing that the investigation would likely conclude with criminal charges, Hinterthuer contacted the family of Larry Anstett.[15]

The family meeting included the deceased's older brother, Ralph Anstett, Jr., his wife, Joan, and Larry's sister, Kathy. The family explained that the bombing death of their brother had taken a toll on their parents. After the incident, Ralph Anstett, Sr. began drinking heavily and passed away a few years prior to the meeting. Larry's mother developed mental health issues and had since been institutionalized.[16]

Retired MPD Lieutenant of Detectives Steve Spingola recalled an incident after Larry's death. During a Catholic Mass at a west side parish, Mrs. Anstett stood up, began shouting incoherently at a priest, and had to be removed. "One can only imagine the mental anguish of having your child's life taken so violently," said Spingola. "In these types of cases, the toughest thing for parents is a belief that they somehow failed to adequately protect their child. It's a place no parent ever wants to go, and even more psychologically troubling because they never had an opportunity to say 'goodbye.'"[17]

At the meeting, Hinterthuer told the Anstett family that investigators had recovered TNT from Machan's farm, which had served as a chop-shop for a member of the Outlaws Motorcycle Club. As Larry's sister sobbed, the detective explained: "Cliff Machan is dead. We think Bushman killed him. We're still building our case, but Bushman will be arrested and charged with murder in the near future." When he left the Anstett home, Hinterthuer noted that, although the Lisbon Avenue home looked very similar to the way it had on that tragic day fourteen years earlier, the lives of the paperboy's family were forever altered.[18]

Meanwhile, the case against Bushman appeared to progress. Hinterthuer and Pete Simet visited a federal prison camp in Duluth to interview Willie Cresca's brother, Jim. In the aftermath of Machan's body being recovered, the detectives learned that Bushman approached Jim Cresca at a car auction and demanded to know the location of 'that fucking snitch brother of yours.' When Cresca replied that he had no clue what the former Outlaws' enforcer was speaking of, Bushman said, 'there's only three people in the world who knew where Cliff's body was; me, Rerun, and your brother, and Rerun is dead.'[19]

As time progressed, however, Hinterthuer's promise to the Anstett family turned to disappointment. During a large meeting at the Waukesha County District Attorney's office, Bucher again lamented that he was having an issue with the identification of Machan and, ultimately, declined to prosecute unless new information, including a positive identification of Machan, surfaced.[20]

Having put their hearts and souls into the murder investigations of Anstett and Machan, investigators voiced outrage. Hinterthuer told the press that Bucher was "afraid" of the Outlaws. "We have it [the Machan homicide] solved," the detective told reporter Jacqueline Seibel, "but no one wants to prosecute it." Hinterthuer echoed the mantra of OMG investigators: "You are not going to get nuns as witnesses in these cases."[21]

In 2003, Willie Cresca's life came to an abrupt end during a stay at the Waukesha County jail. Bucher claimed that Cresca's death would not impact "any future murder prosecution." The detectives who had worked the Outlaws' cases believed otherwise.

Former OMC associate Billy "The Kid" Wadsworth had previously told police that the death of Machan "was linked to about seven Outlaws-related murders," including the homicides of the Drobacs and fifteen-year-old Larry Anstett. Unfortunately, prosecutors in two counties refused to heed the example of Assistant District Attorney Michael Malmstadt and roll-the-dice. As a result, the killers of at least eleven people remained free to, if need be, kill again.[22]

[1]*Milwaukee Sentinel*, September 16, 1988, p. 1.

[2]Frank J. Marine, "Criminal RICO: 18 U.S.C. § 1961 – 1968, A Manual for Federal Prosecutors." Fifth Ed. October 2009 (held by author), 1-2.

[3]Rodney Stich, *The FBI, the CIA, the Mob, and Treachery* (Alamo, CA: Silverpeak Enterprises, 2005), 280; *New York Times*, February 26, 1981, p. A14.

[4]*Milwaukee Sentinel*, September 16, 1988, p. 13.

[5]*United States v. Joseph R. Koller*, Decision of U.S Court of Appeals, 956 F.2d 1408 (7th Cir. 1992); *Chicago Tribune*, September 19, 1990, p. 20; *Milwaukee Sentinel*, March 11, 1992, p. 5A; Berard, interview with author, October 17, 2015.

[6]*United States v. Joseph R. Koller*, Decision of U.S Court of Appeals, 956 F.2d 1408 (7th Cir. 1992).

[7]Ibid.; *Milwaukee Sentinel*, November 4, 1988, Part 2, p. 2; *Chicago Tribune*, September 19, 1990, p. 20; Berard, interview with author, October 17, 2015.

[8]*Milwaukee Sentinel*, July 14, 1988, Part 2, p. 6; *Milwaukee Sentinel*, September 18, 1990, p. 5; *Milwaukee Journal*, March 1, 1989, p. 12.

[9]Roger Hinterthuer, *Justice Delayed is Justice Denied* (Bloomington, IN: iUniverse, 2015), 151.

[10]Ibid., 153.

[11]*Milwaukee Sentinel*, December 9, 1988, p. 6; Hinterthuer, *Justice Delayed is Justice Denied*, 155.

[12]*Milwaukee Sentinel*, December 9, 1988, p. 6; Hinterthuer, *Justice Delayed is Justice Denied*, 155.

[13]Hinterthuer, *Justice Delayed is Justice Denied*, 160.

[14]Milwaukee Journal Sentinel, August 11, 2003, p. 6B.

[15]Hinterthuer, *Justice Delayed is Justice Denied*, 226.

[16]Ibid., 210.

[17]Steve Spingola, e-mail to author, November 20, 2015.

[18]Hinterthuer, *Justice Delayed is Justice Denied*, 211.

[19]Ibid., 230.

[20]Ibid., 269.

[21]Chandler, "Justice Denied," 41; *Milwaukee Journal Sentinel*, August 11, 2003, p. 6B.

[22]*Milwaukee Journal Sentinel*, August 9, 2003, p. 1B.

CHAPTER ELEVEN
RISING STARS

In the late 1980s, rumors swirled that the Hells Angels Motorcycle Club (HAMC) was contemplating an expansion into the heart of the Outlaws Motorcycle Club's turf in Illinois. Tensions between the Outlaws and Hells Angels had existed for over a decade, due, in part, to the July 4, 1979, executions of four OMC members and a thirty-one-year-old woman at a North Carolina clubhouse. Charlotte-Mecklenburg police quickly termed the incident the "July Fourth massacre." Prior to a large Outlaws' funeral procession, Police Officer Walter Hilderman warned the press, "Both groups are in town, and they hate each other's guts." Believing that their southern chapters had previously been outmaneuvered by the Hells Angels, this time around the Outlaw Motorcycle Club's Midwestern leadership was determined to take the fight to their adversary.[1]

In an effort to deter the HAMC's expansion, the Outlaws sought an increase in membership. A surge of members meant accepting bikers from other clubs and, in some instances, lowering standards for mental toughness. A prime example was Charles D. Thomas, a former member of the Confederate Drifters Motorcycle Club and a probate for the OMC. Arrested by the MPD, Thomas told an investigator that he was not particularly fond of his club nickname, "Charlie the Tuna," and was having second thoughts about becoming a member "because as an Outlaw he never had more trouble with the police until he put on that patch."[2]

An increase in members further enabled the OMC to defend and respond to potential HAMC sponsored activity in the Wisconsin-Illinois borderland region. To bolster its ranks, the Outlaws considered patching over an entire club — the Antioch, Illinois-based Booze Runners MC. In Kenosha County and northern Illinois, the Booze Runners had caught the attention of law enforcement. The club's president, Kevin "Spike" O'Neill, was a charismatic individual with a faithful following. The Booze Runners irritable enforcer, Mark "Crash" Quinn, enjoyed a good fight, especially when fellow bikers outnumbered adversaries. "If they [the Booze Runners] were in a tavern and somebody looked at them cross-wise," said Kenosha County Sheriff's Detective Larry Zarletti, "they got smacked."[3]

One example of Quinn's tactics, was the beating of a man at a rural Kenosha County bar. Quinn, along with an unidentified member of the Booze Runners, entered Sprit's Pub, attired in club colors. The six-foot-two, two hundred and twenty-five pound Quinn then approached a man as he finished a game of pool. "Are you Ron Weisinger?" asked Quinn. When the man replied he was, Quinn asked, "Do you remember me?" and punched Weisinger in the face.[4]

Weisinger told responding deputies that he was positive his attacker was Quinn, who he described as a white male with a pony tail and a thick mustache. As the two Booze Runners left the tavern, witness Daniel Svoboda heard one of them shout, "We'll be back! We'll be back!" On November 23, Quinn was charged with battery and a bench warrant was issued for his arrest.[5]

O'Neill's and Quinn's brash behavior and overall disrespect for law enforcement gave the Booze Runners instant street credibility. Still, the Outlaws weighed the pros and cons of having an entire club patch over. The OMC's previous attempt to place a chapter outside Milwaukee crashed-and-burned when Garry Horneck was arrested for his wife's murder in 1976. The Sheboygan experience also included a John Doe probe, a process that left a bad taste in the mouths of the Outlaws' leadership. In theory, a chapter operating in another part of the state would remain under the command-and-control apparatus of the club's Milwaukee chapter. Yet, if a situation presented itself, a spur of the moment decision made by the president of another chapter might have consequences for the entire club.[6]

To test their mettle, the Outlaws' leadership tasked the Booze Runners with an act of urban terrorism. On the evening of November 13, 1990, Kevin O'Neill and Randall Miller, placed an improvised explosive device (IED) at the rear door of the Hell's Henchmen MC's Rockford, Illinois clubhouse, located at 1622 W. State Street.[7]

At about 11 p.m., the club's president, Roger Fiebrantz, and his girlfriend, Cathy Roach, returned to their second floor apartment, located at the front of the clubhouse. As the couple watched "adult films on television," Fiebrantz heard what he thought was a television or a radio on inside the clubhouse. After telephoning the clubhouse and getting no answer, the burly biker — armed with a .38 caliber revolver — went outside to check on the matter.[8]

As he walked a small cement gangway on the lookout for possible intruders, Fiebrantz stopped at the rear door of the clubhouse. Upon opening the screen door, he observed what appeared to be a red fire extinguisher propped up against the interior door. The Hell's Henchmen president bent over to get a closer look and saw wires protruding from the cylinder. He also noticed "a pipe looking thing" protruding from the top of device. After "very softly" closing the door, Fiebrantz immediately told Roach to evacuate the apartment. The couple then walked a block west and summoned the police from a pay phone.[9]

Responding officers evacuated the neighborhood, set up roadblocks, and rerouted traffic. After carefully evaluating the object, at 2:50 a.m., ordnance technicians decided to place the fire extinguisher on a net for transport to a safe location. The IED would then be fed into a fortified steel tube, which would direct a potential explosion "straight up into the air." However, when the fire extinguisher was directed into the tube with a set of ropes, the cylinder rolled on top of the timer and the IED detonated. The blast lifted three bomb squad officers off their feet, "ruptured the inside of the bomb box, bent the trailer's axle, and shattered windows in vehicles and buildings three blocks away." The three officers sustained minor concussions, were treated at a local hospital, and later "returned to duty."[10]

Standing in a car wash two hundred feet west of the clubhouse, Fiebrantz watched as the bomb's shockwave slammed an open door of a nearby car shut. The flames from the explosion shot one hundred feet into the air. A fifteen-year member of the Hell's Henchmen, Fiebrantz told investigators that things had been very "mellow" over the summer and that the club was not having problems with anyone.[11]

Outlaw biker investigators had heard rumors regarding the Hell's Henchmen's realignment to the Hells Angels and, therefore, suspected that the Outlaws may have had a hand in the bombing. A confidential informant further related that the Hell's Henchmen would "not tell the police anything" and would take care of the problem themselves.[12]

While the IED did not directly impact its target, the on-scene explosion put the Hell's Henchmen on notice that their relationship with the Hells Angels carried certain consequences. A month-and-a-half after successfully eluding detection, the Booze Runners officially dropped their club's patch and welcomed in the New Year as the Outlaws Motorcycle Club's Stateline chapter. Having filled the OMC's void on the Wisconsin-Illinois border, O'Neill's crew of ruthless riders willingly assumed the role of point men in the guerrilla-style war with the Hell's Henchmen and the Hells Angels. The charismatic O'Neill, "a man without morals or values," became an unapologetic advocate for the Outlaws' A.D.I.O.S. credo — Angels die in Outlaw states.[13]

The Rockford bomb blast also ushered in a new phase: The OMC's transition from a criminal enterprise to an at-will urban terrorist network. What differentiates organized crime from urban terrorism is motive. The goal of a criminal enterprise is to profit from illicit activities and then launder some of the proceeds. The aim of an urban terrorist is public coercion, which may or may not include a political component. Researcher H.H.A. Cooper defines terrorism as "…the intentional generation of massive fear by human beings for the purpose of securing and maintaining control over other human beings."[14]

Another component of urban terrorism is the intimidation of government officials. In this regard, it took only a few months for the Stateline chapter to adopt the Wrecking Crew's *modus operandi*. In Kenosha, one particular individual stood in the way of the OMC's new chapter: Detective Larry Zarletti, a full-time motorcycle gang investigator with the county sheriff's office. On February 13, 1991, Quinn was convicted of two counts of battery, two counts of intimidating a witness, and one count of obstructing an officer. During the proceeding, Quinn turned and "made a sneering gesture" to Zarletti. After being returned to the jail, Quinn told a corrections administrator that "Zarletti was out to get him" and further stated that the detective owned "an ugly home" and described the dwelling.[15]

On March 22, 1991, Quinn again appeared in court and received a four-year prison sentence. As Zarletti and a colleague exited the courtroom, the detectives walked by a group of Outlaws and overheard one of the bikers say, "We'll have to get ahold of Century 21 and go through that house." Zarletti had just listed his home with the reality company.[16]

Eight days later, a volunteer at the Zarletti's First Assembly of God church provided the detective with three survey cards used to critique an Easter musical — a function that Zarletti and his family had attended. The volunteer found it odd that two of the survey's participants reported that they had heard about the production from "Larry Zarletti's call girl" and "Larry Zarletti's girlfriend." One of the cards was allegedly authored by the now imprisoned Mark Quinn, and the other by Kevin O'Neill.[17]

On April 9, Zarletti interviewed David "Kid" Kadlec, a member of the OMC's Stateline chapter, at the biker's place of employment. Kadlec explained that the Outlaws had visited the church as "payback for all the trouble" the detective had caused the club and noted, "Spike wanted to show you he was not afraid of you."[18]

Another member of the Outlaws, Mark Glass, admitted to detectives that he, along with other members of club, did attend the church musical because "it's a free country, isn't it?" Having heard that Zarletti was slated to participate in the production, Glass's sister, Deanna, obtained tickets for her brother, who then provided a pair to "Kevin O'Neill and a guy named Steve."[19]

On April 20, O'Neill sent a certified letter to Kenosha County Sheriff's Department addressed to Zarletti. In the letter, the president of the OMC's Stateline chapter alleged that the detective had told Kadlec that, should members of the Outlaws ride into his town, Zarletti would "shoot them off their motorcycles." O'Neill further wrote that the Zarletti had "made it personal when you and your henchmen were taking pictures of my wifes [sic] ass outside the courtroom" at Quinn's sentencing hearing. O'Neill carbon copied the letter to several law enforcement agencies, the *Milwaukee Sentinel*, the *Kenosha News*, and the American Civil Liberties Union.[20]

Three weeks later, O'Neill agreed to meet with investigators at the Kenosha County Public Safety Building. The Stateline chapter's president admitted being present at the church musical, but insisted that the harassment complaint was unfounded. The matter was eventually reviewed by the Kenosha County District Attorney, who declined to prosecute.[21]

O'Neill's scurrilous allegations of professional misconduct was just one component of an overall strategy of intimidation. Mark Glass went so far as to telephone a high school classmate, Leonard Giannola, a patrol officer with the Kenosha County Sheriff's Department, at his home. Glass demanded to know why "was Larry Zarletti harassing the Outlaws?"[22]

Similar to the activities of the Milwaukee chapter's "Wrecking Crew," the Outlaws sought to convince the motorcycle gang investigator that pursuing the Outlaws was not worth the headaches. The placement of the IED at the Hell's Henchmen Rockford clubhouse suggested that O'Neill's crew was preparing to take the fight to the Outlaws' adversaries, and the last thing the club needed was an aggressive investigator catching them in the act.[23]

For officer safety purposes, the Kenosha County Sheriff's Department internally disseminated a nine-page information bulletin. Deputies were told that subordinates were "very loyal to O'Neill," and that the club's enforcer, Randall Miller, had "a long, violent criminal history." The report also listed prison inmate Mark "Crash" Quinn as having a "very bad attitude toward law enforcement. Is violent!"[24]

"I can honestly tell you that in twenty-four years of law enforcement nothing has touched closer to home than to have members of the Outlaws appear at my church," Zarletti told the Associated Press. "They were there for one reason — to intimidate me."[25]

The acts of intimidation, the Rockford bomb blast, and the homicides of three one-percent bikers outside an east coast tavern, had served as the impetus for federal legislation. In an effort to coordinate investigations of one-percent bikers at the national level,

U.S. Senator Dennis DeConcini (D-Arizona) introduced *Senate Bill 339, The Outlaw Street and Motorcycle Gang Control Act of 1991*. The bill's provisions increased penalties for the use of firearms and explosives attributed to acts of gang violence. Although S. 339 had bipartisan co-sponsors, the proposed legislation was attacked by the AMA's lobbying arm and *American Motorcyclist* magazine for potentially labeling "as criminals all riders who belong to legitimate motorcycle organizations or clubs." Viewed by civil libertarians as an overreach, S. 339 died in the Senate Judiciary Committee. Forthcoming events, however, would prove DeConcini a visionary.[26]

With the federal legislation quietly tabled, the OMC took aim at clubs allied with the Hells Angels (HAMC). Having previously served as the club's regional president and a national vice president, Harry "Taco" Bowman became the OMC's international president in 1984. Bowman operated out of a clubhouse in Detroit, lived in an upscale suburb, and drove an armor-plated Cadillac. In early 1991, Bowman ordered the assassination of Raymond "Bear" Chaffin, the president of a Warlocks MC, a group that sold drugs for the HAMC in Florida. On February 21, Outlaws' probate Alex Ankerich — armed with .22 caliber pistol outfitted with a silencer — entered a Ft. Lauderdale garage and shot Chaffin four times in the back of the head.[27]

During visits to Florida, club member Christopher Maiale provided protection for the OMC's international president, and later told a court that Bowman delivered valium, marijuana and cocaine to other Outlaws. On one occasion, Maiale watched as Bowman unsuccessfully attempted to sever a man's ear with a dull knife.[28]

During a later visit to Chicago, Bowman became irate after observing a Hell's Henchmen in the vicinity of an Outlaws' clubhouse. He summoned the OMC's Chicago region president, Randy "Mad" Yager, and the OMC's Chicago chapter president, Carl "Jay" Warnecke, to his residence in Detroit to develop a plan of action.[29]

The coordination of a top-down operational plan was a product of the Outlaws Motorcycle Club's military-style command-and-control apparatus, which enabled the group to seamlessly shift strategies in response to real or perceived threats. As the 1990s emerged, the OMC evolved into a Simple Structure organization with a "strategic apex" that coordinated "by direct supervision." The American Outlaws Association (AOA), an umbrella group of sixty-four OMC chapters throughout the United States, operated in "simple, dynamic environments" controlled by "strong leaders." The AOA was divided in to five distinct regions. Chapter presidents reported to the club's regional presidents. Each regional president further reported to the international president of the OMC. This type of organizational structure is adopted by groups "facing severe crises," and was used by Bowman to activate a cell of urban terrorists when the Outlaws saw a need to defend their turf.[30]

The Manson of the Midway

With Mark Quinn in prison, Spike O'Neill elevated Randall Miller to the position of club enforcer. During the probe of the Outlaws visit to the First Assembly of God's Easter musical, Miller telephoned Kenosha County Sheriff Allen Kehl.

"What's we gonna to do to straighten this all out?" Miller asked the sheriff, who recorded the conversation. "I don't know," Kehl replied, "what's the problem?"

"This is getting way out of hand," Miller explained. "Ah, two people who try to push and they don't get nowhere, you know." Miller then reiterated O'Neill's earlier allegation that Detective Zarletti was threatening to "shoot people off their bikes."

"Well, I'll tell you," Kehl explained, "law enforcement's not gonna lose…we have an obligation out here and, ah, and that's to make this community safe."

"I don't disagree with that at all," said Miller, "…but this bickering, and, you know, people saying they're gonna kill people. Nobody ever said they're gonna kill nobody."

The sheriff then laid down the law. "I think, Randy, probably a lot of this started from harassment and attempted intimidation, and I can tell you right up front, you know, this department and nobody in it is gonna be intimidated by anybody, and when you deal with one you deal with all, and I'm not just talking our department, you're talking the surrounding area law enforcement as well."

When Miller voiced concern that the sheriff's department had arranged a meeting with twelve law enforcement agencies regarding the incident at the church, Kehl replied that the "tactics" that the club had employed to intimidate Zarletti "aren't going to fly."

"Okay," Miller replied, "how about the tactics where Larry comes in with his film crew, takes a look at Spike's wife's ass, and says nice, nice…"

The sheriff promised to investigate any complaints and told Miller, "I can police my organization a hell of a lot better than you're policing yours."

Later in the conversation, Miller hinted that the Outlaws had a source inside law enforcement. "Where does Larry Zarletti get off telling city police that are having roll call that there's a, a contract killing on him and his family, you know."

Miller asked for a meeting, but Kehl explained that talking would not resolve the matter and added, "I guess your chapter's gonna have to prove itself." Wise to the Outlaws' good cop, bad cop routine, the sheriff made his position crystal clear, and ended the conversation by telling the biker, "I guess the next move is yours."[31]

The biker's "next move" would not be a good one. Also known as "Madman," Miller's moniker seemed appropriate. On August 24, 1992, a local Racine, Wisconsin marijuana trafficker, Donald "Domino" Wagner, was lured to a boat launch in the rural town of Burlington under the pretense of making a sale. When Wagner arrived, he was greeted by Miller and David "Kid" Kadlec. After robbing the drug dealer, Miller shot Wagner in the head with a .22 caliber pistol. The wounded man then came at Miller, who fired three more rounds into Wagner's torso. A sheriff's deputy on patrol later came upon Wagner's corpse near his still-running Chevrolet Camaro.[32]

A cold-blooded psychopath, the thirty-three-year-old Miller bore a striking resemblance to a similarly-aged Charles Manson. In a 1990 booking photo, the lean five-foot-eleven-inch biker sported a bushy beard and a ponytail. Miller's droopy eyes masked the intensity of a madman. Convicted of a Kenosha County burglary in the early 1980s, Miller — like serial killer Theodore Bundy — hid his nefarious intentions behind the façade of a disarming personality. "Everyone who knows him likes him," said Miller's landlord, Donald Sullivan. "What I saw of him [Miller] and his wife," said another neighbor, "makes me believe they are very nice people."[33]

Like traditional *La Cosa Nostra* organized crime groups, Miller and the Outlaws sought to generate income for the club by engaging in illegal activity. In one regard, however, one-percent bikers are more ruthless than the mob. "Whereas the mafia," said MPD Lieutenant Charles Berard, "…they develop a blood-in-blood-out-type mentality…the public, they didn't care, because the public wasn't part of it." Outlaw bikers, on the other hand, "will go all over the place. The will go into bars, they will go into public venues and they don't care" if innocent people become victims.[34]

The gruesome murders of an elderly Illinois couple are a prime example. On the morning of April 8, 1993, Miller left his Pell Lake, Wisconsin residence and slid into the passenger's seat of a car driven by James "Preacher" Schneider, a fellow member of the Outlaws Motorcycle Club. Soon, the dangerous psychopath and his would-be accomplice had completed the fifteen-mile drive to the Illinois farm of Morris and Ruth Gauger, a semi-retired couple in their seventies. Having heard that $30,000 was stashed somewhere on the property, the two bikers devised a plan to separate and terrorize the couple.[35]

After being greeted at the farmhouse by Ruth Gauger, Miller asked to speak with her husband, who operated a small motorcycle repair shop from a detached garage. Employing a ruse, Schneider stayed behind and accompanied the woman to a nearby trailer. After following her inside, Schneider pistol-whipped Ruth Gauger, who fell to the floor. He then inserted a knife in the woman's neck and slit her throat from side-to-side. Schneider then met Miller outside the garage where the two men entered the repair shop, confronted Morris Gauger, and demanded money. After turning over a small amount of cash, Miller forced the robbery victim into an adjacent room and killed the elderly man by thrusting a dagger into his side. Later, Miller would callously explain that the edged weapon entered Gauger's body "like a knife in butter." Having worn gloves and hairnets under their caps, the two killers felt confident they had covered their tracks. After stopping at a rest stop to destroy evidence, Miller and Schneider visited a Lake Geneva, Wisconsin restaurant and purchased breakfast with the robbery proceeds.[36]

When law enforcement arrived at the crime scene, investigators immediately suspected the couple's son, a recovering alcoholic, who also resided on the family's farm. On the morning of the murders, Gary Gauger awoke at 9 a.m., two-and-a-half hours after Miller and Schneider had fled. A few minutes later, he walked through his parents' home and assumed that his mother and father had left to run errands in nearby Sugar Grove. After smoking marijuana, Gary greeted a few of the family's acquaintances who had stopped by, and then spent most of the day working inside a greenhouse until 6:30 p.m.[37]

Gauger then walked across a field to the family's farmhouse and observed a padlock on his mother's trailer, which was typically secured when his parents left town. He further noticed that the door to his father's motorcycle shop was locked, although a light inside the shop was on. Gauger looked through a shop window, but did not see anything unusual inside. At 10:30 p.m., he returned to the farm house, "became worried," and stayed awake until midnight waiting for a possible telephone call.[38]

The next morning, Ruth and Morris Gauger had yet to return home. At 11a.m., his father's friend, Ed Zander, and his girlfriend, Traci Foskus, stopped by the farm to pick-up a motorcycle part. Gauger then opened an overhead door near the southwest corner of the shop and proceeded to locate the part. When Zander suggested checking a section of the shop where British motorcycle parts were stored, the three entered a small room and discovered Morris Gauger lying on his side in a pool of blood.[39]

After being summoned to the scene, detectives searched the property with Gary Gauger's consent and soon discovered the body of Ruth Gauger inside the trailer. Detained in the rear of a squad car, Gary asked an officer about his mother. When told that Ruth Gauger was deceased, Gary replied, "How could anybody do something like this for money?"[40]

With Detective Beverly Hendle in the front passenger's seat, an officer conveyed Gauger to the McHenry County Sheriff's Department in Woodstock. At 4 p.m., he was placed in a small conference room. The interrogation, which was conducted by Detectives Hendle, Lowery, and Pandre, and spanned eighteen consecutive hours, was not video or audio taped. In regards to the interrogation process, Gauger alleged the following: That Hendle told him there was a stack of evidence pointing to his guilt, including a failed polygraph examination; that Hendle claimed to have recovered a bloody knife from his pocket; that detectives told Gauger his bloody fingerprints were located in his bedroom and that bloody sheets were found on his bed. Gauger further alleged that he specifically told his interrogators that he was exhausted and wanted to sleep, but the detectives said he would not be permitted to do so.[41]

The interrogation then became "very intense," when Gauger asked, "Could it be possible that I did this in a blackout?" When Hendle replied that blackouts are common in family homicides, Gauger added, "What if I construct a hypothetical scenario using the details you have given me of the crime to jog my memory?" Told by his interrogators that police could not lie to suspects during interrogations, Gauger provided a hypothetical scenario of how the murders may have taken place.[42]

Hendle and Lowery offered a different account of the interrogation. Both detectives claimed that, although he had been interviewed in the middle of the night, Gauger did not appear fatigued. Hendle further denied telling Gauger that a stack of bloody evidence was located, but did falsely tell the prisoner that he had failed the polygraph test.[43]

At 10 a.m. the following morning, an exhausted Gauger requested an attorney. The interrogation then ceased and he was placed in a holding cell. Later, when Hendle signed the criminal complaint charging Gauger with two counts of first-degree murder, she knew "of no physical evidence" that linked the suspect to the murders of his parents.[44]

Across the border in Wisconsin, the two Outlaws listened for news regarding the couple's deaths. Two days after the discovery of the bodies, Schneider heard that the Gaugers' son had wrongfully confessed to the murders and passed the details to his accomplice. "That's great," replied Miller, relieved that the two killers had escaped detection. Later, Miller and Schneider would joke that they should author "a book on committing the perfect murder." Still, the conscience of Schneider, a graduate of Wauwatosa East High School, who had joined the Booze Runners in 1990 "because he liked the idea of a crew of guys doing things together," grew heavy. To ease his guilty mind, Schneider "built a wall" to "block out the memory" of the elderly woman he had brutally murdered.[45]

In the interim, the homicide charges leveled against the organic farmer divided the community. "Is Gauger the gentle former hippie his family and friends describe?" asked *Chicago Tribune* reporters Robert Becker and Andrew Martin. "Or is he the malevolent alcoholic with no recollection of the violence he wreaks during blackouts, as prosecutors and his former wife claim?" Just six months after being charged, and absent any physical evidence linking him to the homicides, a McHenry County jury found Gary Gauger guilty of killing his parents. At the conclusion of a January 1994 hearing, a judge sentenced "the gentile former hippie" to die by lethal injection.[46]

[1]Charlotte-Mecklenburg Police Department, official police reports of C.W. Rankin, Case No. 79-91591, July 4, 1979 (held by author); *Kokomo Tribune* (Kokomo, IN), July 5, 1979, p. 18; *St. Petersburg Independent*, July 5, 1979, p. 2A; David Allen Moore, "Question the Queen City: The Outlaws Motorcycle Gang Massacre," *The Clog News & Culture*, April 25, 2014, http://clclt.com/theclog/archives/2014/04/25/question-the-queen-city-the-outlaws-motorcycle-gang-massacre (accessed November 22, 2015).

[2]Milwaukee Police Department, In the Mater of Report: Outlaw Motorcycle Gang Activity, September 21, 1990 (held by author).

[3]*Daily Herald* (Chicago), March 8, 2000, p. 4

[4]Kenosha County Sheriff's Department, Police report of Deputy Kenneth Santelli, Case #90-78818, July 29, 1990.

[5]Kenosha County Sheriff's Department, Police report of Deputy Sturino, Case #90-78818; *State of Wisconsin v. Mark W. Quinn*, Bench Warrant, Case 90CM1375, November 20, 1990.

[6]Larry Powalisz, retired Milwaukee Police Department Detective, e-mail to author, January 9, 2016.

[7]*Rockford Register Star*, November 14, 1990, p. 1

[8]Roger Fiebrantz, interview with Detective Danny Foltz, Case #90-180-255, November 14, 1990.

[9]Ibid.

[10]*Rockford Register Star*, November 14, 1990, p. 1; *Milwaukee Journal Sentinel*, April 25, 2000, p. 3B.

[11]Roger Fiebrantz, interview with Detective Danny Foltz, Case #90-180-255, November 14, 1990.

[12]Officer Sepner, Rockford Police Department, Case #90-180-255, November 16, 1990.

[13]*Daily Herald*, March 8, 2004, p. 4; *Milwaukee Journal Sentinel*, December 23, 2000, p. 5R.

[14]H.H.A. Cooper, "Terrorism: The Problem of Definition Revisited," *The American Behavior Scientist*, 44 (February 2001), 883.

[15]Kenosha County Sheriff's Department, official police reports, Case #91-33206.

[16]Ibid.

[17]Ibid.

[18]Ibid.

[19]Ibid.

[20]Kevin O'Neill, certified letter to Detective Larry Zarletti, dated April 17, 1991, Kenosha County Sheriff's Case #91-33206.

140

[21]Ibid.

[22]Kenosha County Sheriff's Department, Police report of Leonard Giannola, Case #91-33206, April 9, 1991.

[23]Ibid.

[24]Kenosha County Sheriff, Information Bulletin, Case No. 91-33206, November 28, 1991 (held by author); *Beloit Daily News*, June 12, 1997, p. 1.

[25]*Wisconsin State Journal*, June 21, 2000, 2B.

[26]*Washington Post*, November 6, 1991, p. D1; *American Motorcyclist Magazine*, "AMA Takes on DeConcini Outlaw Bill," May 1991, 54; *Outlaw Gang and Motorcycle Gang Control Act of 1991*, S. 339, 102nd Cong., January 31, 1991, https://www.congress.gov/bill/102nd-congress/senate-bill/339/text (accessed December 23, 2015).

[27]*United States v. Henry A. Bowman*, Decision of the United States Court of Appeals, Eleventh Circuit, Case No. 01-14305, August 20, 2002.

[28]*St. Petersburg Times*, April 4, 2001, p. 4B.

[29]*United States v. Henry A. Bowman*, Decision of the United States Court of Appeals, Eleventh Circuit, Case No. 01-14305, August 20, 2002.

[30]Henry Mitzberg, "Structure in 5s: A Synthesis of the Research of Organization Design," *Management Science*, Vol. 26, No. 3 (March 1980): 322; *United States v. Henry Bowman*, Decision of the United States Court of Appeals, Eleventh Circuit, Case No. 01-14305, August 20, 2002.

[31]Kenosha County Sheriff's Department, transcript of telephone conversation between Sheriff Allen Kehl and Randall Miller, Case #91-33206.

[32]*Milwaukee Journal Sentinel*, March 21, 2000, p. 3B; Ibid., April 25, 2000, p. 3B; Ibid., October 13, 2000, p. 3B.

[33]Kenosha County Sheriff, Information Bulletin, Case No. 91-33206 (held by author); *Beloit Daily News*, June 12, 1997, p. 1.

[34]Charles Berard, interview with author, October 17, 2015.

[35]*Milwaukee Journal Sentinel*, April 25, 2000, p. 3B; Gary Gauger and Julie Von Bergen, *In Spite of the System: A Personal Story of Wrongful Conviction and Exoneration* (Lake Geneva, WI: Fourcatfarm Press, 2008), 2.

[36]Ibid., 2-3

[37]Ibid., 5, 9, 11.

[38]*Gary A. Gauger v. Beverly Hendle, Eugene Lowery, and Christopher Pandre in Their Individual and Official Capacities; the Office of the McHenry County Sheriff, and the County of McHenry*, Decision of the Appellate Court of Illinois, Second District, Case #2-10-0316, June 28, 2011.

[39]Ibid.

[40]Ibid.

[41]Ibid.

[42]Ibid.

[43]Ibid.

[44]Gary Gauger and Julie Von Bergen, *In Spite of the System*, 23-24, 27; *Shepherd Express Metro* (Milwaukee), February 24, 2000, pp. 15-16; *Gary A. Gauger v. Beverly Hendle,* et al., Decision of the Appellate Court of Illinois, Second District, Case No. 2-10-616, June 28, 2011 (held by author).

[45]*Chicago Tribune*, March 9, 1999, p. B1; *Shepherd Express Metro*, February 24, 2000, p. 15; *Beloit Daily News*, March 10, 1999, p. 1; Gauger and Von Bergen, *In Spite of the System*, 178.

[46]*Chicago Tribune*, April 17, 1995, p. B1; Gauger and Von Bergen, *In Spite of the System*, 79.

CHAPTER TWELVE

BORDERLAND SKIRMISHES

T he Hell's Henchmen Motorcycle Club had been in existence since the mid-1960s. In 1969, one of the club's members, twenty-four-year-old Vietnam veteran George Greenwood, was shot-and-killed by three members of the Hogan's Motorcycle Club in Chicago. Four years later, officials from three northern Illinois police departments voiced concerns about the Hell's Henchmen and their rivals, the Pagan Saints and Old Stylers motorcycle clubs, after a female informant was beaten. In the two decades since, the Hell's Henchmen had persevered and expanded.[1]

In the latter part of 1993, Hell's Henchmen chapters in Chicago, Rockford, and South Bend, Indiana agreed to prospect for the Hells Angels (HAMC). The bold move into the heart of the Outlaws Motorcycle Club's turf led law enforcement intelligence officials to believe that an unprecedented one-percent biker war was about to begin.[2]

In June, the Harley-Davidson Motor Company held its ninetieth anniversary celebration in Milwaukee. As 60,000 bikers from ten different countries rode into town, outlaw motorcycle gang investigators from a number of jurisdictions monitored the metro area for potential problems. In Kenosha County, a recently promoted lieutenant, Larry Zarletti, told the press that travelers "should not be startled to see as many as one hundred motorcycles coming down the road at any one time," and added that the law enforcement was "not looking to start any problem, but we are ready for any contingency."[3]

With thousands of expensive motorcycles in town, a law enforcement alert instructed officers to keep a watchful eye on rental trucks or other vehicles with ramps. Police in the Milwaukee County suburb of Oak Creek recovered three stolen Harley-Davidson motorcycles from the back of a truck rented by two Florida men. An additional eight motorcycles were reported stolen in Milwaukee.

Although the media gleefully reported that the anniversary bash was peaceful, behind the scenes rumors of possible trouble were brewing.[4]

As one might suspect, the anniversary celebration was also attended by representatives of several one-percent motorcycle clubs. Police received at least one report of a possible group of Hells Angels with weapons. Rumors also swirled that the OMC's international president, Henry "Taco" Bowman, had organized a group to gather reconnaissance on rival clubs.[5]

The purported tensions between the Outlaws and Hells Angels that emanated from the Harley-Davidson bash had yet to reach a zenith. On August 4, two members of the Hells Angels passed through Wisconsin on their way to the annual bike week in Sturgis, South Dakota, an event that serves as a world run for a number of motorcycle groups and is attended by thousands of citizen bikers.[6]

Typically, when a one-percent group travels through a rival's state flying colors, the visiting club would receive permission from the dominant outlaw motorcycle club in the area. However, before stopping at Slick's tavern — a biker hangout in Janesville, Wisconsin — two Massachusetts-based Hells Angels had failed to do so. Upon entering the pub in their club colors, a female bartender — a girlfriend of one of the Outlaws — telephoned Kevin O'Neill, who initiated a call-up of a dozen OMC members. Just prior to the incident, the Stateline Chapter also became known as the Janesville and/or Wisconsin chapter of the Outlaws.[7]

Considered a loose cannon by law enforcement and some elements within the Outlaws, Spike O'Neill was determined to put the Hells Angels on notice. As "Bad Bill" Brock stood lookout, several members of the OMC, including Michael "Studs" Baldwin, Robert "Clay" Kruppstadt, O'Neill, probate David Wolf, and at least eight others, entered Slick's and demanded the Hells Angels' club colors and "the fight was on." During the beating, the Outlaws forcibility took $1,500 and two sets of club colors from the men. Joey "Bad" Badarocco had his nose and jaw broken, and the other HAMC member was also hospitalized. After leaving the tavern, the OMC attackers destroyed the unauthorized visitors' motorcycles.[8]

In regards to the incident at Slick's, the Outlaws "basically went trophy shopping," said OMG investigator Charles Berard. "Anything that said HA on it they wanted it." Upon their release from the hospital, the Hells Angels drove the two battered men to Sturgis in a limousine. "That was just a show of class on their part. The two [HAMC] members refused to identify anybody from the Outlaws that took their colors, but this started the war in the Midwest between the Hells Angels and the Outlaws. It started the newest one [war]. And before that, there had been a lull of six to seven years where they had no violent acts."[9]

Immediately after the incident, the OMC's Chicago region president, Peter "Grease Lightning" Rogers, received a telephone call from a Hells Angels associate, who demanded that the Outlaws return the stolen colors. Rogers promised to look into the matter. Two days later, after receiving a second telephone call, Rogers told the HAMC representative that he didn't know 'what the fuck you're talking about.'[10]

With the robbery proceeds in hand, O'Neill treated the Stateline chapter to dinner at a Lake Geneva restaurant. A few days later, the president of the OMC's Milwaukee chapter paid O'Neill a visit. "Well," warned Edward "Shock" Anastas, "you've opened a whole new chapter on the war going on between us and the Hells Angels".[11]

The beating took tensions with the Hells Angels to new heights. Moreover, in the grand scheme of things, O'Neill's knee-jerk decision to attack was a blunder. While a federal RICO task force was up and running prior to the incident at Slick's, investigators had yet to obtain the required court authorization for wiretaps, telephone traces, and pen registers. The beating became one of the predicate acts of racketeering cited in the government's Title III affidavit.[12]

Retaliatory Strikes

It took less than three months for the Hells Angels to strike back. On October 30, two "improvised" hand grenades were tossed inside the residence of "Fat Wally" Posnjak, the president of the OMC's Buffalo, New York chapter. The ensuing blaze gutted the home. Posnjak had previously served as Taco Bowman's body guard during bike week in Daytona Beach, Florida. Investigators theorized that, with Posnjak on the road for the Outlaws' mandatory Pumpkin Run ride, the Hells Angels selected a soft target to send a powerful, but less than lethal message.[13]

Walter Posnjak was not a stranger to law enforcement. In 1969, he and a co-conspirator had developed a relationship with Michael Levine, an ATF undercover agent. The target of the investigation was anti-government groups, "particularly motorcycle gangs, in upstate New York." Having learned that the agent was looking for explosives, Fat Wally contacted a go-between and learned that the agent was interested in purchasing dynamite. Employed by a company that distributed fireworks, Posnjak had a license to buy and transport explosives in New York.[14]

Levine let it be known that he was procuring the explosives for a group of Cuban revolutionaries "that intended to blow up buildings and people." Initially, Fat Wally provided the agent with one hundred sticks of dynamite. Levine then requested 4,000 more and Posnjak was arrested when he arrived to make the delivery. The biker, however, later caught a break. A federal appeals court ruled that commercial dynamite was not regulated by the *Gun Control Act of 1968* and vacated the conviction.[15]

Eight years later, two Buffalo police officers were dispatched to a report of shots fired near Hazel Place and Main Street, a gritty area on the city's east side. When they arrived, the officers proceeded to frisk a group of men standing outside a recently closed tavern. After the first pat down, Posnjak began walking away, and an officer found a gun in the biker's rear pants pocket. Again, Fat Wally caught another break. An appellate court ascertained that the officer lacked a reasonable suspicion that Posnjak was armed and excluded the gun from evidence.[16]

Posnjak was a clever criminal with a good attorney. Yet, like other gang members, he had more to fear than the law. The war with the Hells Angels was just getting started and Fat Wally was already a marked man. Upset that the biker's family had also been targeted, the OMC made plans to reciprocate.

Just two days later, three members of the OMC's Stateline chapter — Johnson Blake, James "Preacher" Schneider, and Randall Miller — traveled to Richmond, Illinois to get even. When the trio arrived, one of the men shimmied under the truck of Hell's Henchmen member Edward Murphy, which was parked in the lot of the Pease Construction Company. Under stress, the perpetrators failed to adequately secure the sophisticated bomb to the truck's undercarriage. When Murphy attempted to leave work, the IED simply fell from the bottom on the truck and onto the pavement. Murphy told responding officers that "it was the Outlaws who planted the bomb."[17]

The construction company parking lot debacle did little to dissuade O'Neill's crew. Instead, the Outlaws built a larger bomb and — realizing authorities in Illinois and Wisconsin were on high alert — reevaluated potential targets. On December 15, Pat Matter, the president of the Hells Angels Minnesota chapter, returned to his Minneapolis custom motorcycle shop to find his new Chevrolet pickup truck in tatters.[18]

Six months after the purported tensions between the Outlaws and the Hells Angels at the Harley-Davidson anniversary celebration, Spike O'Neill, Randall Miller, and David "Kid" Kadlec transported a six-inch by nine-inch metal aluminum box, packed with plastic explosives to Minnesota. Once outside Matter's shop, Miller attached the bomb to the driver's side undercarriage of the truck. The explosive was outfitted with an activated switch set to explode with significant human movement. Fortunately for Matter, the triggering mechanism was too sensitive and the device detonated when Miller fled. The damage to Matter's new truck was extensive. The upper portion of the front seat had been blown through the vehicle's rear window. The blast also shattered the windows of an adjacent Ford Bronco.[19]

Investigators later learned that the bomb was assembled at the home of the OMC's Milwaukee chapter enforcer, Thomas "Woody" Sienkowski, and then transported to the Twin Cities. After an earlier plan to shoot Matter failed because the Outlaws could "never seem to find the right moment to get the shot off," a decision was made to attach an explosive device to Matter's truck.[20]

The motive for attack was evident. Matter was a leading advocate for patching over the Hell's Henchmen to the HAMC. The former Minnesota club president later described himself as "probably the biggest instigator" of increased tensions with the Outlaws, but sought to keep things "low key because that would draw attention to the business I was in [drug trafficking]."[21]

Fifteen days after the failed Minneapolis bombing, Taco Bowman summoned OMC leaders from around the country to a Ft. Lauderdale, Florida, New Year's Eve meeting. Bowman told those present that the Outlaws would escalate the biker war and "show no tolerance" for the Hells Angels or their allies. The declaration by the OMC's international president would make 1994 one of the most violent years in outlaw motorcycle gang history.[22]

During the first week of the New Year, information had made its way to the ATF that the Chicago, Rockford, and South Bend, Indiana chapters of the Hell's Henchmen had started openly prospecting for the Hells Angels. Agents further learned that the sponsor for the new chapters was the HAMC's Minnesota chapter. The motive for the bombing of Matter's truck was now crystal clear.[23]

In the Midwest, Kevin O'Neill's crew led the charge against the expansionist threat and, once again, Edward Murphy became a target. On February 10, 1994, a van operated by the OMC's apparent designated driver, Johnson Blake, rammed a truck being driven by Murphy in Fox Lake, Illinois. O'Neill and several other members of the Stateline chapter ordered Murphy out of his truck at gun point. The plan to kidnap and torture the rival biker unraveled when a police officer on patrol intervened. A search of Blake's van revealed mace, baseball bats, handcuffs on the floor, and a Smith and Wesson nine millimeter handgun. Prior to the officer's arrival, O'Neill allegedly told Murphy that "the Outlaws had left a little present for the Hells Angel in Minnesota."[24]

Five weeks later, thirty Outlaws from Indiana, Chicago, and Wisconsin, entered J.R.'s Watering Hole, a Calumet City, Illinois tavern frequented by the Hell's Henchmen. The on-duty bartender was the girlfriend of "Big Jerry" Bokina, a member of the Hells Angels' Minnesota chapter and a former Hell's Henchmen.

The Outlaws, who each carried clubs and mace, donned green handkerchiefs on their shirt sleeves to identify each other. After yanking the telephones from the wall, one member of the club pistol whipped the bartender. A member of the Outlaws later said that he was "in awe" by the amount of damage that had occurred in just a matter of minutes. [25]

"Becoming somewhat enthusiastic in their work," a police intelligence report noted, "one of the Outlaws" lopped off the top-third of "one of his thumbs and left some behind on hearing that the police" had been summoned. "We wanted to take a print off of it," said a frustrated detective, but the owner of the bar claimed that "police had been too slow in responding, so she was keeping the thumb." A source later told ATF agents that the attack was organized by the OMC's Chicago regional president, Grease Rogers, and the club's Chicago chapter president. Investigators expected that the Hell's Henchmen would retaliate in-kind.[26]

During the month of April, two suspicious fires broke out at two OMC clubhouses. The first fire occurred at the Outlaws' Indiana chapter clubhouse, located at 3265 Carolina Street, in Gary. The small fire of "undetermined origin" resulted in minor damage. No members of the club were present when the fire started; however, several Outlaws responded to the scene and refused to let fire investigators inside. Some of the Outlaws present told officials that the fire likely started because of "someone who had gone to sleep while smoking."[27]

The second fire took place on Highway 45 near Antioch, Illinois, less than a mile from the Wisconsin border. At the time, the membership of the OMC's Stateline chapter was at a swap-meet one hundred miles to the south, in Peotone, Illinois. The club immediately retained a law firm. Once again, although the clubhouse was vacant, the Outlaws claimed that the fire was likely started vis-à-vis a careless use of smoking materials. Inside the building investigators located several firearms, which were later returned to the club.[28]

In May, the OMC's Stateline-Janesville chapter opened its new clubhouse at 1263 Cherry Street in Janesville. The property was located at the end of the street in a rundown section of town.

When ATF agents stopped by to photograph the club's new digs, they spoke to Ken Peterson, who resided next door.[29]

During this period, Peterson was an interesting character. In early 1992, help wanted ads appeared in Beloit and Janesville newspapers for the Ku Klux Klan. Soon, white supremacist literature was found on the windshields of vehicles parked at prominent public venues. When the *Janesville Gazette* tracked the group's purported leader down, Peterson told a reporter that the Klan had received positive feedback from students and businesses. However, as public scrutiny mounted, Peterson disavowed the Klan and the presumed one-man chapter disbanded.[30]

When questioned by ATF, Peterson alleged that Spike O'Neill had tasked him with "keeping an eye on the clubhouse." Seeking to work both sides of the aisle, the repentant former white supremacist told the agents that he would also keep tabs on the Outlaws.[31]

Then, in early June, two dozen members of the OMC's Milwaukee, Stateline, Chicago, and Joilet chapters traveled to Rockford to meet with five members of the Wheelman Motorcycle Club. The purpose of the visit was to hunt down members of the Hell's Henchmen. During a meeting in a crowded room at a Rockford Motel 6, the Outlaws contemplated visiting Club 51 — a bar frequented by the Hell's Henchman — and beating "the hell out of them." However, since the orchestrated surveillance was poorly organized, the Outlaws failed to locate any members of the rival club.[32]

A month after the Janesville clubhouse opened, the Hells Angels retaliated for the beatings and robberies at J.R.'s Watering Hole. On June 25, after dropping off his personal bodyguard, Peter "Grease Lightning" Rogers, the president of the Outlaws' Chicago region, was preparing to exit the Dan Ryan Expressway at Taylor Street. A red and white pickup truck quickly pulled alongside of the Outlaws' leader and gun shots were fired. Rogers was hit in his stomach and left leg, but pulled off the freeway prior to collapsing. He was rushed to Cook County Hospital for surgery and survived the attack. A day later, during a motorcycle event in Schererville, Indiana, ATF agents spoke with OMC chapter presidents from two adjoining states, including Wisconsin's. The club leaders told the agents that the Hell's Henchmen were responsible for shooting Rogers.[33]

The "permission" for the Hell's Henchmen to take action against the high-ranking Outlaw was given by Pat Matter. "There was talk, ah, about Pete Rogers from the Chicago Outlaws," Matter told a Fox 9 News episode of *The Reporters*, "and I gave the go-ahead to go ahead and, if, ah, they had an opportunity, ah, to come around, they were supposed to take care of it."[34]

Rogers was one of the most influential Outlaws in the country. In 1990, the grizzled club president invited reporter Mary Kiesling to the group's Chicago clubhouse. "You can take it verbatim from me: This club is not based on drug dealing or any other criminal activity," said Rogers. "Basically, the club is a sporting thing - motorcycles, biking and brotherhood — that's what I preach."[35]

During the interview, Rogers claimed that the media's coverage of the Outlaws "has been one-sided, it's always been. You always write what the police tell you, and they're going to blow things out of proportion to get their funding."[36]

With tensions between the Outlaws, the prospecting Hell's Henchmen, and the Hells Angels at an all-time high, law enforcement went on high alert. Just two hours after the Schererville event, police in Gary, Indiana stopped a speeding van. As an officer approached, he observed an empty gun case on the vehicle's roof. After calling for backup, five Outlaws were "removed" from the van, a search of which revealed seven semi-automatic pistols, a shotgun, a "submachine gun," and smoke grenades. Police arrested Milwaukee OMC members Elias Vallejo, Jr., James "Weird" Werdeniuk, Scott "Rhino" Hammond, and Robert J. Paul, as well as Clarence M. Smith, a high-ranking OMC regional president in Florida. Officers said that approximately thirty motorcyclists were "ahead of the van, but they kept going when the van was pulled over." Intelligence officers confirmed that the same vehicle had been present at the Illiana Speedway earlier in the day.[37]

Smith's presence suggested that the Outlaws had put out a call to arms. Known to fellow club members as "Smitty," he had spent almost a decade on death row in Louisiana, where he was the only inmate sentenced to die who walked away free. Tampa Police Department Detective Grady Snyder claimed that Smith was one of the best known "Outlaws anywhere." When asked, the detective declined to comment if the biker was a suspect in four Florida death investigations and a New Orleans homicide.[38]

Clearly, the shooting of Grease Rogers would not go unanswered. Investigators speculated what type of statement the Outlaws would send when the group retaliated.

[1]*Oak Park Leaves*, September 10, 1969, p. 7; *Daily Herald*, March 29, 1973, p. 2.

[2]*Daily Gazette* (Sterling, IL), July 27, 2013, p. 1.

[3]*Milwaukee Sentinel*, June 14, 1993, p. 1; *Kenosha News,* June 9, 1993, p. 4.

[4]*Milwaukee Sentinel*, June 14, 1993, p. 14.

[5]Steve Spingola, retired MPD lieutenant of detectives, e-mail message to author, July 22, 2016.

[6]*Green Bay Press-Gazette*, March 8, 2000, p. 9B; Berard, interview with author, October 17, 2015.

[7]Ibid.

[8]Ibid.

[9]Ibid.

[10]Ibid.

[11]*Shepherd Express Metro*, February 24, 2000, pp. 13-14.

[12]Ibid.

[13]New York State Police, Summation of Case No. 75-1067, October 30, 1993 (held by author); *Shepherd Metro Express*, February 24, 2000, p. 14.

[14]*United States v. Walter Posnjak*, Decision of the U.S Court of Appeals (2nd Cir.), 457 F.2d 1110, March 24, 1972.

[15]Ibid.

[16]*New York v. Walter Posnjak*, 422 N.Y.S.2d 264, Decision of the Supreme Court of New York, Appellate Division, Fourth Department, November 16, 1979.

[17]*Daily Herald*, March 9, 2000, p. 4; *Milwaukee Journal Sentinel*, March, 9, 1999, p. 3B; Illinois State Police, North Central Region, Organized Crime Drug Enforcement Task Force, Midwest Cycle Intelligence Organization, November 18, 1994 (held by author).

[18]Breaking the Code, *Facebook.com,* October 31, 2014, https://www.facebook.com/ BreakingTheCodeBook/photos/a.240930252783960.1073741828.224788274398158/276 468945896757/?type=1&theater (accessed January 27, 2016).

[19]Ibid.; Illinois State Police, North Central Region, Organized Crime Drug Enforcement Task Force, Midwest Cycle Intelligence, November 18, 1994 (held by author). *United States v. Thomas E. Sienkwoski*, Decision of the U.S. Court of Appeals (7th Cir.), 359 F.3d 463, February 20, 2004.

[20]*United States v. Thomas Sienkowski*, 252 F. Supp. 2d 780 (E.D. Wis. 2003.

[21]Ibid., 76; Tom Layden, "Former Minnesota Hells Angel Leader 'Would've Been There' in Waco," *Fox News 9,* May 18, 2015, http://www.fox9.com/news/1974629-story (accessed July 19, 2016).

[22]*Beloit Daily News*, May 9, 2000, p. 1.

[23]Illinois State Police, North Central Region, Organized Crime Drug Enforcement Task Force, Midwest Cycle Intelligence, November 18, 1994 (held by author).

[24]Ibid.; *United States v. Harry A. Bowman.* U.S. Court of Appeals, Decision of the Eleventh Circuit, Case No. 01-14305, August 20, 2002; United States v. *Kevin P. O'Neill, et al.*, Defendants. U.S. District Court for the Eastern District of Wisconsin, 27 F. Supp. 2d 1121 (1998).

[25]*Northwest Indiana Times* (Munster, IN), July 24, 1994, p. 1; Illinois State Police, North Central Region, Organized Crime Drug Enforcement Task Force, Midwest Cycle Intelligence, November 18, 1994 (held by author); David D. Wolf, Interview with ATF Agent Sandra DeValkenere and Rockford Police Department Detective David Ekedahl, April 26, 1995.

[26]Ibid.; Illinois State Police, North Central Region, Organized Crime Drug Enforcement Task Force, Midwest Cycle Intelligence, November 18, 1994 (held by author); *Northwest Indiana Times* (Munster, IN), July 24, 1994, p. 1; *Northwest Indiana Times*, March 9, 2000, p. 1; *Northwest Indiana Times*, February 4, 1995, p. 1.

[27]Illinois State Police, North Central Region, Organized Crime Drug Enforcement Task Force, Midwest Cycle Intelligence, November 18, 1994.

[28]Ibid.

[29]Ibid.

[30]*Milwaukee Journal*, January 15, 1992, p. 1B.

[31]Illinois State Police, North Central Region, Organized Crime Drug Enforcement Task Force, Midwest Cycle Intelligence, November 18, 1994.

[32]David D. Wolf, Interview with ATF Agent Sandra DeValkenere and Rockford Police Department Detective David Ekedahl, April 26, 1995.

[33]*Shepherd Express Metro*, February 24, 2000, p. 14; *Northwest Indiana Times*, October 14, 1994, p. 1; Illinois State Police, North Central Region, Organized Crime Drug Enforcement Task Force, Midwest Cycle Intelligence, November 18, 1994 (held by author).

[34]The Reporters, Episode 3, Fox New 9, *youtube.com*, at 10 min. and 15 sec., August 4, 2014, https://www.youtube.com/watch?v=vh0oUo0rWf8 (accessed July 21, 2016).

[35]*Northwest Indiana Times,* May 11, 1990, p. 1.

[36]Ibid.

[37]Illinois State Police, North Central Region, Organized Crime Drug Enforcement Task Force, Midwest Cycle Intelligence, November 18, 1994 (held by author); *Northwest Indiana Times*, June 27, 1994, p. 1; *Shepherd Express Metro*, February 24, 2000, p. 14.

[38]*St. Petersburg Times*, September 17, 1995, p. 1B.

CHAPTER THIRTEEN

READY TO RUMBLE

The stop of the OMC's "war wagon" may have put the kibosh on a swift, reciprocal attack, but Kevin O'Neill had other plans. "We gotta get these fuckers," the incensed Stateline chapter president told his members. "We can't let this shit with Grease go."[1]

The following day, probate David Wolf was summoned to a Union Grove, Wisconsin clubhouse. Once there, O'Neill instructed Wolf to visit Rockford and, if the opportunity presented itself, to take out Lamont "Monte" Mathias, the secretary-treasurer of the Hell's Henchmen's Rockford chapter. When Wolf asked, "Where do we draw the line?" O'Neill told his prospect to kill Mathias' "old lady," if she was present.[2]

On June 27, at 6:30 p.m., Wolf, fellow Outlaws Motorcycle Club probate Harvey "RV" Powers, and club hang-around "Big Al" McVay, traveled to Rockford armed with a Benelli shotgun, a high-powered rifle, and two pistols that Powers had borrowed from Outlaws' associate Chris Pettengill. The three men snorted cocaine and scouted the location from a map provided by O'Neill. The following morning, the three OMC associates waited in Powers' gray Pontiac outside M.C. Fabrications, a motorcycle shop owned by Mathias.[3]

At 9:30 a.m., Wolf entered the shop, was greeted by Mathias, and purchased a spark plug. Wolf then returned to the Pontiac, which was parked a block away, and told Powers and McVay that Mathias was alone at the shop. Powers then asked, "Are we going to do it or what?" Wolf thought for a second and replied, "Well, fuck it. Let's do it."[4]

With a .45 caliber pistol concealed under a shirt, Wolf returned to M.C. Fabrications. After being met at the counter by Mathias, Wolf explained that he wanted to exchange spark plug for something "hotter." Wolf then followed the shop's owner from behind the counter, pointed the pistol at Mathias, and began firing.

The savvy Hell's Henchmen quickly dove to the floor of a nearby parts room. Although Mathias had been shot in the neck, the two men began to struggle. After the semi-automatic handgun jammed, Wolf pistol whipped Mathias so hard that the firearm's handgrip broke in to pieces. After unsuccessfully attempting to exit the shop's locked rear door, Wolf walked by his victim on his way to the front of the shop. The badly wounded Mathias was still alive and swore at his assailant. Frustrated that the rival biker refused to die, Wolf reached for a nearby screwdriver, stabbed the shop's owner repeatedly, and then jammed the screwdriver down Mathias' throat.[5]

Covered in blood, Wolf made a conscious effort to calmly walk to a nearby McDonald's restaurant and entered a getaway car. The trio then drove to the home of Chris Pettengill, located near Mt. Horeb, Wisconsin. Once there, Wolf's bloody clothes were burned and the .45 caliber pistol was melted with a blow torch. While at the residence, Powers received a telephone call from O'Neill and reported, "One motor's blown, the head gasket is leaking like a sieve." The Stateline chapter's president then replied: "Right the fuck on." [6]

Fortunately for the Outlaws, business was slow at M.C. Fabrications. Two hours after Mathias was murdered, UPS driver David Ulrich entered the shop through the front door to make a delivery. The shop's telephone was ringing and Mathias was not at the counter. Ulrich then went to an office and observed that "Monty" was not present. After opening the rear door and checking the alley, the UPS driver reentered M.C. Fabrications and began thumbing through a magazine. A few minutes later, Ulrich called for Mathias by name and then walked towards the front of the store via the parts room. As he bent down to pick up a fallen placard, the driver saw Mathias on the floor covered in blood. Ulrich walked closer, observed the gruesome injuries to the pummeled corpse, and summoned the police.[7]

Crime scene investigators noted that three rounds had struck Mathias in the neck, another .45 caliber round was lodged in a frame of a door, a fifth round had entered and exited the door frame, and another passed through a filing cabinet. A total of six .45 caliber CCI spent casings were found inside the shop. Blood splatter was observed inside the doorway to the parts room, on shelving, and adjacent to Mathias' face. An autopsy revealed that the Hell's Henchmen had died of blunt force trauma to the head. As the news of murder spread, Bob Brown, an intelligence officer for the Chicago Police Department told the press: "They beat him to death. None of the gunshot wounds were fatal. They were just to slow him [Mathias] down a little. Half his head is caved in. They were whooping him to let others know they [the Hell's Henchmen] ain't coming in [to the Hells Angels]."[8]

Two hours later, Mathias' girlfriend, Brenda Plock, told detectives that her boyfriend of five years had left for work at 7 a.m. On a typical day, Monte would call home before 11 a.m. Finding it odd that she had yet to receive a call, Plock telephoned M.C. Fabrications just before noon. The call was answered by a part-time employee and, based on the terse conversation, Plock believed something was amiss and took a cab to the shop. Once there, she observed the large police response and realized her boyfriend was likely a victim of foul play.[9]

When asked about a possible connection to the shooting of Grease Rogers, Plock indicated that plans for the Hell's Henchman to patch over to the Hells Angels had "been in the works" for several months. As tensions between the Hell's Henchmen and the Outlaws mounted, Mathias had instructed his girlfriend to "watch for strange vehicles with Wisconsin license plates" because there was an "Outlaws' chapter in Janesville, Wisconsin." As a former Hell's Henchmen national president, Plock told detectives that Mathias — a high profile biker, who rarely deviated from his daily routine — was an easy mark for the Outlaws.[10]

Within hours after the incident, investigators learned that, on the evening prior to the murder, Patricia Wolf — the wife of Outlaws' prospect David Wolf — had contacted the Lake County, Illinois Sheriff's office and told an official of the plot to kill a Hell's Henchmen shop owner. For whatever reason, the information was not forwarded to the Rockford Police Department until 11:30 a.m. the following day, about the same time the UPS driver had discovered the bloody corpse at M.C. Fabrications.[11]

The dissemination of the tip concerning the probable killers began with a page from ATF Agent Ron Holmes to Rockford Police Department Detective John Pozzi, both of whom were unaware that Mathias was deceased. Holmes told the detective about the shooting of Rogers and that the Outlaws had planned to retaliate by targeting a high profile member of the Hell's Henchmen's Rockford chapter. The ATF agent was on his way to Rockford and wanted to meet with the Hell's Henchmen to discuss the information obtained by Lake County Sheriff's Detective Gary Govekar. A half hour later, Pozzi heard "radio traffic" concerning a homicide at 714 Broadway, the location of Mathias' shop.[12]

As local, state, and federal law enforcement coordinated security for the Hell's Henchmen's burial, a representative from Avis Rental Car reported that three Hells Angels from New York had procured a vehicle and "demanded several times" that fire and theft insurance be included in the agreement. Two hours later, twenty-four members of the Hells Angels arrived at Rockford's Sunset Funeral Home to "induct Mathias posthumously into their organization." Besides, the Hells Angels, whose members came from as far away as Holland, other one-percent clubs — the Invaders, the Sons of Silence, the Sinners, and the Spartans — also sent representatives to the Mathias' "final farewell." With the large two-day funeral in full-swing, officials registered their concerns. Schererville Police Lieutenant Donald Parker warned that "a real shooting war" between the two largest one-percent clubs was just getting started.[13]

Code Breakers

With the Outlaws Motorcycle Club throwing everything they had at the Hell's Henchmen, outlaw motorcycle gang intelligence officers sought to stop the bleeding. In the late 1970s, investigators from local, state, and federal law enforcement had formed the Midwest Cycle Intelligence Organization (MCIO), a non-governmental group that met privately each month to exchange information on the activities of one-percent bikers. With chapters in several states, the MCIO enabled officers to work around the bureaucratic rules that limited agency-to-agency information sharing. Moreover, when the need arose, the MCIO offered a ready list of knowledgeable investigators from multiple jurisdictions. In early 1993, MCIO member Ron Holmes, an Illinois-based ATF agent, asked Wisconsin MCIO member Charles Berard, a sergeant with the MPD, to join a new multi-state task force led, in part, by Milwaukee ATF Agent Sandra DeValkenaere.[14]

The task force focused on gathering the necessary evidence to obtain court-authorized wire taps, an elaborate process that requires a government agent to compile an extensive affidavit in support of a judicial order. Prior to being reviewed by a federal judge, a Title III application must be signed by a U.S. Attorney, an Assistant U.S. Attorney, and be accompanied by a U.S. Department of Justice authorization memorandum signed by a designated official. The Outlaws Motorcycle Club's brazen beating of the Hells Angels at Slick's tavern, the February 10 attempted abduction of Edward Murphy, and the murder of Mathias, were some of the predicate acts of racketeering offered in support of the Title III application.[15]

Shortly after the murder of Mathias, investigators quietly obtained the cooperation of Patricia Wolf. After learning of a domestic spat between their new informant and her husband, David, task force operatives obtained Patricia's consent to place a lamp — outfitted with an electronic transmitter — inside the couple's home. Within a matter of weeks, O'Neill stopped by to visit and complimented the table lamp's aesthetic design. In short order, investigators procured a similar lamp, which Patricia Wolf then gifted to O'Neill.[16]

The U.S. Attorney's office in the Eastern District of Wisconsin authorized the transfer of the lamp to O'Neill based on U.S. Supreme Court precedent. In *United States v. Karo*, the Court ruled that it was lawful for government agents, with the consent of an informant, to offer an electronic instrument for placement into an area typically protected by the Fourth Amendment. Once O'Neill took possession of the lamp, task force officers applied for and received a Title III judicial order to eavesdrop. The OMC's Stateline chapter president initially placed the lamp inside his home, but later took the listening device to the group's clubhouse. Between the court-authorized wire taps and the placement of the eavesdropping devices, task force members were getting closer to breaking the code of silence.[17]

While the Hell's Henchmen and the Hells Angels contemplated their next move, the Outlaws continued their guerrilla-style offense. On June 12, just ten days after Mathias' funeral, two members of the OMC's Stateline chapter, James "Manson" Hanson and James C. Rostron, drove to Fox Lake, Illinois. Rostron held a Molotov cocktail filled with gasoline between his legs until the two arrived at the residence of Edward Murphy. The rather crude device indicated that the spur of the moment attack was poorly planned.[18]

Once outside of the target's home, Rostron lit a wick and tossed the jar towards a front window, but the Molotov cocktail landed on the roof, shattered, and caused little damage. A neighbor witnessed the errant throw and notified authorities. While trying to flee the area, both Outlaws were stopped by Fox Lake police and charged with attempted arson. Rumors swirled that Hanson and Rostron received light sentences because the club "had set-up one of their best-looking prostitutes with the state's prosecutor."[19]

A similar attack occurred on August 4 when an IED was detonated at the Southwest Tattoo Emporium, a west side Chicago business owned by a former member of the Hell's Henchmen. While no one was injured in the attack, the OMC had created a perception that homes and businesses affiliated with their rivals were unsafe.[20]

Soon, however, it became clear that both the Outlaws and ATF task force operatives had a major problem. In a sensitive intelligence report, a member of the MPD's Criminal Intelligence Division noted that, due to a probable disclosure by an inside source, "…it became apparent that someone had leaked information to Milwaukee Outlaw Sienkowski, who reported it to Edward Anastas, the president. Very soon thereafter it was overheard on thwe [sic] wire that the target's house was tapped." The report further related that "extraordinary steps" had been taken to ensure that other eavesdropping measures had not been compromised. "Title III taps and authorised [sic] pen registers," the report noted, "had recorded Wisconsin President O'Neill calling Milwaukee President Anastas in excess of 28 times."[21]

By mid-summer, information regarding the task force surveillance trickled down to members of the OMC's Stateline chapter. After receiving a page from O'Neill, David Wolf responded to the Union Grove, Wisconsin clubhouse. When he arrived, the chapter's president instructed Wolf to walk around the block because the clubhouse might be "bugged." O'Neill proceeded to tell Wolf that Leslie "Jack" Jensen, the President of the La Crosse, Wisconsin Association of Reformed Motorcyclists' chapter, had gleaned information from "his ATF source" that an "old lady" of an Outlaws' prospect "was a snitch for the government." This source further told Jensen that the "old lady" was going to inform on the two Outlaws' prospects that had killed Mathias. Realizing that the informant was likely his wife, Patricia, Wolf lied and told O'Neill that he had not disclosed any information about the murder to his wife.[22]

The ongoing wire taps further exposed two Outlaws Motorcycle Club plots, the first involved the bombing of a hotel in downtown Chicago. Telephone discussions suggested that a designated OMC member would casually stroll into the hotel, take a seat in the lobby, leave a bag or a satchel next to a chair, surreptitiously exit the building, and then remotely detonate the device from a nearby car. Investigators theorized that a Hells Angels' meeting, which, on rare occasions, took place at hotels, was a possible motive. For whatever reason, the attack never materialized.[23]

The second plan of action involved telephone calls instructing OMC members from the Midwest to travel to upstate New York, where a Hells Angels racing team was set to participate in an event at the Lancaster Speedway. Listening on the wiretaps, investigators heard "a number of things that were being said back and forth."[24]

Prior to the event, O'Neill stressed the need for club members, who could lawfully possess firearms, to team up with club felons. If contacted by law enforcement, the non-felons could then "claim ownership of any firearms" found inside vehicles. Stateline chapter members Randall Miller, Richard Mroch, James "L.J" Meinen, a probate named "Tom," and Wolf, traveled to the event. At 8 a.m. the following morning, four dozen Outlaws from various states, including the Chicago chapter president, Carl "Jay" Warneke, the Indiana chapter's Donald Fogg, and "Fat Wally" Posnjak, rode in a caravan to the New York racetrack.[25]

The September 25 crowd at the Lancaster Speedway included several hundred racing enthusiasts and their families. When the Outlaws arrived at the track, they walked by an area occupied by motor homes and trailers, and were greeted by four members of the

Hells Angels. Representing the OMC's Buffalo chapter, Posnjak stood at the head of the pack and spoke to the Hells Angels. Seconds later, the Outlaws began beating their rivals. A group of two dozen Hells Angels quickly responded, shots were fired, and "bedlam broke out."[26]

Armed with ballpein hammers and handguns, the outnumbered Hells Angels fought back against the knife-wielding, gun-toting Outlaws. "I heard someone yelling cuss words," said witness Carl Pitts. "Then I saw someone clasp their hands together [as if holding a handgun]. Someone shouted, 'Gun!' and I hit the ground." Another witness, Butch Toller, observed a second man lying in his own blood and saw "people come up and drag him away." The shooting victim, Wally Posnjak, collapsed and died at the scene. Michael Quale, a member of the Hells Angels' racing team, whose club colors went missing, had been stabbed to death.[27]

Soon, a "stampede" of Outlaws ran for the track's exit. Living up to his club moniker, Harvey "R.V." (Really Violent) Powers stood over a fallen club member and exchanged gunfire. One of the last Outlaws to leave the track, Powers jumped into a van occupied by Randy "Mad" Yager, "Big Don" Fogg, and other members of the OMC's Gary, Indiana chapter.[28]

In the aftermath of the race track slayings, the vehicle occupied by Powers and the members of the Gary chapter was stopped in Fredonia, New York, about sixty miles southwest of Lancaster. Police discovered Quale's bloody Hells Angels' colors near Fogg's feet. Police seized evidence from the van, fingerprinted the occupants, but then permitted the bikers to leave. Several months later, an informant led investigators to the knife used to stab Quale, which had been discarded near the race track. Although he was ordered to keep quiet by high-ranking Outlaws, Fogg began telling "anyone who would listen" about Quale's murder, a situation that troubled the group's leadership.[29]

Although the OMC's attacks had failed to deter the Hell's Henchmen from prospecting for the Hells Angels, an act of retaliation was in order. Two members of the HAMC's Minnesota chapter — John Derks and Charlie Goldsmith, the former Milwaukee Sinners MC president — were sent to target a southeastern Wisconsin tattoo parlor, operated by OMC Milwaukee chapter member Peter "Debris" Gross — a onetime national club enforcer, Taco Bowman bodyguard, and former member of the Sinners.[30]

Familiar with the metro Milwaukee area, Goldsmith and his colleague proceeded to an Oak Creek tattoo shop, located at 904 E. Rawson Avenue. After the business closed, Goldsmith placed an explosive device on a gas meter behind the building. The ordnance detonated at about 9:30 p.m. and caused extensive structural damage.[31]

Prior to the Oak Creek bomb blast, O'Neill had placed a call to an Outlaws' associate in northern Wisconsin and asked the man to manufacture three improvised explosive devices. On October 10, David Wolf and Harvey Powers stopped by O'Neill's Racine, Wisconsin residence and observed one of the completed bombs inside the Stateline chapter president's garage.[32]

Two days later, O'Neill sent Stateline chapter members Robert "Clay" Kruppstadt and Powers to retaliate. Once outside a Rockford home on Coleman Avenue, Powers attached the explosive device to the undercarriage of a truck owned by Roger Fiebrantz, the chapter president of the Hell's Henchmen. Powers then tied the detonation pin to the vehicle's drive shaft with fishing line. Consequently, if the truck moved just inches, backwards or forwards, the IED would detonate without the vehicle necessarily being started.[33]

Just after 6 p.m., Fiebrantz exited his trailer home, climbed inside his truck, and turned the starter. The minimal movement from the owner's body weight caused the bomb to immediately explode. After hearing the blast, Harold Durham rushed towards the scene and found Fiebrantz still seated inside the cab of the truck. Smelling gasoline and seeing smoke, Dunham and his brother, Ron, extricated the victim, who mumbled "someone help me" and then screamed "something about his leg."[34]

One of the first officers on the scene, Winnebago County Deputy Sheriff Terrance Keegan, secured the area while fire department personnel assisted Fiebrantz, who was lying on the ground between his heavily damaged white truck and a dark colored Cadillac. The Hell's Henchmen's Rockford chapter president had "a large chunk of his right calf missing" and suffered severe "burns on his legs."[35]

The complexity of the ordnance, said Winnebago County Lieutenant Roger Costello, pointed to suspects with "specific knowledge of explosives and the placement of explosives." While Fiebrantz's right leg and right hand were severely injured, Costello noted that the victim was "definitely very lucky he survived."[36]

Three hours later, a Winnebago County Sheriff's detective received a call from a woman, who — fearful of retaliation — agreed to offer information anonymously. Just prior to the explosion, she observed a blackish, gray truck in the driveway where the explosion had occurred. A stocky white male with graying hair, a beard, and a fanny pack around his waist, quickly entered the truck and left the area. After seeing the truck leave, the woman drove to a nearby fast food restaurant. When she returned fifteen minutes later, the explosion had already occurred.[37]

The following day, agents and officers assigned to the ATF task force met at the Winnebago County Public Safety Building, where it became clear that the incident was "a continuation of the rivalry between the Hell's Henchmen Motorcycle gang" and "the Outlaws Motorcycle gang."[38]

In the aftermath of the Coleman Drive bombing, the Stateline chapter kept a close eye on the news coverage of the blast. At a clubhouse in Wisconsin, O'Neill proudly awarded Kruppstadt an Outlaws' "SS" patch, which signified that the biker had committed an act of violence against a rival club. Initially, O'Neill was disappointed that the attack had failed to kill Fiebrantz, however, he later told club members that the Hell's Henchmen's life altering wounds would serve as "a constant remainder" that the Outlaws would not tolerate any club associated with the Hells Angels in northern Illinois.[39]

With retaliatory violence rapidly escalating, task force operatives, as well as their MCIO associates, reached out to possible informants. In an intelligence memo, a detective with the Ft. Atkinson, Wisconsin Police Department reported that, due to a lack of a permit, authorities in Rockford had canceled an October

15 Hell's Henchmen "chili feed." The abrupt revocation, which occurred with Hells Angels from Minnesota, Nebraska, and New York in attendance, served as an impetus to heighten tensions. Later that same day, the detective reported, "Some Hell's Henchmen members had purchased four pounds of C-4 and blasting caps" from a source at a motorcycle shop in Beloit, Wisconsin.[40]

A few days later, rumors began circulating that a decision concerning the Hell's Henchman's final transformation to the Hells Angels had occurred during a meeting in Indiana. In a last ditch effort to discourage an official merger, the Outlaws intensified their offensive. In early November, the OMC's Blake Johnson and Powers arrived in Rockford and strapped a bomb to a Chevrolet Blazer owned by Michael Coyne, the acting-president of the Rockford chapter of the Hell's Henchmen. On November 7, Coyne exited his 15th Street home just before noon, checked his vehicle's undercarriage, and observed a strange object attached to the SUV's drive shaft. From a safe distance, a team of highly trained officers attempted to deactivate the bomb, but the object exploded and destroyed Coyne's vehicle.[41]

Five hours later, the president of the OMC's Gary, Indiana chapter, Raymond "Shemp" Morgan, Jr., drove a red Ford Taurus onto the sidewalk adjacent to the Chicago clubhouse of the Hell's Henchmen, located at 1734 Grand Avenue. Morgan then pulled a cord, which gave him sixty seconds to flee, and entered another vehicle occupied by other OMC members, including O'Neill. Just moments after a school bus passed by, the stolen car, which had been packed with C-4, exploded. The car's rear axle was sent a half-block airborne and the blast left a "four-foot wide and deep" crater in the roadway. A four-hundred pound steel clubhouse door was jettisoned from its hinged supports and became "embedded in another wall on the other side" of the building.[42]

The car bomb also shattered the windows of open businesses and caused structural damaged to other occupied buildings near the clubhouse. In a near miracle, not a single person was injured by blast, which occurred at the beginning of Chicago's rush hour. "In my 17 years as an ATF agent," said Jerry Singer, "this is the largest explosion on a vehicle I have seen. The car was virtually disintegrated."[43]

After the bombing, O'Neill and Morgan arrived at Wolf's residence and seemed "very excited." The three men then watched a 9 p.m. newscast from Chicago that reported on the blast. O'Neill told Wolf that the explosion may have also taken out a car belonging to a member of the Hells Angels. "Man, that fucker really rocked," the giddy Stateline chapter president reported. Five months later, after Timothy McVeigh detonated a truck bomb outside the Alfred P. Murrah Federal Building in Oklahoma City, O'Neill told Wolf, "I bet they got that idea from us."[44]

Investigators later learned that Taco Bowman had approved the bomb plot during a meeting with the OMC's Milwaukee president, Edward "Shock" Anastas. Bowman put the plan in motion by asking the Milwaukee chapter to assemble the components needed for the attack. The explosives were then purchased by Thomas "Woody" Sienkowski with OMC funds, and delivered to Anastas and club member Alan "The Watchmaker" Venus, who assembled the bomb. The device was then conveyed to Sienkowski's residence, where a metal box for the IED was specialty-fabricated. Milwaukee OMC member Scott "Rhino" Hammond then removed a large section of the stolen car's front seat and dash to house the explosive device.[45]

Clearly, the message that the Outlaws sought to send to the Hell's Henchmen was easy enough to understand: Patching over to the Hells Angels is akin to signing one's own death warrant. Yet, with the ATF task force gathering evidence, the Outlaws realized they had to work overtime to deter their rivals before potential federal charges removed O'Neill's crew from circulation.

[1] Illinois State Police, North Central Region, Organized Crime Drug Enforcement Task Force, Midwest Cycle Intelligence, November 18, 1994 (held by author); *Northwest Indiana Times*, June 27, 1994, p. 1; *Shepherd Express Metro*, February 24, 2000, p. 14.

[2] Ibid., 14. David D. Wolf, interview with ATF Agent Sandra DeValkeneare and Rockford PD Detective David Ekedahl, April 26, 1995.

[3] Ibid., 14; Illinois State Police, North Central Region, Organized Crime Drug Enforcement Task Force, Midwest Cycle Intelligence, November 18, 1994 (held by author); *Rockford Register Star*, July 3, 1994, p. 4A; *Rockford Register Star*, July 2, 1994, p. 1.

[4] David D. Wolf, interview with ATF Agent Sandra DeValkeneare and Rockford PD Detective David Ekedahl, April 26, 1995.

[5] Ibid.; Rockford Police Department, statement of witness Joanne Hunt, Case #94-089783, June 29, 1994; Illinois State Police, North Central Region, Organized Crime Drug Enforcement Task Force, Midwest Cycle Intelligence, November 18, 1994 (held by author); *Rockford Register Star*, July 3, 1994, p. 4A; *Rockford Register Star*, July 2, 1994, p. 1; *Shepherd Express Metro*, February 24, 2000, p. 14

[6] Ibid.; David D. Wolf, interview with ATF Agent Sandra DeValkeneare and Rockford PD Detective David Ekedahl, April 26, 1995.

[7] Rockford Police Department, interview of David Ulrich, Case #94-089783, June 28, 1994.

[8] Ibid., *Rockford Register Star*, July 3, 1994, p. 4A; *Rockford Register Star*, July 2, 1994, p. 1.

[9] Rockford Police Department, interview of Brenda Plock, Case #94-089783, June 28, 1994.

[10] Ibid.

[11] *Milwaukee Journal Sentinel*, April 5, 2000, p. 3B; Ibid., April 3, 2000, p. 3B.

[12] Rockford Police Department, Report of Detective John Rozzi, Case #94-088783, June 28, 1994.

[13] Rockford Police Department, Case #94-088783, June 28, 1994; *Rockford Register Star*, July 2, 1994, 4A; *Northwest Indiana Times*, July 24, 1994, p. 1.

[14] Berard, interview with author, October 17, 2015.

[15] Ibid.; 18 United States Code §§ 2510(9) and 2516(1); see also In re United States of America, 10 F.3d 931.

[16] Berard, Interview with author, October 17, 2015.

[17] Ibid.; *United States v. Karo*, 468 U.S. 705 (1984).

[18] Ibid.

[19] Ibid.; Berard, interview with author, October 17, 2015; Illinois State Police, North

Central Region, Organized Crime Drug Enforcement Task Force, Midwest Cycle Intelligence, November 18, 1994 (held by author).

[20]Ibid.

[21]Milwaukee Police Department, In the Matter Of Report: ATF Investigation into the Activities of the Outlaws Motorcycle Club, undated (held by author); Berard, interview with author, November 17, 2015.

[22]David D. Wolf, interview with ATF Agent Sandra DeValkenare and Rockford PD Detective David Ekedahl, April 26, 1995.

[23]Berard, interview with author, October 17, 2015.

[24]Ibid.

[25]*Milwaukee Journal Sentinel*, April 5, 2000, p. 3B; Berard, interview with author, October 17, 2015; David D. Wolf, interview with ATF Agent Sandra DeValkenare and Rockford PD Detective David Ekedahl, April 26, 1995.

[26]Ibid.; *Milwaukee Journal Sentinel*, April 5, 2000, p. 3B Berard, interview with author, October 17, 2015.

[27]Ibid.; *Milwaukee Journal Sentinel*, April 5, 2000, p. 3B.

[28]David D. Wolf, interview with ATF Agent Sandra DeValkenare and Rockford PD Detective David Ekedahl, April 26, 1995.

[29]*Northwest Indiana Times*, June 21, 1999, p. 1.

[30]Charles Berard, interview with author, October 16, 2015.

[31]Ibid.; *Milwaukee Journal*, October 11, 1994, p. 2B.

[32]David D. Wolf, interview with ATF Agent Sandra DeValkenare and Rockford PD Detective David Ekedahl, April 26, 1995.

[33]Ibid.

[34]Winnebago County Sheriff's office, Report of Terrance Keegan, Case #94-049081, October 13, 1994.

[35]Ibid.

[36]*United States of America v. Kevin P. O'Neill et al*, Federal Indictment in the United States District Court, Eastern District of Wisconsin, Case 97-Cr-98 (held by author); *Rockford Register Star*, October 14, 1994, p. 1.

[37]Winnebago County Sheriff's office, Report of Detective B. Harrison, Case #94-049081, October 13, 1994.

[38]Winnebago County Sheriff's office, Report of Detective C. Cowan, Case #94-049081, October 13, 1994.

[39]David D. Wolf, interview with ATF Agent Sandra DeValkenare and Rockford PD Detective David Ekedahl, April 26, 1995.

40Ft. Atkinson Police Department, M.C.I.O. Intelligence Information, October 21, 1994 (held by author).

[41]*Chicago Tribune*, November 9, 1994, p. 2; Illinois State Police, North Central Region, Organized Crime Drug Enforcement Task Force, Midwest Cycle Intelligence, November 18, 1994 (held by author); *United States of America v. Kevin P. O'Neill et al*, Federal Indictment in the United States District Court, Eastern District of Wisconsin, Case 97-Cr-98 (held by author); David D. Wolf, interview with ATF Agent Sandra DeValkenare and Rockford PD Detective David Ekedahl, April 26, 1995.

[42]*United States of America v. Kevin P. O'Neill et al*, Federal Indictment in the United States District Court, Eastern District of Wisconsin, Case 97-Cr-98; Berard, interview with author, October 17, 2015; Illinois State Police, North Central Region, Organized Crime Drug Enforcement Task Force, Midwest Cycle Intelligence, November 18, 1994 (held by author).

[43]*Chicago Tribune*, November 9, 1994, p. 2.

[44]David D. Wolf, interview with ATF Agent Sandra DeValkenare and Rockford PD Detective David Ekedahl, April 26, 1995.

[45]*United States v. Thomas Sienkowski,* Sentencing Memorandum of U.S. District Judge Lynn Adelman, U.S. District Court of the Eastern District of Wisconsin, March 4, 2006 (held by author).

CHAPTER FOURTEEN

G-FORCE

Having withstood the series of attacks and counterattacks, the Hell's Henchmen had proven their resilience. On December 9, 1994, the Chicago, Rockford, and South Bend, Indiana chapters of the Hell's Henchmen officially patched over to the Hells Angels. "They will never again be Hell's Henchmen," said ATF Agent Ron Holmes. "That shrouded ghost insignia, you'll never see it again."[1]

Hells Angels members from New York, Alaska, Massachusetts, and North Carolina traveled to Illinois for the induction ceremony. As the revelers departed, nineteen HAMC members and a female companion were stopped at O'Hare Airport when security officers observed sheaths on some of the bikers' belts. Members of the traveling party told police that they were insusceptible from searches, said Chicago Police Commander William Callaghan, because "they were Hells Angels." All twenty people were arrested and charged with disorderly conduct.[2]

As the bloody year of 1994 came to a close, some members of the Outlaws, frustrated that they had failed to prevent a Hells Angels presence in their own backyard, discussed a planned "Hell's Henchmen hunt." On January 13, 1995, ATF task force members listened as David Wolf, Robert Kruppstadt, and Harvey Powers discussed their next move from Wolf's living room. "If it's in the right spot," Powers mused, "were talking about clunking their knee caps. Spike says fuck that. If we're gonna do that, why not stick the guns in their fuckin' knees and fuckin' blow their knee caps out with a gun, with a pistol."[3]

After Powers suggested that the OMC put "bullet holes in the skulls" of the Hells Angels, Kruppstadt — a church sexton — added, "Cut the head off," and punctuated his rant with, "That's right. Yeah, yeah, I love being an Outlaw."[4]

After a meeting at the Janesville, Wisconsin clubhouse,

several Outlaws, as well as members of the Wheelmen — a group that was seeking to patch over to the OMC — traveled to Rockford on the lookout for Hells Angels. Standing by at a Rockford hotel was Powers' girlfriend, Theresa Sprosty. When the Outlaws arrived, they had the woman don a set of Hells Angels' colors taken during the robbery at Slick's tavern, and drove her to Club 51 — a known Hell's Henchmen hangout. From a pay phone, O'Neill called the Hells Angels clubhouse to report that a woman attired in HAMC colors "was shooting her mouth off at the bar." The Outlaws then laid in wait, but the Rockford chapter refused to take the bait.[5]

With the large scale federal investigation looming, the Indiana leadership of the Outlaws recognized a need to eliminate loose ends. On January 29, at 12:30 a.m., the body of Donald Fogg, the enforcer for an OMC's Indiana chapter, was found outside his pickup truck on a vacant wooded lot in the city of Gary. Fogg had sustained gunshot wounds to his head and face. Physical evidence indicated that Fogg was shot a third time while on the ground. The slain six-foot-six-inch, two-hundred and eighty-pound biker's .45 caliber pistol was still inside his jacket pocket.[6]

A theory quickly emerged that Fogg was killed by the Outlaws. Crime scene detectives observed two sets of footprints, which led from the driver's and passenger's side doors to the rear of the truck, where Fogg was executed. The lack of a struggle suggested that the perpetrator was a person who the deceased had trusted. Another telltale sign: None of Fogg's Outlaws' paraphernalia — considered trophies by rival clubs — had been taken. An autopsy revealed that Fogg was shot with two different firearms — a .38 caliber and a nine millimeter. Footprints showed that, after shooting Fogg, the assailant walked to another car that had pulled into the lot. Since "Big Don" had been present at the Lancaster speedway, and "Mad Mike" Quale's bloody Hells Angels' colors had been found at his feet, his testimony could have pointed "all the way to the top to Taco Bowman, including the Midwest," said MPD Lieutenant Charles Berard, "which would have been Grease Rogers, would have been Kevin O'Neill."[7]

At 8:30 a.m. the following morning, O'Neill paged David Wolf, who was in the midst of a liaison with a new girlfriend at the

Fantasy Suites Motel in West Bend, Wisconsin. O'Neill explained that Fogg had been murdered and asked Wolf to accompany him to Indiana. When the two Stateline chapter members arrived at the Gary clubhouse, both were surprised to see Fogg's club brothers reclined in chairs watching television and an acting very "nonchalant about the murder." O'Neill became very upset when he learned that none of the Gary chapter's members had visited the crime scene, located less than a mile from the clubhouse. After being chauffeured to the dead end road where Fogg was murdered, O'Neill observed a set of small footprints and speculated that Big Don's "old lady, Shelly," was a possible suspect. A member of the Gary chapter told O'Neill that a Gary police officer may have shot Fogg.[8]

In an attempt to cover their tracks, task force officers believed the Outlaws employed a tactic from the Drobac slayings' playbook, and held a large funeral to deflect attention away from the club. While speaking from the podium at the Engel Funeral Home, the OMC's Chicago region president, Randy "Mad" Yager, criticized the press for suggesting that Fogg's murder was an "inside job." Ironically, investigators considered Yager a strong suspect.[9]

"The fact that he [Fogg] had his own handgun in his pocket, never touched, never brought out, no shots fired," said Berard, meant that the suspect had to "be somebody that could get extremely close, and the closest one that could get to him is Randy Yager."[10]

According to Yager, law enforcement's assertion that Fogg was killed by the Outlaws was, "Just a lot of bull — they have said, and the press has printed it without bothering to check it out. If anybody thinks they know something, let them prove it. If they don't, then let them drop it."[11]

As Gary police probed the murder of Fogg, the Outlaws took another crack at the Hells Angels. In the early morning of March 3, HAMC member Jack Castle entered his Lincoln Centennial after leaving a coffee and donut shop on Chicago's northwest side. A black Chevrolet then pulled alongside the Lincoln and a dozen gunshots rang out. After pulling Castle's bullet-ridden corpse from the car, medical personnel found eleven entry wounds. "We're looking at this as part of the ongoing war between the Hells Angels and the Outlaws," said Chicago Police Department Commander Phillip

Cline.[12]

An informant told the ATF that members of the OMC's Chicago chapter, as well as the leadership of the prospecting Wheelmen, did most of the surveillance for the Castle assassination. However, the black Chevrolet used by the shooter to roll up on the victim belonged to the Wisconsin Stateline chapter. After the murder, O'Neill — aware that the fingerprints of several Outlaws would likely be found inside the vehicle — called the OMC's Chicago region president, Carl "Jay" Warneke, to check on the Chevrolet's whereabouts. Told that the vehicle was abandoned near the crime scene, a livid O'Neill immediately traveled to Chicago to investigate.[13]

When O'Neill arrived, he located the Stateline chapter's vehicle parked in a handicapped zone just three blocks from the scene of the homicide. In the interim, the vehicle had accumulated several parking tickets. If the out-of-state Wisconsin license plates had peaked the parking enforcement officer's curiosity, the shell casings from the firearm used in the hit would have been found lying in plain view on the vehicle's floorboard.[14]

After retrieving the shell casings, wiping the car of prints, and retrieving an insurance card from the glovebox, O'Neill contacted a member of the OMC's Joliet chapter. The Chevrolet was then taken to a salvage yard and crushed.[15]

Suddenly, however, the OMC's attacks against the Hells Angels subsided. The motive for the undeclared ceasefire was the noose of the federal dragnet tightening. In a March 29 telephone conversation, Patricia Wolf offered the pager number of Assistant U.S. Attorney Paul Kanter to her husband. "Oh, Tricia, no, don't do this, Tricia," said a sobbing David Wolf, who became so distraught that he vomited. Having previously informed O'Neill that he told absolutely no one of Mathias' murder, Wolf was concerned that his wife's cooperation with law enforcement may cost him his life.[16]

Aware that their telephones may be wiretapped, OMC members began meeting in private places to discuss club business. In late April, O'Neill — unaware that the lamp inside his Racine home was transmitting conversations — told Robert Kruppstadt about the lack of respect that he had received at a recent Outlaws' national meeting. "Them fucking hillbillies, I couldn't believe it... they started saying, well, how'd this whole war [with the Hells Angels] start anyways? Everything was fine, you know."[17]

With his voice rising, O'Neill told his vice president, "They basically said that they're not gonna go to war with them Angels down in the Carolinas and Tennessee because they feel like they'd lose." O'Neill reportedly told the forty leaders of the Outlaws present at the summit, "I don't know if you think we started this war or what the deal is up there in Wisconsin. I said those Angels were circling around us." Believing that the Outlaws' southern leaders lacked intestinal fortitude, O'Neill noted, "...when we got in this club we were told that any chance we got at those fuckers coming through our fucking state, to go for it — that's the way I was brought up."[18]

While O'Neill and his crew pondered their next move, stringent federal sentencing guidelines caused one member of the Outlaws Motorcycle Club to rethink his options. On August 31, Mark "Crash" Quinn, the former enforcer for the Booze Runners, and a member of the OMC's Stateline chapter, contacted ATF Agent Sandra DeValkenaere from the DuPage County jail. During a meeting three days later, Quinn offered a startling revelation: Randall Miller and James Schneider were the persons responsible for the murders of Morris and Ruth Gauger.[19]

On the day that the couple's bodies were discovered, Miller had told Quinn that Schneider and he were responsible for the Gaugers' deaths. Now aware that an innocent man was incarcerated at Illinois' infamous Statesville prison, DeValkenaere recognized that Quinn's statement alone would not suffice to free Gary Gauger and convict Miller and Schneider.[20]

While waiting for Quinn to complete his jail sentence, the ATF notified McHenry County officials of Gauger's possible innocence, but the state's attorney's office declined to alert the convict's legal counsel. Instead, Larry Marshall, of the Northwestern University Innocence Project, readied Gauger's appeal, which was heard by the Illinois Second Court of Appeals on February 6, 1996. Aware of the information unearthed by the ATF task force, an

Illinois appellate prosecutor clung to the convict's confession and claimed: "It defies belief that anyone who had lived with his parents for years and worked on the same farm as they did every day would not immediately go to the two most logical places they would be found."[21]

Fortunately for Gauger, the appeals court chose not to focus on guilt or innocence, but on the admissibility of his statements to investigators. Finding a lack of "temporal proximity between detention" and Gauger's confession, the Court held that the "defendant's inculpatory statements were the fruits of an illegal arrest." The justices then vacated Gauger's conviction and ordered a new trial. As Marshall petitioned to have his client freed on bond, Gauger's cell block was locked down after an inmate stabbed a prison guard.[22]

After being released from jail, Quinn assumed the risk of frequenting OMC haunts and surreptitiously struck up conversations captured on task force wires. On one occasion, Randall Miller told Quinn: "There's not one bit of my evidence there [of the Gaugers' murders]. I had stuff on, I kept my fuckin' hair clean . . . I had all this shit covered. There's nothing, there's no way they could ever put me there. I'm not even worried about that. Somebody could say, 'Hey, I saw him there,' and the cops would laugh at him 'cause there's no physical evidence from me there; there's none."[23]

Nearly five months after the Illinois Court of Appeals had vacated his conviction pending a new trial, the evidence procured by the ATF task force and Quinn compelled officials to release Gauger. On August 8, 1996, prison guards escorted the inmate from his cell and turned him over to Marshall. On the trip back to his family's farm, Gauger and a group of the Innocence Project's law students stopped at an ice cream parlor in Hebron, Illinois. After almost two years on Statesville's execution-row, the organic farmer was finally a free man. Three years later, Gauger's wrongful conviction served as a catalyst for Governor George Ryan's "moratorium on the death penalty" in Illinois.[24]

Waiting for the Hangman

By late March 1996, the Outlaws realized that the federal government had the evidence to indict several of the club's members. Since Patricia Wolf suggested that her husband contact an assistant U.S. attorney, David Wolf decided to discuss the matter with O'Neill. "I had a guy rat on me," said the Stateline chapter president, as he sought to reassure Wolf. "He fuckin' knew the whole fuckin' deal and I got a witness to cover every situation. It took me a year to do it, but I did it."25

In April, O'Neill's second-in-command offered his strategy to beat the federal rap. "I'm gonna tell 'em that I ain't an Outlaw," said Kruppstadt. "Just because I'm wearing a patch on my back, and belt buckles or whatever, I'll tell them on the fuckin' witness stand that I got the shit at a rummage sale. Outlaws, that's the thing of the 60s. I bought this from an old guy who used to be an Outlaw in the 60s."26

O'Neill contemplated a different plan: Drumming up an allegation of police corruption. "Say, say a girl I met in a bar told me that, ah, that's she been prostituting for ah, ah, male and female ATF agents, on the job for years, you know, that they come in there on investigations, and she, they do weird sex things." Based on her conversations with the agents, the factious prostitute would then allege that ATF agents had conspired to burn down an Outlaws' clubhouse.27

With the Outlaws under surveillance and laying low, the Hells Angels retaliated for the murder of Jack Castle. On April 14, between six and seven a.m., an explosive device was detonated outside the OMC's clubhouse in Chicago. "The blast blew in the front door and superficially injured" a member of the Outlaws, who did not seek medical treatment and declined to contact law enforcement. After the incident, thirty to forty Outlaws met "behind closed doors" at a swap meet in Racine, Wisconsin. Although the FBI believed a reprisal against the Hells Angels was imminent, the OMC declined to respond in-kind.28

Instead, realizing that several members would likely face substantial prison sentences, the Outlaws focused on camaraderie.

In early December, the OMC's Milwaukee chapter held their annual Pearl Harbor Day party. During the event, the MPD received a report of gunshots emanating from inside the large clubhouse. When police arrived, the Outlaws refused to allow officers entry. On December 9, MPD detectives executed a search warrant at the S. 2nd Street clubhouse. Investigators found ten firearms in a safe and a switch blade knife collection located in an area controlled by the chapter's president, Edward "Shock" Anastas. Unable to identify any persons previously involved in gun-play, officers arrested Anastas for possessing the illegal knives.[29]

With rumors of indictments swirling, the OMC sought to portray a kinder, gentler image. A few months after the raid, Larry Powalisz, a detective assigned to the MPD's Intelligence Division, jotted down the license plate numbers of vehicles parked adjacent to the Milwaukee clubhouse. When Powalisz made a Y-turn at the dead end road, a thin layer of ice prevented his unmarked squad car from traversing the small S. 2nd Street hill. As a result, the detective — alone and stuck just outside the fortified clubhouse door — realized, "They [the Outlaws] had me by the balls." Suddenly, two of the OMC's leaders, Anastas and Sienkowski, emerged from the clubhouse, approached Powalisz, and asked if there was a problem. When the detective told the two men that his vehicle was unable to negotiate the icy incline, the two Outlaws' leaders pushed the unmarked squad from behind until the rear tires gained traction.[30]

Behind the scenes, prosecutors in the U.S. Attorney's downtown Milwaukee headquarters had impaneled a federal grand jury. With nearly 30,000 pages of documents to process, presenting reams of evidence to grand jurors took several months. On May 30, 1997, the grand jury returned a fifty-one-page indictment of seventeen members of the Outlaws Motorcycle Club. Eleven days later, after a two hundred-strong posse of local, state, and federal officers had rounded up all but one fugitive, Randy Yager, the thirty-four count indictment was unsealed.[31]

Besides a dozen acts of violence, the federal government alleged that members of the OMC had conspired to distribute controlled substances, unlawfully transported stolen Harley-Davidson motorcycles overseas, and counterfeited U.S. currency.

Besides O'Neill, Miller, and other members of Wisconsin's Stateline chapter, the indictment also included OMC members from Illinois and Indiana. "This is one of the largest indictments because it involves more than one chapter," said Thomas Schneider, the U.S. Attorney for the Eastern District of Wisconsin. "The Outlaws are more than just a motorcycle club. They are a sophisticated and dangerous organized crime group, which has repeatedly resorted to bombings and murder to protect their ongoing criminal enterprise."[32]

Since many of the Outlaws under indictment faced sentences of twenty-five-years to life, members of the task force believed that a handful of the seventeen charged would cooperate with the government. One of the first to flip was James "Preacher" Schneider, the man responsible for the murder of Ruth Gauger. "I pulled a gun out of my pants," Schneider calmly told officials, "I hit her over the head twice. I lifted her up by her hair, lifted her head up, then I cut her throat." Schneider further told investigators that Randall "Madman" Miller had stabbed Morris Gauger to death.[33]

Having agreed to turn informant prior to the indictments, Mark "Crash" Quinn told investigators that Miller related that he had almost severed Morris Gauger's head in the attack that killed the elderly farmer. Quinn further reported that Miller had confessed to killing Donald "Domino" Wagner after a drug rip-off at a rural Racine County boat launch.[34]

As the U.S. Marshal's service continued its search for Randy "Mad" Yager, the thirteen remaining OMC members from Wisconsin, Illinois, and Indiana, prepared for Milwaukee's "biggest racketeering trial case since the prosecution of Milwaukee mob boss Frank Balistrieri in the mid-1980s." By the time jury selection began in March 2000, five additional defendants had entered guilty pleas. The eight remaining OMC members — O'Neill, Carl "Jay" Warneke, Raymond "Shemp" Morgan Jr., Kruppstadt, Richard Mroch, David Kadlec, Randall Miller, and Leslie "Jack" Jensen — believed that they had little to lose and proceeded to trial.[35]

A short time later, Taco Bowman was indictment by a federal court in Florida. When word on the sealed indictment leaked, Bowman went into hiding. The FBI then offered a $50,000 reward for information leading directly to his arrest. In June 1999, two years after appearing on the FBI's most wanted list, Bowman was arrested in an upscale Detroit suburb. In the Midwest, the government alleged that the OMC's international president had orchestrated the conspiracy to attack the Invaders at the Indiana speedway and gave Carl "Jay" Warneke and Randy "Mad" Yager permission to bomb the Hell's Henchmen's Grand Avenue clubhouse in Chicago.[36]

During the three-year gap between the arrests and the start of the Outlaws' Milwaukee trial, the ATF task force gathered additional information for a second round of federal indictments. One of the targets was Thomas "Woody" Sienkowski, the enforcer for the OMC's Milwaukee chapter. Sienkowski was also a committeeman for Steelworkers Local 1343 — a closed shop of union employees at Bucyrus Erie, a company that manufactured heavy mining equipment at a plant in South Milwaukee.[37]

In the late 1990s, as Sienkowski held various leadership positions with the OMC's Milwaukee chapter, he ran for, and was later elected, vice president of the local union. One veteran Bucyrus Erie employee believed that having a member of a notorious motorcycle club on the union's executive committee would "help us out," but soon regretted his decision. Another worker at the plant, who had a disagreement with the union, alleged that Woody ominously drove by his home on his Harley-Davidson flying Outlaws' colors.[38]

"Seinkowski is cold blooded," said former ATF task force member Charles Berard. "If you ever shake his hand, look at eyes, his eyes are black — it's like death."[39]

As some of the Outlaws under indictment offered information, investigators alleged that Sienkowski was a co-conspirator in the bombing of Pat Matter's truck in Minneapolis, was present during the Rockford, Illinois "Hell's Henchmen hunt," and further conspired to murder members of the Invaders Motorcycle Club at an Indiana speedway.[40]

Linked to Kevin O'Neill vis-à-vis wire taps and pen registers, the OMC's Milwaukee chapter president, Edward Anastas, blamed the government and the press for the predicaments of his indicted club brothers. "As a spokesman for the Milwaukee Chapter of the A.O.A. (American Outlaws Association), we support the claims of innocence of those indicted and are confident of their eventual acquittal in this case," wrote Anastas in January 3, 2000 letter to the U.S. Marshal's office. "The biased, slanted `profiling' of all Outlaw members by law enforcement and the media is mean-spirited and blatantly unfair."[41]

On March 8, 2000, the jury selection for the Outlaws' racketeering trial began in Milwaukee. The voir dire examination took nearly three-and-a-half months. Opening arguments finally began in late July. Some of the most damning evidence during the three-month-long proceeding came from fellow Outlaws James "Preacher" Schneider, David Wolf, and Mark "Crash" Quinn, as well as the words of O'Neill, Kruppstadt, and Harvey "RV" Powers, surreptitiously captured via electronic eavesdropping. When the trial concluded, jurors were presented with one-hundred and seventy-five pages of instructions associated with the thirty-four count indictment. In less than a week, the jury gave federal prosecutors "nearly everything they asked for" and convicted all eight OMC defendants.[42]

At sentencing, Chief U.S. District Judge J.P. Stadtmueller saved his harshest words for two members of the OMC's Stateline chapter. The judge noted that O'Neill had the "rather ignominious distinction" of registering the highest federal sentencing guideline score — fifty-five — that Stadtmueller had witnessed during his thirteen-years on the bench. Under federal law, a life sentence is mandated a level forty-three.[43]

The judge minced even fewer words while sentencing the Manson of the Midway. Randall "Madman" Miller, said Stadtmueller, had committed an "incredible series of barbaric attacks we only find in Third World, uncivilized societies" and was "richly deserving of the death penalty." Ironically, Miller's life was sparred not by the judge, but by U.S. Attorney Thomas Schneider, an appointee of President Clinton, who opposed the death penalty for federal crimes prosecuted in the Eastern District of Wisconsin. Before sentencing Miller to life in prison, Stadtmueller added, "I go home on an everyday basis thinking about the lives that were taken."[44]

Just six months after O'Neill was sentenced, the U.S. Attorney's office in the Eastern District of Wisconsin unsealed more indictments. Undergoing cancer treatment, Alan "The Watchmaker" Venus, one of the club's bomb makers, opted to cooperate with the government so he could spend some time with his grandchildren.[45]

Once again, however, the U.S. Attorney's office learned that an inside source had tipped-off the Outlaws. Caught on a wire, Anastas was overheard telling another indicted member, Ronald "Rotten Ronnie" Talmadge, that he would be leaving the area. On June 7, Talmadge told a judge that he also had gleaned information about the indictment before it was unsealed.[46]

The other Outlaws included in the indictment were Anastas, Sienkwoski, Scott "Rhino" Hammond, and fifty-one-year-old Orville Cochran, a member of the OMC's Chicago Southside chapter. The government alleged that Anastas and Cochran were co-conspirators in the Outlaws rampage at the Lancaster speedway on September 25, 1994.[47]

At least for the time being, the Outlaws Motorcycle Club's reign of terror in and around Wisconsin was over. The racketeering convictions of Kevin "Spike" O'Neill et al appeared to discourage the "barbaric attacks" witnessed during the tumultuous 1990s. Yet it took thirty-seven years, a task force of local, state and federal officers, and strict federal sentencing guidelines to rein in the club's most violent members.

[1] *Rockford Register Star*, December 12, 1994, p. 1.

[2] Ibid.

[3] *Milwaukee Journal Sentinel*, April 5, 2000, p. 3B.

[4] Ibid.

[5] David D. Wolf, interview with ATF Agent Sandra DeValkenaere and Rockford PD Detective David Ekedahl, April 26, 1995.

[6] *Northwest Indiana Times*, February 3, 1995, pp. 1, 5.

[7] Berard, interview with author, November 17, 2015; *Northwest Indiana Times,* June 21, 1999, p. 1.

[8] David D. Wolf, interview with ATF Agent Sandra DeValkenaere and Rockford PD Detective David Ekedahl, April 26, 1995

[9] *Hammond Times*, February 2, 1995, p. A4; *Northwest Indiana Times*, February 5, 1995, p. B2; Berard, interview with author, October 17, 2015.

[10] Ibid.

[11] *Northwest Indiana Times*, February 5, 1995, p. B2.

[12] *Shepherd Express Metro*, February 24, 2000, p. 13; *Chicago-Sun Times*, March 4, 1995, p. 11.

[13] David D. Wolf, interview with ATF Agent Sandra DeValkenaere and Rockford PD Detective David Ekedahl, April 26, 1995.

[14] Ibid.

[15] Ibid.

[16] *Milwaukee Journal Sentinel*, April 5, 2000, p. 3B.

[17] *Shepherd Express Metro*, February 24, 2000, p. 13.

[18] Ibid.

[19] *Gary A. Gauger v. Beverly Hendle, et al*, Decision of the Appellate Court of Illinois, Second District, Case No. 2-10-616, June 28, 2011.

[20] Ibid.

[21] Gary Gauger and Julie Von Bergen, *In Spite of the System: A Personal Story of Wrongful Conviction and Exoneration* (Lake Geneva, WI: Fourcatfarm Press, 2008), 155-156.

[22] Ibid., 163-164.

[23] *Chicago Tribune*, April 25, 2000, B1.

[24] Gauger and Von Bergen, *In Spite of the System*, 171; *New York Times*, December 17, 2001, p. 22A.

[25] *Milwaukee Journal Sentinel*, April 5, 2000, 3B.

[26] Ibid.

[27]Ibid.

[28]Federal Bureau of Investigation, Rockford, IL, Teletype Regarding OMC Clubhouse Bombing, April 17, 1996 (held by author).

[29]Detective Larry Powalisz, MPD Memo Book Entry, December 9, 1996 (held by author).

[30]Powalisz, e-mail to author, November 13, 2015 (held by author).

[31]Bruce Vielmetti, "Brother of Outlaws Leader Charged in Milwaukee Found Dead in Burning House," *Milwaukee Journal Sentinel*, June 8, 2015, http://www.jsonline.com/blogs/news/306507541.html (accessed December 29, 2015); *Racine Journal Times*, June 11, 1997, p. 1.

[32]Ibid.; *United States of America v. Kevin P. O'Neill et al*, Federal Indictment in the U.S. District Court for the Eastern District of Wisconsin, Case 97-Cr-98 (held by author).

[33]*Beloit Daily News*, March 10, 1999, p. 1.

[34]*Milwaukee Journal Sentinel*, April 25, 2000, p. 3B.

[35]*Shepherd Express Metro*, February 24, 2000, p. 13; *Racine Journal Times*, June 6, 2000, p. 1.

[36]Harry Joseph Bowman, Poster authored and distributed by the FBI, Wanted for RICO conspiracy, July 1997 (held by author); *United States v. Harry Bowman*, decision of the U.S Court of Appeals (11th Cir.), Case No. No. 01-14305, 302 F.3d 1228, August 20, 2002.

[37]*Milwaukee Journal Sentinel*, July 12, 2003, p. 1B.

[38]Ibid.

[39]Berard, interview with author, October 17, 2015.

[40]*United States v. Thomas Sienkowski*, decision of the U.S. District Court for the Eastern District of Wisconsin, Case No. 01-CR-108, 252 F. Supp. 2d 780, March 19, 2003.

[41]*Racine Journal Times*, March 8, 2000, p. 1.

[42]Associated Press, "Opening Statements Filed in Outlaws Motorcycle Club Trial," *Quad-Cites Online*, March 16, 2000, http://www.qconline.com/news/illinois/opening-statements-filed-in-outlaws-motorcycle-club-trial/article_fbca420c-420f-549f-bde5-734774b051ec.html (accessed January 3, 2016); *Racine Journal Times*, June 6, 2000, p. 1; *Racine Journal Times,* June 15, 2000, p. 1.

[43]*Milwaukee Journal Sentinel*, December 23, 2000, p. 5R.

[44]*Milwaukee Journal Sentinel*, October 13, 2000, p. 3B.

[45]Powalisz, e-mail message to author, May 23, 2016; *Milwaukee Journal Sentinel,* June 8, 2001, p. 3B.

[46]Ibid.

[47]Ibid.

CONCLUSION

PAST & PRESENT

Over the course of four decades, the Outlaws Motorcycle Club in Wisconsin morphed from a ragtag band of former Milwaukee Gypsy Outlaws to an influential component of an international organization with one hundred and twenty-four chapters in twenty-three countries. As the OMC's Milwaukee chapter transitioned from a group of ruffian tormenters to deadly eradicators, law enforcement's response to the Outlaws also evolved.

From the mid-1960s – 1972, as the Outlaws moved through the club's development phase, the MPD's Special Assignment Squad classified the group as a facilitator of public disorder. As a result, Police Chief Harold Breier implemented a street-level suppression strategy. Near the end of the 1972 riding season, the Outlaws entered a consolidation phase; whereby, acts of violence and intimidation were used to disassemble and/or absorb other one-percent motorcycle clubs in southeastern Wisconsin.

After an explosive device left for an OMC rival killed a fifteen-year-old *Milwaukee Sentinel* paperboy, the MPD implemented a plan of organizational disruption. During this period, detectives searched for evidence of any crimes to jail club members. By removing influential leaders from the Outlaws Motorcycle Club's command-and-control structure, law enforcement hoped to foster a level of organizational maladroitness and cultivate informants. This approach was met with mixed results. While some OMC members were convicted of sexual assault, weapons offenses, and drug charges, several major crimes went unsolved.

In the 1990s, as the Outlaws prepared to defend their established turf in Illinois and Wisconsin, law enforcement advanced an organizational dismantle strategy by assembling a task force of local, state, and federal officers. Comprised of knowledgeable outlaw biker investigators, the creation of a multi-agency unit enabled agents to circumvent the rules of federalism. Moreover, the virtually unlimited resources of the national government, as well as the leverage afforded by punitive U.S. sentencing guidelines, enabled prosecutors to develop informants and obtain the court authorized wiretaps necessary to build unbeatable cases.

Another facet of this book addresses the OMC's evolution from a criminal enterprise to an at-will urban terrorist network. To bring the classification of the Outlaws' structure into focus, an examination of three critical areas — command-and-control structure, organizational motives, and tactics — demonstrated that the club operated along the lines of a quasi-military unit. The Outlaws gathered intelligence on the activities of other organizations, as well as governmental entities, such as law enforcement. In at least two instances, the OMC obtained sensitive information from police sources. At the direction of the club's hierarchy, Outlaws traveled to various locales and conducted surveillance of rivals in preparation for future attacks. This military-style command-and-control apparatus collected and passed critical information to the OMC's international president, who formulated a strategic response to real or perceived threats.

Through this confederation, from 1990 – 1996, the Outlaws Motorcycle Club perpetrated eighteen documented incidents of intimidation-based offenses against the Hell's Henchmen and/or the Hells Angels. The vast majority of the violent attacks occurred in the aftermath of a December 31, 1993 meeting in Ft. Lauderdale, Florida. At this gathering, the OMC's international president, Taco Bowman, told those in attendance to "show no tolerance" for clubs allied with the HAMC. The high-profile criminal acts orchestrated by members of the Outlaws, which included public beatings, bombings, and homicidal fierceness, are atypical of secret societies principally concerned with operating "illegal enterprises to produce large profits" and then converting "profits into channels of influence and legitimate enterprise."[1]

The 1990s incident study further illustrates that the OMC's primary motive was the protection of club turf vis-à-vis intimidation. Although the Outlaws Motorcycle Club fits the federal government's definition of a criminal enterprise, the majority of the group's violent activities were directed towards public bullying.

Another objective of urban terrorism is diminishing the public's trust in government institutions. By committing attacks on chosen targets, the urban terrorist creates an atmosphere of instability. The OMC's scheme to deny the Hells Angels a foothold in Illinois was premised on increasing the opportunity costs of the Hell's Henchmen and their associates. The effectiveness of the Outlaws' strategic plan of action hinged on the perception that, should the Hell's Henchmen patch over to the Hells Angels, death or great bodily harm was a distinct possibility. The voices of police officials, as portrayed in various newspaper articles, reinforced a perception that the government was unable to deter outlaw motorcycle gang violence.[2]

Urban terrorism is also distinguished, part-in-parcel, by tactics. A key component of the Outlaws' campaign of intimidation was the possibility of collateral damage. "For every established patch wearer," said Berard, "you have to figure that there are ten to fifteen people that are his core network."[3]

This member-to-associate ratio suggests that the Hell's Henchmen's Chicago, Rockford, and South Bend, Indiana chapters may have had two hundred and fifty loyal associates acting as the club's "eyes and ears." By targeting racing venues, taverns, private vehicles, and clubhouses, the OMC's attacks produced a certain chilling effect designed to reduce the number and collaborative efforts of Hell's Henchmen associates. When attaching bombs to the undercarriages of vehicles, and by using a car as an ordnance delivery system, the Outlaws employed "semi-strategic weapons" to secure and maintain control over other human beings. In essence, the OMC's "poor man's air force" became an integral part of the club's strategy to dissuade the Hell's Henchmen from patching over to the Hells Angels.[4]

While seeking to define the conduct of Outlaws Motorcycle Club members, the 1997 federal indictment offers a telling source of tangible data. Of the thirty-four counts alleged in the charging document, forty-seven percent were related to urban terrorism. An additional thirty-five percent of the acts cited in the indictment pertained to crimes committed by various club members. Based on the 1990s incident study and an analysis of the indictment, it is reasonable to conclude that members of the OMC were engaged in racketeering-based activities. Yet, when the Outlaws Motorcycle Club's Midwestern hegemony was threatened by the Hells Angels, the organization's command-and-control structure used urban terrorism in an effort to emasculate their rivals.[5]

In anticipation of the federal indictments, the Outlaws

began a process of establishing outposts throughout Wisconsin. On February 15, 1997, the OMC's La Crosse chapter was formed when members of the Association of Recovering Motorcyclists (ARM) patched over. The chapter's first president, Leslie "Krazy Jack" Jensen, who had previously procured information from an ATF source concerning the Mathias homicide, was indicated two months later. In 1998, several members of the Regulators MC dropped their club's patch and reemerged as the OMC's Sheboygan chapter, which later relocated to Green Bay. In the small village of Dousman, several members of the Trogs MC morphed in to the Outlaws' Waukesha chapter. In 2003, when two members of the Capital City Riders Motorcycle Club began prospecting for the Hells Angels Rockford chapter, the Outlaws opened a clubhouse near Madison. The OMC later added a chapter in Eau Claire, just ninety miles to the east of Minneapolis, the home of the Minnesota chapter of the Hells Angels. These outposts form a ring around the Badger State and serve as an intelligence gathering network for the president of the Outlaws Motorcycle Club's gold region.[6]

Just a decade-and-a-half has come-and-gone since the conclusion of this history regarding the Outlaws Motorcycle Club. Many professional historians believe that a minimum of fifteen years must pass before an event is studied through a historical lens. This passage of time, notes University of Manchester Professor Paul Fouracre, enables a researcher to examine an incident in "terms of significance and consequence" by using "all possible relevant information." In regards to the Outlaws, however, there are several loose ends and persons of interest that tie the past to the present. One such individual is John W. Bushman, the former enforcer of the OMC's Milwaukee chapter.[7]

Several investigators have linked Bushman to the deaths of at least eight people, including two children — Larry Anstett and Brock Drobac. Now seventy-one-years old, Bushman still roams free. In 2008, "Flapper 1%er" flashed a smile in a photograph that later appeared in an Outlaws Motorcycle Club pictorial. Nonetheless, the aging biker has never left the radar screen of retired detective Roger Hinterthuer.[8]

During a meeting in May, Hinterthuer explained that a prosecution of Bushman for the murder of Clifford Machan is still possible, but not probable. For whatever reason, Hinterthuer mused, Waukesha County prosecutors seemingly want no part of bringing

John Bushman to justice. The retired detective further noted that the federal grand jury testimony of deceased persons, namely Willie Cresca and Billy Wadsworth, would still be admissible at a state trial. Wadsworth passed away on May 24, 2010. Inside the Beulah Church Cemetery in Opp, Alabama, the moniker "Billy the Kid" is etched in to the tombstone of the former fastest car thief in America.[9]

Just days before meeting with Hinterthuer, I contacted the office of the Waukesha County Medical Examiner in an effort to obtain Machan's death certificate, a document that is needed to file a Freedom of Information Act request with the FBI. Deputy Medical Examiner Katie Dougherty promptly returned my call and explained that the bones recovered from the Letko farm have yet to be positively identified. Consequently, a death certificate for Machan does not exist. Instead, this box of bones has collected dust for almost twenty-eight years. Dougherty explained that Machan's children have refused to provide a comparative DNA sample, and the medical examiner's office has been unable to locate other living relatives of the deceased Outlaws' associate.

The following day, with the use of two University of Wisconsin system library databases, it took me less than an hour to locate relatives of Machan's. I then telephoned one such relative. After explaining the purpose for the inquiry, the relative agreed to submit to a comparative DNA sample. When I telephoned Dougherty with an update, she enthusiastically agreed to pass the relative's information to an investigator from the Waukesha County Sheriff's office.

Unfortunately, it took almost two weeks for the case detective to contact the relative. Whether it was this passage of time or former Waukesha County District Attorney Paul Bucher's unwillingness to prosecute Bushman, the relative — as of this writing — has refused to provide DNA until the case detective assures her that criminal charges are forthcoming.

Two days later, I explained the situation to Hinterthuer, who chuckled and remarked, "Well, you've really opened up a can of worms for Waukesha." The lack of a positive identification of the bones unearthed at the Letko farm was the primary reason Bucher gave for refusing to prosecute Bushman. "Sometimes," Hinterthuer lamented, "law enforcement is its own worst enemy."

Another loose Outlaws-end is Randy "Mad" Yager, a former regional OMC president who, in June 1997, just happened to be in Las Vegas when a posse of local, state, and federal officers conducted the roundup of wanted Outlaws. Seventeen-years later, Yager was apprehended outside a Baja California, Mexico *taberna*. "While Randy Yager attempted to evade federal law enforcement for nearly two decades," said Special Agent in Charge of the St. Paul Field Division James C. Modzelewski, "today's arrest signifies ATF's relentless pursuit of violent criminals across the nation."[10]

When Yager disappeared, so did his girlfriend, Margie Jelovcic. On October 15, 2014, as Mexican officers moved in to apprehend Yager, his long-time girlfriend fled and became involved in a high-speed vehicle pursuit. Mexican officials reported that Jelovcic lost control of her vehicle, "which rolled over several times before coming to a stop," and was dead on arrival at a local hospital.[11]

Prior to his arrival in Milwaukee, a federal grand jury issued a superseding indictment that charged the fifty-nine-year-old Yager with racketeering and racketeering conspiracy. After his initial court appearance, Yager received access to some of the government's 50,000-pages of discovery. On June 6, 2015, Yager's sixty-eight-year-old brother, Gerald, was found dead inside a burning home on Washington Street in Gary, Indiana. Gerald Yager's hands were bound and his throat slashed. "All indications show it was arson," said Lake County Sheriff John Buncich. "Gas cans were found in the residence." A relative told investigators that Gerald Yager had received death threats that emanated from his incarcerated brother.[12]

On April 4, 2016, Randy Yager entered a guilty plea regarding his role as a coconspirator in the murders and various bombing plots that targeted the Hell's Henchmen and Hells Angels. In accordance with the plea deal, Yager received a fifteen-year prison sentence; however, the death investigation of the convict's brother is still ongoing.[13]

Another link to the past and present debunks the myths behind a large biker funeral. After the Drobac family slayings and the murder of "Big Don" Fogg, the Outlaws held large burial processions. By doing so, the club hoped to generate public sympathy for their fallen brothers and minimize suspicions that the hits were inside jobs. Last year, a third instance of an Outlaw funeral being coopted for subterfuge materialized.

On July 8, 2015, Major Cam Selvey, of the Charlotte-Mecklenburg Police Department, explained that the four Outlaws and one woman killed during the July 4 massacre thirty-six years earlier were slaughtered by members of their own organization. "One of the suspects had a confrontation with one of the victims," Selvey told the press. The four victims, all of whom witnessed the first homicide, lost their lives for simply being in the "wrong place, wrong time." With Taco Bowman leading the pack, the Outlaws held a half-mile long funeral procession through Charlotte and, in a *de facto* sense, tolerated the rumors that the Hells Angels had committed the murders.[14]

Sadly, another connection to the past is no longer with us. During his tenure as the Kenosha County Sheriff's full-time biker investigator, Detective Larry Zarletti kept tabs on arguably the most dangerous group of one-percenters in American history — the Outlaws Motorcycle Club's Stateline chapter. In 1996, Zarletti was elected Kenosha County Sheriff and retired from the post ten years later. On July 8, 2013, the tenacious former detective — a man despised by Spike O'Neill's rogue riders — suddenly and unexpectedly passed away at a Kenosha hospital at sixty-years-of-age.[15]

When comparing the past to the present it is imperative to gage the conduct of the Outlaws Motorcycle Club to other hideous acts of terrorism. Investigators with the ATF believe the November 7, 1994 explosion outside the Hell's Henchmen's Chicago clubhouse was the third largest car bomb in U.S. history. Only the 1993 al-Qaida parking garage bomb beneath New York City's World Trade Center and Timothy McVeigh's 1995 rental truck blast just outside Oklahoma City's Alfred P. Murrah Federal Building rank higher.

Regardless of the law's shortcomings, the *USA Patriot Act* has increased penalties for bomb makers and has deterred outlaw bikers from using explosive devices. Still, with the wars in Iraq and Afghanistan winding down, scores of returning military veterans will — like their predecessors after World War II and Vietnam — gravitate towards the one-percent subculture. As a result, the saga of the Outlaws Motorcycle Club in and around Wisconsin will continue for the foreseeable future.

[1]*Beloit Daily News*, May 9, 2000, p. 1; Denny F. Pace and Jimmie C. Styles, *Organized Crime: Concepts and Control* (Englewood Cliffs, NJ: Prentice-Hall, Inc., 1975), 20.

[2]G.J. Ashworth, *War in the City* (New York: Routledge, 1991), 84.

[3]Berard, interview with author, October 17, 2015.

[4]Ibid.; Mike Davis, *Buda's Wagon: A Brief History of the Car Bomb* (New York: Verso, 2007), 2-5.

[5]United States of America v. Kevin P. O'Neill et al, Federal Indictment in the U.S. District Court for the Eastern District of Wisconsin, Case 97-Cr-98, June 10, 1997 (held by author).

[6]Powalisz, e-mail to author, June 21, 2015.

[7]Matt Elton, "When Does History End?," *historyextra.com*, October 28, 2009, http://www.historyextra.com/feature/when-does-history-end (accessed August 8, 2016).

[8]Beverly V. Roberts, *Portraits of American Bikers: The Flash Collection* (Birmingham, MI: Flash Collections, LLC), 172.

[9]William Jay Wadsworth, 1947-2010, *findagrave.com*, created by Anita Ellis, June 16, 2013, http://www.findagrave.com/cgi-bin/fg.cgi?page=gr&GRid=113914197&ref=acom (accessed August 6, 2016).

[10]James L. Santelle, United States Attorney for the Eastern District of Wisconsin, "Outlaw Motorcycle Gang Member on the Run for 17 Years Arrested in Mexico," *atf.gov*, October 17, 2014, https://www.atf.gov/news/pr/outlaw-motorcycle-gang-member-run-17-years-arrested-mexico (accessed August 8, 2016).

[11]*Northwest Indiana Times,* October 20, 2014, p. 1.

[12]Katie Delong, "Second indictment: "Outlaws Motorcycle Club" Boss Randy Yager Faces Life in Prison on Racketeering Charges," *fox6now.com*, May 13, 2015, http://fox6now.com/2015/05/13/second-indictment-outlaws-motorcycle-club-boss-randy-yager-faces-life-in-prison-on-racketeering-charges/ (accessed August 8, 2016); *Northwest Indiana Times*, June 7, 2015, p. 1; Bruce Vielmetti, "Brother of Outlaws Leader Charged in Milwaukee Found Dead in Burning House," *jsonline.com*, June 8, 2015, http://archive.jsonline.com/blogs/news/306507541.html (accessed August 8, 2016).

[13]John Diedrich, "Fugitive Outlaws Leader Takes Plea Deal in Milwaukee," *jsonline.com*, April 4, 2016, http://archive.jsonline.com/news/crime/fugitive-outlaws-leader-takes-plea-deal-in-milwaukee-b99699857z1-374527321.html (accessed August 8, 2016).

[14]Mark Washburn, Joe Marusak, and Jane Wester. "How Police Solved 1979 Biker Massacre," *The Charlotte Observer*, July 8, 2015, http://www.charlotteobserver.com/news/local/crime/article26725426.html (accessed August 5, 2016).

[15]Larry Zarletti, "Obituary," *legacy.com*, July 10, 2013, http://www.legacy.com/obituaries/kenoshanews/obituary.aspx?pid=165764427 (accessed August 7, 2016).

INDEX

28996601R00114

Made in the USA
Lexington, KY
24 January 2019